PRAISE FOR **HEALING RESISTANCE**

"Kazu Haga's deep, nuanced, and princ[...]
has challenged and inspired me and m[...]
of encountering his work."

—**MICHELLE ALEXANDER**, author of *The New Jim Crow: Mass Incarceration in the Age of Colorblindness*

"To resist today's violence exploding everywhere, in ways that can actually heal our world, seems a pipe dream—until Kazu Haga makes it real. In his wry, funny, and utterly grounded fashion, he helps me believe we can do it and begin to become the Beloved Community. We need this book like oxygen."

—**JOANNA MACY**, author of *World as Lover, World as Self: Courage for Global Justice and Ecological Renewal*

"Kazu Haga broadens the landscape of nonviolence from an idealistic, often passively perceived, aspiration into a practical path of being deeply engaged and lovingly transformative of our world. Beautifully accessible and profound, Haga is a masterful teacher connecting our internal and external experiences of intending, of doing, and of being—living together with care and justice."

—**LARRY YANG**, core teacher at the East Bay Meditation Center, member of the Spirit Rock Teachers Council, and author of *Awakening Together: The Spiritual Practice of Inclusivity and Community*

"Kazu Haga has written an accessible, thorough, and deeply personal introduction to nonviolence as a power for personal and social transformation. He reflects upon common myths about nonviolent resistance, offers practical insight from his own experiences, and challenges readers to consider a radical, healing approach to confronting injustice. An inspiring read."

—**ERICA CHENOWETH**, Berthold Beitz Professor in Human Rights and International Affairs at Harvard Kennedy School and coauthor of *Why Civil Resistance Works: The Strategic Logic of Nonviolent Conflict*

"An inspiring book about the power of nonviolence—living it in our lives and using it in our work for social transformation. Kazu Haga brings to life Martin Luther King Jr.'s six principles of nonviolence and his six steps for building powerful nonviolent campaigns. Read this book, feel empowered, and help build the Beloved Community."

—**DAVID HARTSOUGH**, author of *Waging Peace: Global Adventures of a Lifelong Activist* and cofounder of Nonviolent Peaceforce and World Beyond War

"*Healing Resistance* breathes life into the often misunderstood study and practice of nonviolence. Kazu Haga simply and beautifully articulates the nuances, the grays necessary to be and build the Beloved Community. Haga exemplifies our value that the Beloved Community is not just a destination but the journey. It's how and why we do the work and yet it is the work itself."

—AINKA JACKSON, executive director of the Selma Center for Nonviolence, Truth & Reconciliation

"Kazu Haga has offered us his heart and soul, inviting us to liberation from a domination system fueled by unconsciousness. He effortlessly dispatches the myopias associated with nonviolence in the only way he knows how—through love and accessibility."

—ANTHONY K. ROGERS-WRIGHT, author of *IntersectionALL: Missed Opportunities and New Possibilities for the Climate Community*

"*Healing Resistance* is one of the most accessible, convincing cases for the effectiveness and necessity of nonviolence to date. Kazu Haga draws on years of experience in movement work to offer a grounded and deeply inspiring blueprint for how to build a more just world—one that reflects deep empathy and wisdom beyond his years. He is one of our brightest lights in this dark time, and his book is a gift to us all."

—ERIC STONER, cofounding editor of *Waging Nonviolence*

"Peace is messy, and nonviolence is the work of the courageous. In *Healing Resistance*, Kazu Haga takes on the why of violence, breaks it down, and then builds us up for the work we need to do now."

—MUSHIM PATRICIA IKEDA, Buddhist teacher, author of "I Vow Not to Burn Out," and racial justice community activist

"*Healing Resistance* is an incredibly authentic and embodied work. Author Kazu Haga shepherds us by his own example. This work is an example of loving inquiry and analysis, not ideology or theory, toward the healing of people and planet. With empathic humility and generosity, he shows us that the nature of being human means that reconciliation, peace, and wholeness, in all of their variegated forms, are always a possibility."

—REVEREND LYNICE PINKARD, pastor, activist, and author of *Revolutionary Suicide: Risking Everything to Transform Society and Live Fully*

"*Healing Resistance* is a beautiful book that allows us to think about how to reduce harm and live in harmony. It is a tool for sustaining movements and movement builders. The pages hold not only past movements and philosophy but the possibility for a better future."

—SUSAN BURTON, founder of A New Way of Life Reentry Project

"Few people are as grounded in the tenets and traditions of principled nonviolence as Kazu Haga. Any of the thousands of people that Haga has trained in nonviolence can attest to the great wisdom, care, and talent he brings to his craft. He is informed by a rich spiritual practice, deep practical experience in social movement organizing, and years of careful research into nonviolent campaigns. It is a rare combination that he brings to his writing, and we can all be grateful that Kazu has given us this offering."

—**PAUL ENGLER**, coauthor of *This is an Uprising: How Nonviolent Revolution is Shaping the 21st Century*

"At a time when the literature is often divided between advocates of nonviolence out of principle and advocates of nonviolent action for strategic and utilitarian reasons, Kazu Haga puts forth a compelling argument as to why both are important to challenge the forces of oppression and build a better world."

—**STEPHEN ZUNES**, professor of politics and international studies at the University of San Francisco and author of *Nonviolent Social Movements*

"*Healing Resistance* is a powerful window into the world of Kingian Nonviolence. In these times, when our species is weak in its reciprocity with Mother Earth and with each other, this great tradition illuminates the need for reconciliation, struggle, and personal transformation. Haga honors this tradition by sharing a moving account of his personal journey with us."

—**CARLOS SAAVEDRA**, founder of the Ayni Institute

"If anyone ever thought that enough has already been written about nonviolence, they haven't read Kazu Haga's book. What this book accomplishes is nothing short of making nonviolence accessible, hopefully to many more people than have previously engaged with it. This is a clear and friendly book, never compromising depth for simplicity, nor losing courage because of the core optimism woven through it. We learn about Haga himself, about the world, about power, about conflict, and about how all of us can increase our capacity to respond effectively to a world gone awry."

—**MIKI KASHTAN**, author of *Reweaving Our Human Fabric: Working Together to Create a Nonviolent Future*

"Kazu Haga has written an insightful, thought-provoking exploration of the impact of violence and the personal and political power of nonviolence based on his own experiences. This practical guide for building Beloved Community can inspire activists, organizers, and trainers to go deeper in our efforts."

—**JOANNE SHEEHAN**, War Resisters League

"As a serious meditator, Haga's sharp insights point to poignant details about the subtle reality of nature, building on a new human dimension to the adage 'hurt people hurt people; healed people heal people' by adding and embodying with his fierce care 'loved people love people.' *Healing Resistance* is a celebration of our collective healing and a priceless intergenerational gift for all of us, the Beloved Community!"

—PANCHO RAMOS-STIERLE, full-time ServiceSpace volunteer and a proudly undocumented and unafraid migrant organizing in Fruitvale, East Oakland, California and Tijuana, Mexico

"In a compelling, honest, and often humorous manner, Kazu Haga guides you through the philosophical and practical dimensions of Kingian Nonviolence in today's world. He unflinchingly addresses some of the complexities of our times, including racism, classism, police brutality, privilege and oppression, and other social injustices. As a strategist for nonviolent movements, I found new depths and insights into the dynamics of struggle and conflict—lessons that will be applied in my work many times over."

—RIVERA SUN, nonviolence trainer and author of *The Dandelion Insurrection: Love and Revolution*

"I have read a number of books on conflict resolution and community organizing. Most of them are like kale: I consume them because I know they are good for me. Kazu Haga's book was like cake: I enjoyed every bit of it and wished there were more. *Healing Resistance* is so accessible and enjoyable to read that I found myself imagining a world where enough of us read this book that peace could be normalized all over the world. I cannot recommend it highly enough."

—SANDHYA JHA, author of *Transforming Community: How People Like You Are Healing Their Neighborhoods*

"Whether he's accompanying us behind prison walls, on walking pilgrimage with Buddhist monastics, or into the streets for head-on direct action, Kazu Haga seamlessly illustrates the indivisibility of personal and societal transformation and our desperate need for both at this pivotal moment in history. We're deeply fortunate to have this inspiring new offering from one of the most powerful contemporary thinkers and doers in the field of nonviolent social change."

—CHRIS MOORE-BACKMAN, author of *The Gandhian Iceberg: A Nonviolence Manifesto for the Age of the Great Turning* and producer of *Bringing Down the New Jim Crow*

"Kazu Haga has devoted his life to the training and organizing that our world most needs, in a philosophy that transforms both the activist and society on the path to Beloved Community. This book brings alive Haga's inspiring personal story, as well as his spirit, energy, deep inquiry, empathy, dedication, and down-to-earth teaching of the fundamentals of nonviolent transformation."

—DONALD ROTHBERG, PhD, author of *The Engaged Spiritual Life: A Buddhist Approach to Transforming Ourselves and the World* and member of the Spirit Rock Meditation Center Teachers Council

"With very human stories—his own and others'—simple and relatable language, and engaging humor, Haga lays bare the power of nonviolence: what it is, what it isn't, and what it takes to get to a more just, thriving, and beloved world. For those struggling to see ways forward for healing harm and repairing relationships in these polarizing times, this book will guide you."

—SHILPA JAIN, executive director of YES!

"*Healing Resistance* is refreshingly honest and direct in its approach. It is a homage to the experiences and teachers that shaped Kazu Haga and the reality that none of us arrive to greater consciousness alone. Drawing from his depth of experiences in movements in just thirty-eight years, Kazu is like a sponge, absorbing everything he can to be more healed, to fight for liberation and justice with a wealth of experience, tools, and knowledge behind him."

—SONYA SHAH, founder and director of the Ahimsa Collective

"First there was Gandhi's autobiography: *The Story of My Experiments with Truth*. Now there's Kazu Haga's *Healing Resistance*. Like Gandhi, the author drills down into the depth of his life experience to reveal the world-shaking power of active nonviolence, all delivered with riveting clarity, fearless intimacy, and over-the-top truth-telling. If you want to get to the bottom of nonviolence, check out *Healing Resistance*—and risk changing your life and your world."

—KEN BUTIGAN, PhD, educator in the Peace, Justice, and Conflict Studies Program at DePaul University, and executive director of Pace e Bene Nonviolence Service

"With clarity and humor, *Healing Resistance* offers each of us an opportunity to reexamine our deepest commitments, our goals for society, and our strategies for achieving them. Informed by his wealth of experience in resistance movements, strategy sessions, and many other spaces, Haga confronts us again and again with the proposition that, in crafting solutions to even the most serious of conflicts, that there are no substitutes for compassion and love."

—SHERRILYNN BEVEL, PHD, cofounder of the Addie Wyatt Center for Nonviolence Training and director of training and special projects at the Nonviolence Institute

HEALING RESISTANCE

HEALING
RESIST
ING
ANCE

Kazu Haga

A RADICALLY DIFFERENT
RESPONSE TO HARM

My Life and Training in the Nonviolent Legacy of Dr. King
Foreword by Dr. Bernard LaFayette Jr. and David C. Jehnsen

**PARALLAX
PRESS**

BERKELEY, CALIFORNIA

Parallax Press
P.O. Box 7355
Berkeley, California
94707

parallax.org

Parallax Press is the publishing division of Plum Village
Community of Engaged Buddhism, Inc.

Printed in Canada by the union workers of SCEP 145

Cover and text design by Joshua Michels

Author photo © Cyndi Kuiper

Text printed on 100 percent post-consumer fiber manufactured using
renewable energy - Biogas and processed chlorine free.

Library of Congress Cataloging-in-Publication Data

Names: Haga, Kazu, 1980- author. | LaFayette, Bernard, Jr., writer of
    foreword. | Jehnsen, David C., 1943- writer of foreword.
Title: Healing resistance : a radically different response to harm / Kazu
    Haga ; foreword by Dr. Bernard LaFayette Jr., David Jehnsen.
Description: Berkeley, California : Parallax Press, [2020] | Includes
    bibliographical references. | Summary: "Offers a practical training in
    Kingian Nonviolence, a step-by-step approach to conflict inspired by Dr.
    Martin Luther King Jr. during the Civil Rights Movement, which
    transforms not only unjust systems but all broken relationships;
    combines Kingian Nonviolence with the author's experience in activism,
    prison work, mindfulness, and Buddhist studies to present a holistic
    view of social change"— Provided by publisher.
Identifiers: LCCN 2019027098 (print) | LCCN 2019027099 (ebook) | ISBN
    9781946764430 (trade paperback) | ISBN 9781946764447 (epub)
Subjects: LCSH: Nonviolence. | Social change.
Classification: LCC HM1281 .H34 2020 (print) | LCC HM1281 (ebook) | DDC
    303.6/1—dc23
LC record available at https://lccn.loc.gov/2019027098
LC ebook record available at https://lccn.loc.gov/2019027099

2 3 4 5 / 24 23 22 21

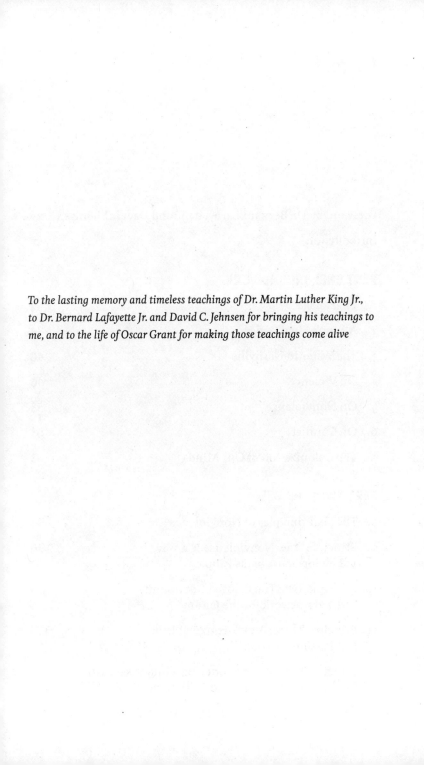

*To the lasting memory and timeless teachings of Dr. Martin Luther King Jr.,
to Dr. Bernard Lafayette Jr. and David C. Jehnsen for bringing his teachings to
me, and to the life of Oscar Grant for making those teachings come alive*

Contents

PART THREE: THE SKILL

APPENDIXES

Foreword by Dr. Bernard LaFayette Jr. and David C. Jehnsen

Throughout the course of our lives, there has been no greater educational experience than our association with Dr. Martin Luther King Jr. We did not know that we were making history then, nor did we know that we were working with a man who would ultimately have a federal holiday dedicated to his memory. But we were always aware of his historic significance and that the wisdom we were learning from him was going to be with us for the rest of our lives.

Bernard LaFayette Jr. began his work with Dr. King in 1958 as a young Baptist seminary student in Nashville, Tennessee, and David C. Jehnsen in 1962 as a conscientious objector from the Church of the Brethren sent down to assist in the movement in Albany, Georgia. We remember fondly when the two of us first met each other. It was the summer of 1964. We both found ourselves at an annual activist institute in Wisconsin organized by the American Friends Service Committee. Bernard had just been hired onto their staff, and David was working with the Westside Christian Parish. Standing in the water on the lake in our bathing suits, we found out that we were both preparing to launch a nonviolent campaign in Chicago.

We decided then that we might as well be working together. Fifty-five years later we find ourselves still fulfilling that promise. Since our earliest conversations, our partnership was centered on training and leadership development. Together, we developed our own style of training, but when Dr. King was assassinated, we reread all of his writings and dedicated ourselves to educating people about his philosophy.

In 1971, activists George Lakey and Bill Moyer organized a gathering of more than one hundred activist trainers in Pendle Hill, a Quaker retreat center outside of Philadelphia. At that gathering, Student Nonviolent Coordinating Committee (SNCC) leader Diane Nash made a suggestion that we reframe "nonviolence" as "agapic energy," after the Greek word *agape*, which describes the unconditional love for all of humanity that Dr. King spoke of.

The two of us had a long discussion that night, and we decided that rather than finding a different term, we would work to reframe how people understood the term "nonviolence." The word, despite the countless nonviolence misunderstandings about it that exist, connects us with an important lineage of social movements. Not just with Dr. King but with Mahatma Gandhi, Susan B. Anthony, Jesus of Nazareth, and the historical Buddha. The teachings of nonviolence, when understood in their proper context, have been and will always remain timeless.

Yet, any lineage must continue to evolve with the times. While continuing to stand on a foundation of timeless and universal principles, historical knowledge must continue to adapt, learn from contemporary thought, and be applicable in the context of current social issues. That is what *Healing Resistance* does. It takes the timeless, universal teachings of nonviolence and builds on them with a fresh perspective, making them relevant to today's issues.

Years ago when we wrote the Kingian Nonviolence Leaders Manual, and its corresponding training curriculum, we wanted to share the richness of Dr. King's philosophy and strategy with others. Time and events have carried us beyond what we could have ever anticipated. The Kingian Nonviolence curriculum has spread to all corners of the world, with thousands of trainers across multiple continents. It is being applied in social movements and educational institutions ranging from elementary schools to universities, prisons, law enforcement agencies, churches, and community centers. It has been translated into multiple languages and has benefitted countless individuals dedicated to creating a peaceful culture.

The manual was never meant to be a meticulous academic study on nonviolence, to be taught and debated in the halls of academia. It was meant to be a point of departure toward a long-term journey of real-life application. It was meant for the practitioner, for people dealing with real-life issues.

Haga illustrates this perfectly in the pages that follow. His training ground in nonviolence has not been a classroom. The lessons in these pages were forged in the field from working in violent prisons to leading social justice movements—the stories come from real-life application of, and experimentation with, the principles. This is how we know that nonviolence works.

From the earliest stages of education, students are taught to accept violence as a normal and necessary part of our culture. We learn from history class that we are a violent nation. We learn about the history of war and violence with little attention paid to understating the underlying social, psychological, and political causes and conditions that lead to violence.

Violence, despite the countless ways in which it has destroyed lives and communities, despite the dignity that it rips away from people, despite the perpetual and cyclical nature in which it continues to harm society, is constantly justified and excused as acceptable behavior and even admirable behavior. Its tentacles stretch into every aspect of our lives. It is in our homes, our work, our sports, our music, our children's toys. Without knowing it, we have been trained to respond to conflict with violence.

We view nonviolence not as the opposite of violence but as its antidote. Nonviolence is about resisting the nature of violence and healing from its impact. Nonviolence challenges the seemingly "peaceful" nature of unjust conditions. When we are sold a story that war is an effective path to peace, we must resist that narrative. We must rebel.

Dr. Martin Luther King Jr. was arrested for being a troublemaker. Socrates was convicted for stirring up doubt in the minds of young people. Jesus was crucified for speaking out against the dominant paradigm. Nonviolence comes from a long tradition of disturbing the peace and challenging the accepted norm.

Healing Resistance continues that important tradition by disturbing many people's understandings of what it means to work for peace. Haga has added to what we initiated with the publication of the Kingian Nonviolence Leaders Manual. He has experimented with it and adapted it, and this book is the documentation of that process.

For those already exposed to Kingian Nonviolence, we hope this will be a catalyst for you to experiment and document your own work. For those new to Kingian Nonviolence, this will be an invaluable introduction. Haga's writing style avoids the theoretical ways in which nonviolence is oftentimes discussed. You will be able to see yourself in the stories told in these pages and engage directly with this book.

When the Leaders Manual was first published, some saw it as an endpoint. But for us, we saw it as the beginning of a process of institutionalizing this knowledge. Institutionalization is not a static process that takes place in a university. It is a constantly evolving process. It is what is happening now at the East Point Peace Academy; at the Addie Wyatt Center for Nonviolence Training; the Selma Center for Nonviolence, Truth, and Reconciliation; the Connecticut Center for Nonviolence; and so many more centers that have sprung up.

Each of those centers has its roots in the Kingian lineage but are blazing their own tradition based on their local needs. There is no cookie-cutter blueprint for social change. It can have common standards and foundations, but it needs to evolve separately from there. We need to be open to that fluidity.

Readers should keep this in mind as they read *Healing Resistance*. In the same manner that Haga has found ways to incorporate Kingian Nonviolence into his life, we encourage you to find how you can incorporate the lessons in these pages into your own situation. If we all take it upon ourselves to do so, perhaps we will reach the mountaintop that Dr. King got to witness in his dreams.

Dr. Bernard LaFayette Jr. and David C. Jehnsen
Coauthors of the Kingian Nonviolence Leaders Manual
June 1, 2019

Introduction

I started facilitating nonviolence trainings when I was nineteen years old. In groups like the American Friends Service Committee and ad-hoc organizations that would come together in preparation for major demonstrations, I would work with diverse groups of people preparing them for protests, preparing them for possible arrests and discussing direct action tactics. As a shy, insecure, and quiet kid who grew up not believing that I had anything to offer the world, being at the front of a room teaching a group of people *anything* was a seductive thrill.

Yet, after a couple of years of facilitating these workshops, I stopped. I still remember a conversation I had with Jo Comerford, then the coordinator of the local American Friends Service Committee and someone I consider to be one of my first mentors. We had just wrapped up a training and, though we both felt it had gone well, we also felt like we were not having the depth of dialogue we needed to touch a deeper, almost spiritual component of nonviolence. It would not be until years later that I would realize this. While I couldn't quite place my finger on it then, it bothered me enough that I quit doing the trainings. While I remained active in social change work, I stayed away from any relationship with the concept of "nonviolence" for many years.

That all changed when I discovered Kingian Nonviolence Conflict Reconciliation, a training curriculum that grew out of the legacy of Dr. Martin Luther King Jr. A simple, two-day introductory workshop I took when I was twenty-seven years old changed my life forever. By that point, I had spent ten years of my life on work dedicated to social justice. Even with all my experience, I realized that weekend that I knew *nothing* about who Dr. King was, what he stood for, or what he meant by "nonviolence."

Actually, I take that back. I had in a sense always known. I remember telling Jonathan Lewis, who facilitated that workshop, that this was stuff I *always* knew—in the very core of my being. I just didn't have the language to articulate it.

I realized during that workshop that the stuff I had been teaching at nineteen wasn't, in fact, nonviolence. It was nonviolent civil disobedience. I had been training people to go into mass demonstrations without throwing a punch. While that is certainly one application of the theory of nonviolence, I realized how limited of an understanding I had. If nonviolence is simply a set of strategies and tactics that do not use physical violence, then the Ku Klux Klan could argue that they are using nonviolence when they rally. Neo-Nazis could argue that they are using nonviolence when they march. And that doesn't feel right. Something about the work of nonviolence has to be fundamentally different from the work of the KKK or neo-Nazis.

Fifty years after his assassination, Dr. King has taught me that a commitment to nonviolence is a commitment to restoring relationships and building Beloved Community: a world where conflict surfaces as an opportunity to deepen in relationship, a world where all people understand our interconnectedness, and a world where—as stated in the Kingian Nonviolence training curriculum—"all people have achieved their full human potential." Nonviolence as an ethical choice stems from a deep understanding about the impact that violence has on all people—those who experience it, those who perpetuate it, and those who witness it. It is about acknowledging that violence itself is the enemy that we need to defeat, not the people who are caught up in its cycles. Nonviolence is a worldview that speaks to the impact of violence, harm, oppression, and injustice on the human condition. It is about the dynamics of conflict and how to transform it. It is about an unwavering faith in the goodness of people and an undying commitment to healing ourselves and society. It is about stripping away the layers of trauma and separation and remembering the core of who we are. It is about coming home.

Since that weekend workshop, I spent another ten years studying Kingian Nonviolence, eventually becoming a senior trainer. This book loosely follows the Kingian Nonviolence training curriculum, into which I have infused my own stories, experiences, and the lessons I have picked up from Buddhist practice, social justice organizing, restorative justice, and trauma healing work inside of our country's prison system.

Wisdom evolves as it gets passed down through generations. I have tried to honor the legacy of this special curriculum while adding new information and adapting it to our current times. Dr. King's teachings—ultimately a set of timeless, universal principles that came to me through the words of Dr. King and the training I've received from people like Dr. Bernard LaFayette Jr.—helped me synthesize two areas that I see are disconnected from each other in most of our movements for change.

On one side, many activist movements have the courage to put their bodies on the line and the militancy to shut down highways, occupy government buildings, and resist and blockade injustice in its tracks. Yet, I find too often that the very cycles of harm that we are trying to fight get replicated within those same movements. I have known too many people who have been traumatized in one way or another in social justice spaces. From large organizations like Amnesty International to the smallest, most grassroots groups, people are getting harmed by a "woke" activist culture that has become toxic. We can bring down the entire system and have a worldwide revolution, but if we haven't healed our traumas and learned how to be in authentic relationship with each other, we will corrupt any new system we put in its place.

On the other side, there are many communities of healers, meditators, and community builders who are doing the vital work of healing trauma, bringing us back to the present moment, building and restoring trust between people, and cultivating love for all of humankind. Yet, we've seen too often, those communities are disconnected or not in solidarity with people who are risking it all to fight for justice. We can heal every person's trauma, but if we haven't begun to dismantle the structures still in place that perpetuate injustice at a systemic level, we'll replicate the conditions for new traumas to constantly be created.

I have a deep yearning to be in a community that is engaged on both fronts. A community committed to personal transformation as well as social and structural change. A community that understands we need to work on healing our traumas and transforming our relationships. If we don't upend unjust systems, we will spin our wheels forever. We need a movement that is, in Dr. King's words, "nonviolent, but militant, and as dramatic, as dislocative, as disruptive, as attention-getting as the riots" but also understands that the goal of such a movement is to bring humanity together and heal. This is "healing with teeth," as my friend Rev. Samantha Wilson calls it.

I believe that the laws that govern conflict and harm are fractal in nature. adrienne maree brown's book *Emergent Strategy* got me into fractals. A fractal is a shape, a design, or a pattern that repeats over and over, and each small section has the same exact characteristics as the whole. From seashells to ice crystals, snowflakes, ferns, and Romanesco broccoli, there are examples of fractals all throughout nature. What's possible at the smallest scale is possible at the largest scale. Whether we are talking about intrapersonal conflict within our own hearts; interpersonal conflict between two people; or large-scale global conflicts between nations; the principles, practices, and strategies that guide the transformation of conflict are the same at every scale.

In my work in prisons, I've had the privilege to witness the transformation of countless people who have committed the most horrific acts of violence—including homicide—into the most compassionate, dedicated peacemakers I know. I've had the honor of witnessing healing dialogues between people whose lives were brought together by tragedy. Between the person who almost beat another to death in a mugging and the survivor of that crime. Between mothers and the people who took away their children. Between two men who killed each other's best friends. I have come to believe that if these depths of healing are possible on those scales, then there is no conflict that is too large for us to transform. In each of those cases, it has been through love and understanding, not shaming and punishment, that transformation was made possible.

I am not naïve enough to think that social transformation is possible without a powerful movement that will need to use militant forms of nonviolent direct action to push for change. But even in nonviolent movements, direct action oftentimes begins with an assumption of separation. "We" are the good people, and we need to use direct action to harness power so we can overpower "those" other people. It is still about forcing our will over the "bad" people. Our language and thinking are still couched in the worldview of separation and domination.

I have to believe that it is possible to do things differently. That it is possible to build a movement as "disruptive as a riot," yet deeply grounded in love and understanding. A resistance movement that sees its purpose as healing the wounds of society. This fractal nature of conflict is one of the reasons why we have been able to use the same exact curriculum of Kingian Nonviolence in institutions like prisons and schools, in

Whether we are talking about intrapersonal conflict within our own hearts; interpersonal conflict between two people; or large-scale global conflicts between nations; the principles, practices, and strategies that guide the transformation of conflict are the same at every scale.

movement settings where activists are working on systemic transformation, or in community settings where people simply want to get along with their families.

I encourage people to keep this in mind as they read this book. I will be sharing examples of conflict on all levels of our social lives to demonstrate that each principle, each step, each theory in nonviolence applies on all levels equally. When I'm talking about a large-scale organizing campaign, see if you can spin the story and apply the teaching to an interpersonal conflict you are having with someone in your life. Similarly, if I use the example of violence within a family to illustrate a principle, see if it holds true to a mass movement.

There is no separation between the personal and the global. A holistic understanding of nonviolence presents us with an opportunity much greater than what either a movement of healing or a movement of resistance can accomplish on its own. We need that. I am sick of fighting for crumbs. I have been part of countless movements and campaigns where we have spent so much time and resources fighting for one policy change, only to look up and see that we are still swimming in injustice. I have been part of so many circles in prison where incredible healing has taken place, only to look up and see two million more incarcerated souls that need healing, with more on the way every day.

I am convinced that only a movement that is grounded in a *principled* approach to nonviolence can get to where we need to go. A principled approach to nonviolence has an explicit goal that is big enough (not just revolution but the realization of Beloved Community) and tactics that are militant enough to create the systemic changes that we need without perpetuating harm while engaging in it. We need resistance. We need to resist injustice, we need to resist violence, we need to resist our own tendency to fall into blame, resentment, greed, hatred, or despair. But we need to do it in a way that is healing to *everyone*.

It is my deepest and most sincere hope that this book can contribute toward creating that type of movement. It's not all for selfless, altruistic motives. It is largely because being part of such a movement is something I have been searching for my whole life. I want so badly to see and experience a movement that will never waver in its commitment to the fullness of nonviolence.

I am in the minority on this. Most people aren't going to buy into nonviolence as a way of life. I get that. It's much easier to convince people that nonviolence is an effective strategy for social change and much harder to get people to commit to a lifestyle and worldview that centers reconciliation above all else, refuses to dehumanize any individual, and cultivates loving compassion for all beings no matter how much harm they have caused.

Years ago, I met an elder who used to be a part of the Student Nonviolent Coordinating Committee, or SNCC, the youth arm of the Civil Rights movement. When I mentioned that I had been trained by Dr. Bernard LaFayette Jr., coauthor of the Kingian Nonviolence curriculum, this man's response was, "Oh Bernard? Yeah, he's great. He was always the principles guy. I believed in nonviolence as an effective strategy, but Bernard was always talking about nonviolence as a principle." I let out a little laugh. In that moment, I felt proud to have been trained by the "principles guy." For this elder, and for so many activists today, nonviolence simply describes a set of strategies that doesn't include violence. But for Dr. King, Dr. LaFayette, and people like myself, nonviolence is a worldview and a way of being.

*

This book is obviously about nonviolence, but I want to say a few words about violence first. I do not believe that the role of a committed practitioner of nonviolence is to cast moral judgment on those who choose to use violence, especially as a form of resistance or self-defense or self-preservation. This judgment is oftentimes teeming with privilege; it's easy to give a blanket disapproval of violence when your life is not being threatened on the daily or if your community hasn't suffered the pain of oppression for five hundred years.

It is easy to judge people who engage in direct, physical acts of violence, instead of truly grappling with how much modern society has saturated our daily lives with violence. We all contribute to systems of violence each and every day, whether it's the wars that we fund with our tax dollars, the violence embedded in the food we eat, the wars fought over the petroleum products we put into our cars, or the suffering built into the coltan inside the computer I used to write this book.

As controversial as this may be to write, I don't believe that violence and nonviolence are necessarily mutually exclusive. Nonviolence is a long-term commitment to building Beloved Community, but it is not a false sense of purity, naiveté, or a dogmatic commitment to certain tactics that come at the expense of realism. Violence can feel like a cathartic release from a lifetime of pain and oppression.

A few years ago, I was speaking to someone serving a life sentence for a homicide he committed as a young man. When he was describing his story, he said that every time he pulled the trigger, it felt like he was throwing his pain at his victim. It was a visceral, vivid image that I will never forget. This young man held so much pain inside—a lifetime of poverty on top of generations of oppression suffered by his ancestors—that it had to be released in some way, and it was released on his victim.

During the Oscar Grant movement, I found myself in a moment of civil unrest between a bank window and a young man trying to smash it.[1] However he may have interpreted my act of intervention, I was more concerned about him than the bank window; there were dozens of riot cops just around the corner, and the last thing I wanted to see was for him to end up in the hands of law enforcement.

I remember looking into his eyes as he told me to come to his neighborhood. "We don't have movie theaters. We don't have malls. We don't have shit to do," he explained. "Give us something to do and we wouldn't be out here smashing windows." I realized

---

1. Oscar Grant was the young man who was shot and killed on New Year's Day by a transit policeman in Oakland, California, in 2009. Widespread protests followed.

then that if society doesn't provide safe spaces for people to release their legitimate anger, it's going to get released on bank windows or on other people. Who are we to judge when it is we who participate in a society that built the systems that caused those harms and have failed to provide safe spaces for people to heal?

As ineffective a *strategy* as it may be, violence is oftentimes an expression of a yearning to heal. It is a cry for peace. As Marshall Rosenberg says, "violence is the tragic expression of unmet needs."[2] Needs for healing. Needs for release. Needs to be seen or to be heard. Needs for pain to be legitimized. Violence may not always be the most effective strategy to meet those needs, but some of us don't have access to strategies that might work better.

Violence is used every day by people as a matter of survival. This is the case in interpersonal relationships, and it may be the case for entire communities of people who are facing annihilation. Violence can be very effective in keeping you alive or protecting those in danger, and there is great value in that. If a woman who is getting attacked or an Indigenous community that is facing annihilation believes that violence is their *only* option for survival, or their *most effective* option for survival, then I believe they should have the right to engage in it without being judged.

In terms of the use of violence for self-defense or for the protection of life, I want to point out three things:

1. The first has to do with the spirit with which we engage in that violence. Sometimes, we romanticize violence and make it "fun." In some of our movement work, we go to rallies looking for a fight, gearing up for it with a sense of excitement. There's a "Yeah, we're gonna fuck the other side up" attitude. At times, the level of violence we witness in our society is so great that we may have no choice but to use violence to stop the escalation. But that is no cause for celebration. If a conflict escalates to that level, force should be used with a spirit of mourning that we allowed things to get so out of hand that human beings had to be harmed.

2. Rosenberg is the founder of Nonviolent Communication.

I once had to call the police on someone who was threatening someone dear to me. It was a decision that I knew would lead to his incarceration. In that moment, it was the only thing I could think to do to protect the life of somebody he was threatening. I was 3,000 miles away, and it felt like the only option available to me. While it would be easy for me to demonize this person and celebrate the fact that he had to suffer for hurting somebody that I cared about, it was far from a moment of celebration for me. I made the call with a deep mourning that my actions would cause harm to someone.

2. The second is Rosenberg's idea of "protective use of force," which is about using the minimum amount of force necessary to stop the immediate harm. The intention is not to hurt anyone but to stop harm. This is in contrast to "punitive use of force," which is about punishing or controlling someone by harming them. As a society, we rarely think about what the minimum amount of force could look like, nor do we realize that the more we train ourselves, the more options we have for what that minimum amount could be. That's why, as a practitioner of nonviolence, I am also a strong advocate for martial arts training.

3. The third point is that I believe that there is *always* a nonviolent response to violence that is at least as effective as a violent response.[3] The challenge here is that a nonviolent response to violence usually takes much more training and creativity than violence. It's easier to shoot someone than learning to subdue them. It can be easier to hurt an attacker than using nonviolence to keep yourself safe. And some groups have more access than others to that sort of training.

So, violence does have its place. It is often an expression of unheard and unseen pain, and it can keep us safe. All that said, violence is limited in one very important way, and that is that violence can never create, restore, or strengthen relationships. Violence can never bring us closer to reconciliation or closer to Beloved Community, which, in a principled approach to

3. Some examples will follow throughout this book.

nonviolence, is always our long-term goal. If we're ultimately not working to heal relationships, communities will always be at odds, and the threat of violence, injustice, and domination will continue. Any peace we create will be temporary.

Again, violence may be a necessary tool in some moments. It's hard to reconcile with someone as they're beating you. You certainly can't reconcile with someone if they've killed you. You need to survive in order to build a relationship. But we can't simply stop there. If our goal is to end these cycles of harm, then violence will never be enough. If we find we need to use violence to protect life, then we need to double our efforts at reconciliation afterward. This book is not about casting judgment on violence or criticizing those who use it. It is an acknowledgment that if we are to ever defeat injustice, then we need more than violence. It is an exploration about what that "more" looks like.

Violence can never create, restore, or strengthen relationships.

*

There is a Zen Buddhist teaching that says, "Words are fingers pointing at the moon, but it's not the moon itself." Words are nothing but sounds we make with our vocal cords or symbols we jot down on a page to communicate a message. Language is a tool that we use to try to point at something, but it is not the thing itself.

When two people are making the same sounds, we assume they are pointing at the same thing. Someone may be pointing at the moon, but from where you stand, it may look like they're pointing at Venus. From your perspective, you may be right. You might end up getting into an argument as opposed to trying to understand what the other person is pointing at. Other times, two people are using different words but pointing at the same thing. It doesn't matter if we're using our pointer finger or our pinky, a laser pointer or a broomstick. We could all be pointing at the moon, and we get stuck arguing over the right finger or the right tool to use to point to the moon.

In workshops that I've facilitated, I see people get tripped up over the use of certain words. Sometimes we see or hear certain words, dig our heels in about *our* understanding of those words, get into a conflict about the meaning of those words, and completely miss the spirit of the teaching. Language is not static or uniform. It evolves over time, and it differs based on culture and context. Dr. King's words come from a culture from a specific time in history. He only referred to men in most of his writings and speeches. He used the word "negroes," a word that people today would find offensive, because that was the common vernacular at that time. To truly understand his message, we need to try to understand the *spirit* of what he said and not get caught up in the specific language he used.

Similarly, I'm aware the words I write in these pages are coming from a very specific time and have passed through the lens and filter of my personal worldview. Perhaps you will disagree with some things you read in these pages. If that happens, my request is that you try to understand the spirit of my words before automatically disagreeing. Perhaps I'm using a word differently from how you understand it, but perhaps I'm still pointing at the same moon.

I often use words like "militant" nonviolence or speak to the need for an aggressive movement for change. I often compare the process for social transformation to a battle or a fight. I know that not everyone resonates with that language, but those words are tools I use to communicate a spirit, and it's the spirit that matters. In the end, there will likely be some things in this book that you simply do not agree with, but I hope that you will read on with an intent to understand, take what benefits you, and leave the rest behind.

*

I consider myself a student of Dr. King, even though I obviously never met him (he died twelve years before I was born). I have pictures of him up on my walls, items of clothing displaying his face, and I have invested more than a decade of my life to spreading his teachings and his legacy. As much as I idolize Dr. King, I know he was not perfect. By many accounts, he was not always a great family man, and his attitudes toward women were troubling. He was a Southern Baptist preacher in the 1950s, so part of the equation is that his faults reflected that particular culture and era.[4] While that may explain some of the questionable things he said or did, it does not excuse or condone them.

We need to be real about all of our idols, past and present. It is important that we do not romanticize them or put them on pedestals where they don't belong. No one is perfect. From Gandhi to Che Guevara to Mother Teresa, everyone has faults. As dangerous as it is to put people on pedestals, it can equally be dangerous to refuse to learn anything from their lives and teachings because of their imperfections. Dr. King's faults do not negate his brilliance, nor do they nullify his contributions to the work of justice. Dismissing him would be a huge disservice not only to his legacy but to our own struggles for freedom.

After having studied the work of the German philosopher Georg Wilhelm Friedrich Hegel, Dr. King came to see himself a Hegelian thinker. Hegel was one of the most influential thinkers in the field of dialectics: the study of conflicts and contradictions to arrive at truth by synthesizing seemingly opposing perspectives. The fact that Dr. King considered Hegel one of his biggest influences is itself a great example of Hegelian thinking, because Hegel held, among other things, incredibly racist views. That didn't stop Dr. King from learning what he could from Hegel's work. He

---

4. While views on gender within the Civil Rights movement were certainly a "sign of the times," I also don't want to discount the powerful work of women like Ella Baker, who offered insightful criticisms from within the movement, as well as Audre Lorde, whose struggles as a woman within the movement inspired her to pioneer the concept of intersectionality.

studied his philosophy with a critical lens, took the things that benefitted him, and left the other stuff behind. He synthesized what resonated from Hegel's work and left the rest behind.

It is true that Dr. King's behavior was at times less than stellar. It is also true that he was a brilliant man who sacrificed his life for the liberation of all people. It is important to hold both of these truths and not sanctify him or negate his work because of a part of who he was. This brings us to the last thing I want to ask of you as you read this book. Read the following pages with your own critical dialectical lens. Read this book, try to understand it, criticize it, and synthesize the parts that ring true to you. You don't have to take everything offered in a buffet, and you don't have to believe everything I write.[5]

It is true that there is something odd and potentially even problematic about a Japanese guy writing a book about the teachings and legacy of Dr. King. Dr. King's teachings are universal, and at the same time, the legacy of the Civil Rights movement belongs to the Black people who led it. I am aware of that dynamic and sometimes still struggle to understand how to sit with it. It is also true that this is the position that I have found myself in, and I hope that whoever the messenger is, the teachings can benefit all people.

---

5. I love to eat almost as much as I love justice, and I would eat every item in a buffet if I could. But I know that's not healthy. We need to be critical with our appetites, gastronomically and intellectually.

PART ONE
GROUNDWORK

CHAPTER 1

Pilgrimage

This book contains nothing new. No new knowledge, no new insights, no new wisdom to speak of. Perhaps not the best words to begin a book with, but it's the truth.

INK

Against my mother's best wishes, I've been a lifelong fan of tattoos. I don't have anything below the sleeve, so most people don't realize I have been collecting them since I was eighteen. Every once in a while, I'll be at a beach or a swimming pool without a shirt on, and someone will compliment me on my ink. I'm never quite sure what to say. "Thank you?" It feels awkward to accept praise for my tattoos, since they are not my art. All I did was sit there while someone more talented than me graced my body with their artwork.

I've always felt the same with any wisdom I may have to share. It's not my wisdom. I don't own it, nor did I come up with any of these words independent of all of the people who have touched my life. Whether it's the ink on my body or the ink on these pages, they are gifts that have been handed down to me by someone with more talent and wisdom than I have. My job is to simply carry them and pass them on.

What follows is not a list of obligatory acknowledgments that simply shows up as a preface to flip past to get to the real content of this book. This is the first section of my book, the one that will tell the story of how this knowledge was shared with me and by whom. It's gonna be a few pages. But it's deeply important to me to start here, to honor all of the teachers I've had along the way.

IN THE BEGINNING

I was born in November 1980 in Tokyo, Japan, to a loving, wealthy, and powerful family. My great-grandfather, Hitomi Enkichi Tomei, was a well-known poet who started a college that is now one of the largest and most prominent women's universities in Japan. My early childhood was everything a kid could ask for. I had a loving and supportive family, a large and comfortable home, big family gatherings on holidays, and annual vacations to Hawaii.

My parents belonged to a small offshoot of the Shinto religion and had an altar upstairs in our house. We chanted and prayed to it every day, sometimes twice a day. From an early age, I learned the value of silence, discipline, and sitting *seiza* while communing with the sacred.[1] Every Christmas, the whole extended family would gather at our house for a feast. Somehow, I always managed to *just* miss Santa Claus as he flew by our house.[2] "There he is, there he is! Come out quick!" my mom would shout out as she pointed above our roof. Of course, he would be gone by the time I ran out to look up at the night sky. Later on, after we moved to the United States and lived in a house with a chimney, I set traps for him and slept in the living room. I once tied a web of strings with bells attached to them inside the fireplace and slept next to it with a net. I never managed to catch him, but I was never disappointed at the gifts he would bring me each year.[3]

One year during Children's Day, my older sister begged to get a pet duck.[4] Not a puppy, not a kitten, but a duck. We had gone to

---

1. A formal and traditional style of sitting while kneeling, folding your legs underneath your thighs. It hurts when seiza is held for a long time, so it involves a certain degree of stoicism.
2. Despite my family being practitioners of a small offshoot of the Shinto religion, and Japan being largely a Shinto and Buddhist culture, Christmas is a major holiday there. Capitalism and Western influence moved in quickly after the end of the war. For whatever reason, the fast-food chain KFC has cornered the market on Christmas. I always figured it was because Colonel Sanders looks like Santa.
3. I wasn't trying to steal the presents. I just wanted to get a glimpse of him, I promise.
4. Children's Day is an annual Japanese holiday celebrated on May 5th.

the department store a few days prior, and the pet store there had a baby duck for sale. That duck became the first animal to live in our house. The fact that we had a yard large enough to keep a duck in downtown Tokyo was a privilege that I was not aware of at the time. We named him "Happy." Or "Hup-pee," as we pronounced it. His name was symbolic of my life at the time. Everything was good. Everything was innocent. Life was Hup-pee. The threat of violence was the farthest thing from my mind.

Everything changed for me in 1988 when I was seven years old. My parents had a falling out with my mother's side of the family. The details of what happened are complicated. I am still not sure if I understand the full story, but it involved some illegal activity that my father was involved in, and it ended up with my mother being disowned and our having to leave the country.

"We're going on vacation," my parents told my two sisters and me. We never once had a conversation about moving to the United States. My parents believed that things would eventually get better and that we would be able to go back to Japan. The United States was great at first. Through a complicated series of events, we ended up living in a six-bedroom mansion on a private beach in Massachusetts. Even though we lived in a large house back home by Tokyo standards, this place felt like a castle. Before we knew it, we were enrolled in school, and our vacation turned into a story of immigration.

A few years later, everything changed again when my father, at age forty-three, was diagnosed with pancreatic cancer. I remember him telling my sisters and me that he had six months to live. I couldn't comprehend it. I couldn't fully grasp it even when he passed away just a few months later. I was eleven years old.

Looking back, I can't imagine what it must take to tell your own children that you have only a few months to live. I don't remember him shedding a single tear—his stoicism a character trait revered in Japanese culture. Stoic. Honorable. Controlled. It wouldn't be until decades later that I would come to see the repression of emotion as an act of violence we perform against ourselves and see all of the ways that internal forms of violence can manifest. I often wonder now in what ways a lifetime of repressed emotions may have contributed to his cancer.

Within a couple of years, we went from living in the multi-million-dollar mansion on the beach to briefly experiencing homelessness. I went from being in a loving and stable family to witnessing my mother struggling in an abusive green-card marriage to my stepfather. I went from a happy childhood to experiencing denial and depression. I turned to drugs and alcohol to drown out the reality of what my life had become.

My freshman year of high school in New Hampshire, I had my first opportunity to be in service to community, and I failed miserably. It was Community Service Day at school, and some students went to the food bank to serve food, some went to the fire department to wash trucks, and others went to the senior center to spend time with elders.[5] I skipped out with some friends, stole some beer from the local grocery store, and spent the day getting drunk at the park. We made it back in time to take the buses home, still a bit tipsy.

One day when I was fifteen, some friends and I skipped school after lunch, went to a friend's house, and finished off the stolen bottles of vodka and whiskey we had been working on the night before. As we walked to town, I got sick and threw up in the bathroom of a pizza shop. I somehow managed to get home, passed out, and woke up with the worst headache of my life. That ended up being one of the last times in my life I got drunk, though it would be another couple of years before my life started to change for the better.[6] I ended up dropping out of school shortly thereafter at age fifteen, signaling the end my formal education.[7]

5. How sad it is that spending time with our elders has to be considered "community service."
6. Yes, I quit drinking when I was fifteen.
7. Little did I know that it would also begin the process of my life education. It was when I dropped out of school that I learned that I had a passion to learn.

By this point, my home life had completely unraveled. I barely came home, preferring to spend nights on the floor of a friend's house or sleeping in the woods. When I was home, I rarely came out of my room other than to eat. My days consisted of waking up late, hitchhiking to town, meeting up with friends, trying to score some weed, LSD, mushrooms, or whatever else could help me escape for the night, and trying to figure out where I was going to sleep.

My mom, my two sisters, and I were all going through our own challenges and dealing with our traumas in our own ways. It wasn't just the constant fighting and the difficult relationship with my stepfather that I was avoiding. It was our inability to talk about it. As a culturally Japanese household, we were not good at addressing conflict, and we didn't have the skills to have the difficult discussions about what was hurting us. I wouldn't learn about the concept of "negative peace," the absence of open tension at the expense of real peace and harmony, until years later.[8] I didn't realize at that time how hurt and broken I was, but I was a mess. Sometimes the original pain of something doesn't hurt nearly as much as the ways in which that pain goes unacknowledged. Having to bury it and not being able to give words to it can exacerbate it, and having our pain feel invalidated can be one of the most hurtful things we can experience.

Even through these challenges, my mother somehow managed to be the epitome of compassion. Though she was never an activist in the political sense, she was the one who instilled in me the values of compassion and forgiveness. That she managed to transmit those values to me in the midst of the most tumultuous years of her life is a miracle. I've had many great teachers and incredible life experiences, but all of those things only helped to nurture the seeds that were planted in me by my original teacher. So it's only

---

How sad it is that for so many, our educational system beats the passion of learning out of our students.
8. We'll discuss this key concept later in the book on page 56.

right that the first gratitude in these pages goes to my mother, Naoko Hitomi.

IT WAS THE MONKS AND NUNS

May 30, 1998, was a day I will never forget. It was the first day of the Interfaith Pilgrimage of the Middle Passage. I was seventeen years old. Rewind a couple of weeks. I was telling myself I was having fun, living the life. No responsibilities, partying every night. But I knew that inside I was bored, and I was looking for a way out.

At that point in my life, I probably would have taken *any* opportunity to leave town. Had I met a military recruiter, I would have joined the army and gone off to war. Had I met a charismatic cult leader, I would have joined a cult. Had I lived in a city with street gangs, I would have joined a gang. Anyone who reached their hand out to give me a sense of community, purpose, and adventure would have won me over. Luckily, it was the monks and nuns.

Someone had told me about this pilgrimage to retrace the transatlantic slave trade by *walking* from Massachusetts to New Orleans, through the Caribbean and Brazil, then down the coast of Western Africa. It was being organized by the folks at the New England Peace Pagoda, a nearby Japanese Buddhist temple, which belonged to Nipponzan Myohoji, a small offshoot of the Nichiren sect of Buddhism. Members are sometimes considered outcasts in Japan because of their outspoken stances on social issues. They are deeply committed to nonviolence and social change.

Initiated by a white Buddhist nun, Sister Clare Carter, and an African American artist-activist, Ingrid Askew, the vision of the pilgrimage was to uncover the true legacy of slavery, begin a discussion about how it still impacts this country today, and embark on a process of reversing it by walking *from* the United States *back* to Africa. Sister Clare and Ingrid believed that the slave trade and the genocide of the Indigenous peoples of this land are the original sins of this country—sins that have never been healed and therefore the wounds are still open. Racism today is a direct result of those legacies, and until we reconcile ourselves with the history of how the United States came to exist, we will not resolve the challenges we face in our society today.

Being seventeen and never having been involved in activism, I could not begin to comprehend the scale of that vision. My analysis on racism at the time amounted to, "Yeah, racism sucks." But I was bored. Plus, I heard it was a drug- and alcohol-free walk, and I figured it would do me some good to sober up for a while. I planned to join for the first week of walking from the Leverett temple to Boston. Coincidentally, my friend Jacob Singh was also considering joining for the first week. So, we took off for a week. I wouldn't come home for a year and a half.

On the third day of the walk, we were walking towards the Peace Abbey in Sherborn, Massachusetts. We were on a rural country road with the woods to our right and a railroad track running parallel to our path. I was holding a prayer drum and chanting along with the crowd. I looked down at my own feet, with the right foot in front of the left, and at this moment, I knew I was meant to stay on the walk. I talked to Jacob that night, and he told me he had also decided to stay.

Over the next year, Jacob and I became best friends, building the type of bond that only comes from sharing crazy life experiences like walking hundreds of miles with a bunch of crazy monks and nuns, hitchhiking through the Deep South while tripping on acid in between two major interstate highways, and getting stranded overnight in a storm in the Himalayas.[9] We almost died together several times, and yet each time, we were able to laugh through it all. I wouldn't have made it through those experiences without him. Of course, I probably wouldn't have been in those life-threatening situations to begin with if not for him, but still.... At such a pivotal time in my life, when *everything* was changing, it was a blessing to have someone to process with—who would call me on my shit.

9. We were saved by some sheep herders. A story for another book at another time....

Jacob and I participated in the first six months of the walk along with about sixty people who were there more or less that entire time. We were a ragtag bunch. Picture a group of Buddhist monastics wearing bright orange robes drumming and chanting, African Americans holding Pan-African liberation flags, a dozen Japanese followers who could barely speak English and traveled halfway around the world to join the walk, hippies in dreadlocks, church elders in button-up shirts, scruffy war veterans smoking cigarettes at the tail end of the march, a bunch of college kids, and a few teenagers scattered about walking through your town. We turned heads everywhere we walked.

To this day, it is still one of the most diverse communities I have ever been a part of. On any given day, we would walk 10-20 miles, sleeping on church pews and gymnasium floors. We walked to the sites of slave rebellions, plantations, lynching trees, and prisons. Most nights, the local community would host and feed us. We chanted a lot. We cried a lot. We laughed a lot. We ate a lot of fried chicken. We popped a lot of blisters. And we argued. *A lot.* Here we were: sixty tired, sweaty, and smelly people, uncovering the legacy of one of the worst forms of systemic, institutionalized violence to ever take place in our world. Some days, we simply didn't have the capacity to take it in. So we took it out on each other.

Though the walk remains the greatest and most impactful experience of my life, it wouldn't serve anyone to romanticize it. There is nothing fun about learning the legacy of slavery in such a deeply embodied way. This was not an academic experiment, but a brutal spiritual pilgrimage attempting to purge the country from this ugly legacy.

Between the forgings of some lifelong friendships, we would argue with each other for hours. One night, I remember a meeting where we screamed at each other for four hours about whether or not to carry an American flag that was printed in the Pan-African liberation colors of red, black, and green—a gift given to us by a local African American artist. But before we began *that* meeting, we got in a heated debate about whether or not to move a desk that was in the middle of the room. The argument about the desk got so heated that people left in tears.

We were all holding a lot, and some of our debates got unspeakably heated and painful. We were all committed to the idea of racial healing, but we did not have the skills to carry out such a massive undertaking. It was one of my earliest lessons about the importance of training. *Desire and will alone cannot bring about the changes that we need.* We need training and skill.

Some of our arguments were about race. Other times it was about the food. But ultimately, they were all about us trying to heal the pain of generations. It was on this walk that I first learned that violence of that magnitude passes on unspeakable trauma for generations. It was on this walk that I began to understand the concept of intergenerational trauma, even before I heard that exact framing. As a young person brand new to this work, it was hard for me to understand intellectually why our arguments were getting so escalated. I could feel in my body that the pain being spoken was not ours alone.

> **Desire and will alone cannot bring about the changes that we need. We need training and skill.**

We held a healing circle at the site of a slave rebellion where dozens of Africans had been slaughtered. I heard their pain screaming through their descendants who were with us. It was a pain deeper than anything I had ever heard. It hit me for the first time in that moment that people *benefitted*—and still benefit to this day—from that level of violence. It broke me. In that circle, I cried in public for the first time since I was a kid.

The blisters on our feet were nothing compared to the open wounds in the soul of this nation. Generations upon generations of human trafficking, enslavement, torture, cultural genocide, families being ripped apart, and slaughter—all in the name of profit. That is what this country needs to heal from.

While I was too busy that day trying not to choke on my own

tears to articulate it, I realized that nonviolence is not only about refusing to shoot somebody. A commitment to nonviolence means a commitment to heal the open wounds in our hearts, our families, our communities, and our world. As the walk approached New Orleans, interpersonal dynamics had splintered the group. Most of the people I had become close with were leaving, so rather than continue on for the African leg of the journey, I decided to end my pilgrimage in New Orleans. I had also begun to question my role in a pilgrimage that was focused on the legacy of the Middle Passage. *What's the role of an immigrant Japanese teenager in all of this?*

I wasn't going to Africa, but I couldn't go home. It had just been six short months, and I wasn't ready. I knew that if I went back, I'd start hanging out with the same group of friends, and I would quickly fall back into the same aimless, depressing, and self-destructive patterns. I felt scared and lost. Again.

As the end of the walk approached, the anxiety of not knowing what I was going to do next was killing me. So why not help speed up the process? I went outside of the small church we were staying at in rural Mississippi and chain-smoked more cigarettes than I had ever smoked in my life. I wasn't keeping count, but I remember that at some point I ran out, so I went back inside to grab another pack, and by the time I went back inside again the second pack was nearly empty.

Afterward, I was sitting in a chair in the middle of the hall where we were sleeping with my head in my hands. *What am I gonna do?* I asked myself. The moment I asked myself that question, Jun-san, a very well-respected Japanese nun from the order, approached me with an offer.

"Kazu-san, after New Orleans, I go to temple in Lumbini, Nepal, where Buddha born. We build big temple there, biggest peace pagoda in the world. You want come with me?"

The following day, I got a one-way ticket to Kathmandu. I didn't know where Nepal was, what language they spoke there, or what I would be doing when I got there, but I knew it was where I was meant to be. I spent the next year living in Nipponzan Myohoji's temples throughout Nepal, India, and Sri Lanka, as well as taking a month-long peace walk through Cambodia with the Buddhist order there. Jun-san became like a second mother to me, though much stricter than my own. She is another person to whom I am deeply indebted. In addition to giving me the opportunity to travel through Asia, knowing her has allowed me to participate in many other life-changing projects, including a walking pilgrimage to Big Mountain years later.[10] I spent the majority of my time—about four months—based in Lumbini. Our days looked like this:

Prayer 5 a.m.–7 a.m.
Breakfast 7 a.m.–8 a.m.
Construction work 9 a.m.–5 p.m.
Prayer 5 p.m.–7 p.m.
Dinner 7 p.m.–8 p.m.
In bed 10 p.m.

Seven days a week.

Construction meant picking up a plate of wet concrete, putting it on a cushion on our heads, carrying it up two flights of stairs, dumping it, and going back down for another plate. Seven days a week, breakfast consisted of dried rice cereal with honey and a piece of chapati, a simple flat bread. Lunch *and* dinner were rice, a simple dal, potato, and cauliflower curry. If we were lucky, we would get an onion. How I looked forward to those onions!

I sometimes joke that life in a monastery is not unlike being in a prison labor camp.[11] The rigid schedules, the strict environment,

---

10. Big Mountain is on the Black Mesa in Arizona. It is sacred land to both the Diné (Navajo) and Hopi peoples. It is also the largest coal deposit in North America. Traditional families who live on that land have been fighting the coal industry for years.

11. Obviously, I *chose* to live in monastery, which is the major distinction. As someone who has some idea of the horror of prisons from my work, I never want to undermine the violence of incarceration.

the hard work, the discipline, the social solitary. And yet, that is the place where I found liberation. I had never felt more free. I'm not saying I want to go back to that lifestyle, but at that time, it's exactly what I needed. When you don't have to make any decisions throughout the day, you're completely free to simply ... be. Monastic life is not for everyone. But for me, at that period in my life, it saved me.

To all the monks and nuns who taught me to be free, thank you. As I didn't go on to college afterward, I always consider that year and a half to be my "higher education." While formal education certainly has value, I am reminded of the Mark Twain quote, "Don't let schooling interfere with your education."[12] I am proud of the education I have received in my life, despite not having any letters after my name beyond my GED.[13] I had planned to stay in Asia continuing my spiritual path for the remainder of my life, but my mom wasn't having it. My green card was about to expire, and if I stayed outside the United States for more than a year, I would lose what my mom had gone through hell to get for us. I was still young and didn't comprehend what this meant to her. I didn't care about a green card. I wanted to stay, but after some hard thinking, I came back to the United States 364 days after I left, one week after my nineteenth birthday.[14] My plan was to come home, see my friends and family, and make some money so I could go back to Asia. Before I knew it, I had a car, a job, an apartment, a girlfriend, a dog, and a garden.... Twenty years later, I have not been back to Nepal.

---

12. I still sometimes dream of going to college and getting a degree.
13. A General Education Diploma is a high school equivalency certificate for those who did not complete high school. Not being in school allowed me to have a wealth of experiences that no amount of school loans could have given me. My GED is a Global Educational Degree, and I am grateful and wear it proudly.
14. I was trying to get out of my trip at the very last minute. I still remember the customs agent looking at me like I was crazy. "What if you had missed your flight?" he asked.

INTRODUCTION TO ACTIVISM

I didn't go back to my old life either. Instead, I got into activism. I joined the Prison Book Project, a volunteer-run project that sends free books to people behind bars. I became involved in the movement to support political prisoner Mumia Abu-Jamal and got arrested in my first act of civil disobedience in Washington, D.C. The group that I was arrested with became a permanent affinity group called Mass Resist, and we organized together for a couple of years to support Leonard Peltier, Shaka Sankofa, and other political prisoners.

In the fall of 1999, I participated in a weeklong fasting ceremony outside of Abu-Jamal's prison outside of a small town in Pennsylvania with Jun-san. One morning, a group of youth from the Bruderhof community came to support us.[15] I had heard on the news earlier that there had been some riots in Seattle the night before.

"Those weren't riots," they said, "They were peaceful protesters being attacked by the police. The media is spinning it and blaming the protesters, but they were all being peaceful!"

Like most people at the time, I had never heard of the World Trade Organization prior to the WTO protests being on the news.[16] After the fast was over, I dug into its history and got deeply involved in the anti-globalization movement of the late 1990s and early 2000s.

Following the events in Seattle, the next large mobilization was during the meetings of the International Monetary Fund and World Bank in Washington, D.C. Working with a group of mostly student activists, we took several busloads of people to

15. The Bruderhof is a Christian movement that lives in intentional community and practices nonviolence. One of their communities was near the prison where Abu-Jamal was held in the late 1990s, and one of their elders served as his spiritual advisor.

16. The protests that shut down the WTO meeting on November 30th of 1999 launched the anti-globalization movement into national consciousness. For many activists of my generation, this movement was where we cut our teeth as we learned about the complexity of international trade and finance, as well as the thrills and challenges of mass mobilizations.

D.C.[17] The months leading up to April 16, 2000, or "A16," was my first time being involved in a mass mobilization. This was also the first time I began facilitating nonviolence trainings. I laugh about it now, how a group of fairly inexperienced activists were able to mobilize several hundred people from our little area of western Massachusetts. We had no idea what we were doing, but we pulled off training, transporting, housing, and offering logistics support for the largest group I've ever helped to organize.

A16 was a turning point. It was the first time I had ever been in the streets with tens of thousands of people. There were so many people downtown that we had taken over the streets. I remember blockading an intersection with about twenty people, staring down a row of police in riot gear. A major march of thousands that had been walking past us stopped to stand in solidarity behind our line. It was exhilarating. As exhausted as I was after going days without sleep, these were some of the most inspiring and empowering moments of my young activist life. I'm blessed to still be in community with people like Paul Engler, Kai Newkirk, and others who were in that small circle of young activists.[18]

Around the height of the anti-globalization movement, I met another person who became a key figure in my life. Jo Comerford was, at the time, the coordinator for the local chapter for the American Friends Service Committee (AFSC). She was one of the first people to see something in me and put me in real leadership positions. I was ultimately named clerk of that chapter of the AFSC and would work with Jo on many different projects. There were times I was scared out of my mind about the positions she would put me in (talking to the media, facilitating meetings, representing AFSC at different events), but I am so grateful for the faith she had in me. Jo was one of the first models I saw of servant leadership,

---

17. Most people at the time assumed that I was also a student because of my age and the fact that I spent most of my time organizing on college campuses.
18. Shout-out to Paul and his brother Mark Engler's book, *This Is an Uprising*. A must-read for any activist.

an example I still try (and fail) to live up to today.

All of this work eventually led to my employment at a small public foundation called the Peace Development Fund (PDF). I started as a temp doing data entry in January of 2002 and left ten years later as the program director. As a funder, PDF was unique in that we grappled with questions like, "How do we build relationships with our grantees that aren't based on the money we give away?" and "What does it mean for a funder to actually share power with its grantees?" We worked with groups from the most marginalized communities in the country. This meant I had the privilege of witnessing the founding of the first national movement of formerly incarcerated peoples, All of Us or None, from the ground floor. It meant that I consider some of the founders of this country's environmental justice movement as my mentors. It meant that I was able to build relationships with grassroots leaders from across the country, relationships that have lasted to this day.

I learned and grew a ton in my ten years at PDF, learning from elders like executive director Paul Haible and board chair/spiritual grandmother Teresa Juarez. I learned the importance of centering relationship in organizing. I learned the ins and outs of the world of philanthropy, including many of its pitfalls. I learned about the importance of honoring our elders and empowering our youth. It was an education that no college degree could ever give me.

In addition to all these life lessons, PDF gave me an opportunity to move to California in 2006. I was ready for another change in my life, and I had heard rumors that California doesn't really have winters. So, I packed my car, loaded up my black lab terrier, and drove west.[19] Toward the end of my time at PDF, we entered into a partnership with movement elder Harry Belafonte and his organization, The Gathering for Justice. The Gathering, for me, was yet another game changer.

Mr. Belafonte, or "Mr. B," as he is lovingly known by those around him, started The Gathering after watching a news story about a

19. RIP to the faithful Ebony....

four-year-old girl getting handcuffed and arrested for being unruly in kindergarten. The project was a national effort to bring communities together to end child incarceration. Mr. B began by hosting a gathering of African American youth and elders in the South, white communities in Appalachia, Indigenous communities on Onondaga land, Latino communities in Northern California, and Asian and Pacific Islander communities in Southern California. All of this was leading up to a national convention to be held in Oakland, California, for which I played the role of convention coordinator.

What followed were months of conference calls and very little sleep, culminating in a gathering of close to one thousand young people from around the country. I will never forget that weekend and the sleepless nights I shared with the team of Malia Lazu, Carmen Perez, and Jonathan "Globe" Lewis. By the time it was over, I was delusional and running on pure adrenaline. I collapsed into my mentor's arms in tears in the hotel lobby. We had pulled it off! While organizing such a gathering was in and of itself an unforgettable experience, it was what happened later on, when I was a member of The Gathering's executive committee, which changed my life again and set me on a course to eventually write this book.

KINGIAN NONVIOLENCE

The Gathering had adopted a philosophy and training methodology called Kingian Nonviolence Conflict Reconciliation as one of its main programmatic offerings as well as its core organizing strategy. Carmen, then the Gathering's national director of organizing, and Jonathan, our national director of nonviolence training, traveled around the country offering this training to local communities. The first two-day workshop in Kingian Nonviolence held in Oakland was hosted in October 2008 at the Intertribal Friendship House, a historic site filled with the stories of Indigenous communities throughout the San Francisco Bay Area.[20] As a

20. The San Francisco Bay Area was one of the sites of the forced relocation

member of The Gathering's executive committee, I felt obligated to check it out. I was one of only six participants.

This training helped me to realize everything that was missing in the nonviolence trainings that I had been conducting earlier in my life. In just two days, this workshop changed the ways I viewed nonviolence, violence, conflict, and social change. Forever. While I have learned—and continue to learn—a great deal about social change and conflict reconciliation, Kingian Nonviolence still remains the foundation, the lens through which I view the world. If such things as civil disobedience, nonviolent communication, restorative justice, community organizing, and various healing modalities are tools for the tool belt, then Kingian Nonviolence is the belt itself.

Many people have contributed to my understanding of Kingian Nonviolence, not least of all Dr. Bernard LaFayette Jr. and David C. Jehnsen, the curriculum's two coauthors. But no single person contributed more in my development as a trainer and practitioner of Kingian Nonviolence than Jonathan Lewis, who led that fateful Oakland workshop. Since both Jonathan and Carmen were staying at my house that weekend, I stayed up until 2 a.m. after the first day of the workshop picking Jonathan's brain about this philosophy. He and I went on to become the closest of friends. He eventually helped me become a trainer, and we traveled the country together for the next couple of years planting the seeds of nonviolence.

---

programs of the 1950s that forced Native peoples from all over the country to move to urban centers to "assimilate," another word for cultural genocide. The Friendship House opened their doors to serve the needs of those families. Historic events like the occupation of Alcatraz Island and the original Longest Walk were largely organized out of this space. In addition to political organizing, the House hosted weddings, birthing ceremonies, community celebrations, and memorial services. I spent a period of time on its development committee, and I used to refer to it as the "living room of the Bay Area Indigenous community." It is one of the treasures of the Bay Area.

THE LIFE OF OSCAR GRANT

I was at my mom's house watching the news the morning of New Year's Day 2009. On the news ticker across the bottom of the screen I saw, "Transit passenger shot and killed by police in Oakland, CA." I remember thinking, "Shit, another one...." Even in the pre–Black Lives Matter period before the proliferation of mobile devices, police shootings in Oakland were not unheard of. I didn't realize then how different this one would be.

I got a text message a few hours later from Malia Lazu, The Gathering's executive director. This was followed up by a phone call. "Hold on, I'm gonna conference you in with Tshaka," she said. Tshaka was another member of The Gathering's executive committee who also lived in Oakland.

Tshaka jumped on the call. "Yo, did you see the video?"

His name was Oscar Grant. A twenty-two-year-old African American father who had been out celebrating New Year's Eve with his friends in San Francisco. On their way home, there was an altercation on the BART train.[21] The police were called. When the train reached Fruitvale Station, BART police pulled Grant and his friends off the train and sat them down on the station platform.

Future investigations showed that the BART police were poorly trained, did not follow their own procedures, and contributed to escalating the situation. Chaos ensued. Everyone was yelling, including the police who were screaming out commands along with racial epithets. Grant found himself being held on the ground by an officer.

At that point, BART police officer Johannes Mehserle, himself only twenty-six years old and a recent father, stood over Grant and shot him in the back. Grant died in the hospital hours later. As gruesome as this was, it was no more horrifying than the untold number of police killings of unarmed Black men that happens

21. Bay Area Rapid Transit, the regional train system.

frequently in the United States.[22] The difference was that, for the first time, this shooting was captured on camera.

Grant's death touched a nerve in Oakland. I've never felt the emotions of a city like I did in Oakland for the next six months. You couldn't be in Oakland and not feel it. There have been an outrageous number of similar videos that have surfaced since then, but this was raw. Those emotions came pouring out into the streets and into community meetings and town halls. Hundreds attended organizing meetings, and thousands showed up to rallies. I joined the steering committee of CAPE, the Coalition Against Police Executions, and devoted the first six months of 2009 to this struggle.

The Kingian Nonviolence workshop just two months prior sparked my intellectual curiosity and commitment to nonviolence. But these six months deepened that commitment to the core of my being. It was through this campaign that I became a practitioner of nonviolence. Of course, at the time, I was only a white belt practitioner, a beginner. I had only just taken an introductory workshop in what I realized was a lifelong practice. I could feel the need for nonviolence in my heart, but I couldn't articulate it with my tongue. I tried, and ended up becoming an inarticulate advocate for nonviolence and an unpopular voice in some circles within the movement.

I remember a suggestion made at one community meeting that we print posters of Mehserle's face with a bullseye over it for an upcoming protest. I remember feeling something in the deepest pit of my gut and raised my hand to respond. I remember saying something along the lines of not believing that Mehserle woke up that morning wanting to kill somebody—he's not sitting around somewhere happy about what he did. I remember the chorus of boos as those words stumbled out of my mouth.

---

22. A 2014 study by the Malcolm X Grassroots Movement showed that in 2012 a Black person was killed by police, private security, or vigilante every twenty-eight hours in this country. Every incident is documented in the report, available at www.operationghettostorm.org.

I was surprised. I had never been booed like that. I wasn't sure how to feel. It would not be the last time I was booed for advocating for nonviolence, but each time, it only deepened my resolve to better articulate what I felt in my heart. How could I communicate to a community that has suffered so much that we needed to see the humanity of Mehserle? How could I explain that the more we direct our anger at Mehserle, the more we are letting *the system* off the hook? How could I communicate all this while centering the life of Grant?

At times I felt guilty that I didn't have more hatred in my heart for Mehserle. I almost felt obligated to hate him. But I remember one day receiving a call from Dereca Blackmon, one of the leaders of the movement. She had just come out of a court hearing for Mehserle. I remember her telling me, "I was in court looking at his face, and I realized … that I don't hate him!"

She probably has no idea what an important call that was for me to receive in that moment. It made me feel like I wasn't crazy, or at least that I wasn't alone in my craziness. One of the biggest lessons I learned in those six months was that while anger can be a powerful force to spark movements, it cannot sustain them. If we try to fuel our movements with anger, it will eventually burn us out from the inside. Anger alone is not sustainable fuel.

During this campaign, I reread Dr. King's famous "Pilgrimage to Nonviolence," and this quote stuck out to me: "The nonviolent resister not only refuses to shoot his opponent, but he also refuses to hate him." This reminded me of another quote of his: "I have decided to stick with love…. Hate is too great a burden to bear." These two quotes were central in my committing to nonviolence at that time.

While anger can be a powerful force to spark movements, it cannot sustain them.

CERTIFIED

I knew I needed to learn more. The gap between what I felt in my heart to be true and the chorus of boos I was hearing at those community meetings made that clear. I still remember countless meetings trying to convince CAPE's steering committee to study Kingian Nonviolence, the committee asking me why, and not being able to explain it to them.

So that summer, I traveled to the University of Rhode Island's Center for Nonviolence and Peace Studies and immersed myself in a one-hundred-hour certification training in Kingian Nonviolence. Those two weeks were some of the best times of my life. I will never forget how much more sleep I could have gotten if not for the unforgettable late nights I shared with people like Jonathan, Lori LeChien, Tiffany Childress-Price, and Nick Katkevich.

This is where I first met Dr. Bernard LaFayette Jr., or "Doc" as everyone calls him. He has also been called a national treasure, and I quickly found out why. Doc got his start in the Civil Rights movement as one of the leaders of the Nashville Sit-Ins. He went on to become one of the cofounders of SNCC, a senior staff member of the Southern Christian Leadership Conference (SCLC), one of the early organizers in Selma, and national coordinator for the Poor People's Campaign. One of the great honors in my life has been to study, work, and train alongside him. How many of us get to hear countless stories that begin with, "Well, this one time I was having dinner with Dr. King and...."

A team of senior trainers (shout-out to Paul Bueno de Mesquita and Rich Tarlian, who showed me that a different way to do policing is possible) led the sessions during the day, and we would spend most evenings with Doc. I filled up notebooks transcribing every word that came out of his mouth. His teachings felt that valuable and insightful. I had never understood nonviolence to be as deep as a philosophy and so thoughtful as a strategy.

Carmen and Malia had driven down to join us for the celebration. I remember driving with them to a celebratory dinner after our graduation ceremony, where we had received our certificates officially branding us "Level I Kingian Nonviolence Trainers." As a high-school dropout, it was the first time I'd ever received a piece of paper formally announcing that I knew something.

"So how do you feel?" Carmen asked from the backseat. I thought about it, and one word came to mind.

"Certified."

After coming back from the University of Rhode Island, I was gung ho to change the world. I set out to organize as many trainings as I could. Joanna Macy, an elder in Buddhist and environmental circles, gave me, along with my friend Arthur Romano, my first opportunity to present during one of her workshops.[23] I've never prepared so hard for a ninety-minute presentation.

This was followed by a series of short presentations all over Northern California. My first several two-day workshops involved a ton of one-on-one outreach. I basically bought a cup of coffee for everyone I knew, begging them to come, promising them it would change the world. I was still figuring out the marketing side of things. As much as I loved my job at PDF, and as much as I grew from my time there, it began to feel more and more like employment. It was where I rented my time to earn a paycheck. I knew that I needed to pursue nonviolence full time.

I decided to go back to school. Or rather, I decided to go *to* school. I had not been in a classroom since I was fifteen years old. Everything was pointing me to the University of Rhode Island and its Center for Nonviolence and Peace Studies. I had begun to make arrangements. I worked to get over my insecurities about being a thirty-year-old college freshman. I even got as far as looking for housing in Rhode Island. I dreaded the winters, but at least I'd (a) be near Dunkin' Donuts and (b) be surrounded by Celtics fans.

Then, my best-laid plans were occupied by a group of activists camping out in New York City's Zuccotti Park. Like many movements, Occupy Wall Street started out small. I was in Massachusetts

---

23. I would later go on to receive training from Joanna directly and become a trainer for her curriculum, the Work That Reconnects. Another great honor in my life.

for a series of meetings when it started, and I was keeping an eye on it every morning. September 29, 2011, was the day I realized that Occupy was going to be big. That was the day United Airlines pilots went to the park in full uniform to show their solidarity. That was the moment that it became more than a bunch of radical activists protesting corporate power.

From 3,000 miles away, I began hearing that my community of activists in Oakland were planning our own Occupy encampment. On October 10, the same day I flew back home to Oakland, Occupy Oakland was born. Thinking back, I can still feel the excitement in the air on the first night of camp as I walked through what became renamed as Oscar Grant Plaza.[24] I had never been to a rally without big name speakers. There was simply a large crowd and a megaphone being passed around. The seeds of a "leader-full" movement were being planted right on the corner of Fourteenth and Broadway.

There were only a few tents at first, but over time Occupy Oakland became one of the largest Occupy encampments in the country. We organized multiple mobilizations, including the country's first general strike in decades.[25] It was beautiful. Occupy Oakland wasn't just an act of resistance. It was a celebration. Without anyone's permission, we built the world we wanted to live in, right there in front of City Hall. Our camp had kitchens, a free library, a school, bicycle-powered electricity, a children's area, a holistic healing center, and an interfaith tent. It was also a mess. There

---

24. This was one of many controversies within Occupy Oakland. "Oscar Grant Plaza" was a name given to the site that is officially known as Frank Ogawa Plaza. Frank Ogawa was a Japanese American activist and former city council member who was interned with his family during the war and fought for racial justice. Members of Occupy Oakland renamed the plaza not knowing the significance of who Ogawa was and not having had any conversations with the local Asian American community. Ironic and sad that a movement named "Occupy" would unilaterally change the name of a local park without knowing its full history.

25. A general strike is a labor strike with participation from people in all sectors of society. The last general strike, fittingly, also happened in Oakland in 1946.

was rain and mud, arguments over drug use, endless debates over tactics, arguments over the name (Occupy vs. Decolonize), and an abundance of personal conflicts and ugly arguments on Facebook.[26] But through it all, Occupy was perhaps the most jubilant form of resistance I had ever seen. I learned then that you can't inspire a movement simply by talking about all the things you're opposed to. You have to show people an alternative to the status quo and inspire hope in people. The early days of Occupy did that.

I remember the night that the camp was evicted (the first time). It was the night Scott Olsen was shot. Olsen was an Iraq War veteran and an activist with Veterans for Peace. He was at the encampment when police shot him in the head with a lead-filled beanbag, fracturing his skull. This incident is what catalyzed the decision to organize a general strike a week later, which would become the height of Occupy Oakland and the largest mobilization during its run.

When we recaptured the camp, I saw on social media that activists had reclaimed the Plaza, and there was to be a celebratory gathering. I ran to the Plaza as soon as I could. When I got there, I saw only about a dozen people milling about. I was heartbroken. I thought I must have missed the celebration. As I turned to go home, a march of what must have been a thousand people walked right past me. I joined them as we marched throughout the city in jubilant celebration. I will never forget marching past an apartment building where a couple of people were cheering us on from their fourth-floor balcony. The entire march stopped and began chanting, "Join us! Join us! Join us!" I was brought to tears when I saw them run in to join us outside.[27] After what had been a somewhat slow start in my effort to introduce Kingian·

---

26. Social media, by the way, is a *terrible* place to try to resolve conflicts. I am convinced that this contributed greatly to the demise of Occupy.

27. I bought a camera when I realized we were witnessing history. I documented this moment, and much of what I experienced at Occupy, on video. This exact moment, worth watching, is at 2:53 of the video titled "Occupy Oakland Victory Parade," available at youtu.be/opM22oaOxlo.

Nonviolence to Northern California, interest in the training exploded with the emergence of the Occupy movement. At one point, Jonathan was living on my couch as we facilitated two-day workshops every weekend. We were literally turning people away and could not keep up with the demand. We had also established a working relationship with staff at the San Bruno jail during the same time period. The staff, as well as the men inside, had fallen in love with the training. There were times Jonathan and I would facilitate workshops in the jail Monday and Tuesday, go back to facilitate another workshop on Thursday and Friday, and then facilitate a workshop for Occupy activists on Saturday and Sunday. Sometimes this schedule lasted weeks at a time.

I realized then that I could not leave Oakland for Rhode Island to go to school. I had spent so much time trying to create momentum around Kingian Nonviolence, and now there was no way I could leave. While I decided not to go to school to further my study of nonviolence in a formal setting, these years were critical in deepening my commitment and understanding. Not only because of the countless trainings I was able to lead, the conversations I had with similar minds, or the experience of organizing on the ground, but because of the countless, oftentimes heated but just as often loving conversations I had with anarchists and many others who opposed my views. It was humbling to learn that I could build deep, meaningful relationships with those that I ardently disagreed with. I will always be grateful for the hours of endless debates I had with people like Bettina Escauriza and Gen Lamont D'Belle, even though neither of you will probably ever read this book, LOL.

As others have said more articulately than I can, Occupy was far from a failure. Not only did it inspire an entire generation of activists, but it was largely because of Occupy that people in relatively mainstream spaces began to openly challenge the idea of unbridled capitalism. That is a *major* cultural shift, the impact of which is hard to measure. The lessons that we learned and the relationships we forged are alive in so many of today's communities, organizations, and movements. The work I've been able to do since then, much of which is captured in this book, is a result of that time.

At the time, all of our nonviolence workshops in Oakland were being hosted free of charge by the East Bay Meditation Center (EBMC), a center known as one of the most diverse meditation communities in the world. After spending so much time there teaching nonviolence, I decided to check out one of their workshops: "Beginning a Meditation Practice." The course was led by Mushim Ikeda-Nash, an early attendee of one of our nonviolence workshops. Mushim has since become the most significant figure in my path in meditation, one of the biggest cheerleaders for my work, and someone I am honored to call a friend.

Another early participant in one of the workshops hosted by EBMC was Chris Moore-Backman, a Gandhian nonviolence trainer and author of the book *The Gandhian Iceberg*.[28] He came to our workshop, and Jonathan and I went to his. We have been collaborating ever since, and I am now humbled, honored, and privileged to sit with him every day and call him my friend and colleague.

EAST POINT PEACE ACADEMY

After several months of riding the wave of Occupy, I decided in the summer of 2013 to start my own organization. There was simply nothing else I wanted to do more with my life, and I no longer wanted to compromise. I was all in.

The idea of the East Point Peace Academy—a counterpoint to the Military Academy at West Point—has been bouncing around the Kingian world for years, but no one had formalized it.[29] There is a scene in the documentary *A Force More Powerful* in which Dr. LaFayette is reminiscing on the intensive trainings they received in preparation for the Nashville Sit-Ins.[30]

---

28. A book I *highly* recommend.
29. East Point is based on the West Coast, but this works out since West Point is actually on the East Coast.
30. More on this later.

"We were warriors," he remembers. "We had been prepared. This was like a nonviolent academy, equivalent to West Point."

Equivalent to West Point.

There have been no shortages of moments in my life where I've been in community with people who were deeply committed to fundamental social transformation. There have been moments where our movements have captured the imagination of the entire nation. Yet none of them led to the types of changes that I longed for. I began to wonder if part of our problem was a lack of training and preparation.

We held a workshop once inside a unit in a county jail that exclusively housed war veterans. One of them told us that no matter what background they came from, each one of them had to go through a boot camp that lasted at least six months before being sent off to war. The military invests heavily in training and in preparing their troops to use violence effectively. Yet in many of my own experiences with movement work, we were trying to bring about fundamental shifts in society but only asking people to show up for a two-hour workshop the day before an action. I began to see how unprepared we were for building the type of movement that I dreamt of.

I called Theresa Guy Moran, one of the people who came through our workshops during the height of the Occupy movement. A lawyer-in-recovery who at the time was leading forgiveness workshops, but didn't take shit from anybody, her first words to me after the workshop were, "So, how can I help?" We schemed together and a couple of months later organized our first public visioning meeting to launch this little experiment we call the East Point Peace Academy.

It has been an amazing, humbling thing, watching our work grow. I still remember sitting down for lunch with Leah Pearlman, founder and author of *Dharma Comics*, and being blown away by her belief in my work and her commitment to supporting it. This bewilderment continues to this day, as Leah's support has been instrumental not only in building East Point but in helping to write this book. I will never be able to fully convey the depth of my appreciation to her.

I have learned over time that nonprofit organizations are typically built on traditional, corporate models that only perpetuate systems of hierarchy and domination.[31] Even if our mission is to undo those systems, without creating intentional and alternative structures that allow us to practice operating differently, we inevitably revert back to the same ways of relating to each other that got us into this mess. So, the work of East Point is not just about the *what*, but equally about the *how*. As an organization committed to building a new way of being in the world, we are experimenting with a 250-year work plan: not having job titles or job descriptions; practicing full financial transparency; counting vacations, family time, meditation retreats, and self-care as work hours; committing to offering all of our programs on a gift economy basis and never charging a dime; not accepting funds from most traditional sources of nonprofit funding (including most foundations); and, most important, placing relationships above all else.

Much of the *what* of our work happens inside California's prisons and county jails. I've always had the belief that if we are to build a culture of peace, the voices of those most directly impacted by violence has to be in leadership. I am proud to have worked with close to a hundred incarcerated men who have dedicated themselves to the long process of becoming Kingian Nonviolence trainers and have learned from them as they have exposed thousands more incarcerated people to this philosophy. No one understands the impact of violence better, no one understands what their communities need more, and no one has a bigger stake than the people I've met inside these institutions.

I remember one of the first times walking into a prison in California. It was through the invitation of Barrios Unidos founder

31. I would recommend books like *The Revolution Will Not Be Funded* and *Reinventing Organizations* for more on this theme—see Resources for details.

Daniel "Nane" Alejandrez, someone I met during my time at the Peace Development Fund and someone who has gone on to become a mentor in my work. Nane is a pioneer in the fields of prison programming and gang intervention. He has blazed the trail for so many of us who work inside the system.

I remember watching him walk down the long corridor of the prison as each person—incarcerated men *and* prison guards—approached him with a smile and a greeting. They were all genuinely happy to see him. I remember admiring so much the type of person you would need to be to earn that level of respect from everyone in the prison. I've been trying to follow in those footsteps ever since.

Working in prisons and jails is a privilege and an honor that I do not take lightly. It's a strange thing, really, to go inside and receive so much gratitude from incarcerated people about coming in and running programs. I understand, of course, and accept their gratitude with humility, but I wonder if they can ever understand how much I've learned from them and how healing it has been for me to be in their presence. After several years of working inside the system, it was through meeting Sonya Shah, founder of the Ahimsa Collective, that I truly understood what restorative justice is and the depth of healing that is possible.

To hear the stories of people who have been through so much trauma, witness remarkable levels of transparency and accountability from those who have committed unspeakable harm, meet people who have been branded as the "worst of the worst," and learn that these same people are some of the most compassionate, dedicated peacemakers I have ever met, gives me so much faith in our resilience as a species. I go inside to be inspired about the nature of humanity. I won't list the names of those behind bars, but if you are reading this, know that I am eternally grateful for your wisdom, your commitment to peace, and the stories you have shared with me.

COLLECTIVE, INTERGENERATIONAL WISDOM

There is a concept in psychiatry called "cryptomnesia," which describes two very common and closely related phenomena. The first is when a forgotten memory resurfaces into your conscious mind without any awareness on your part that it is an old memory. It appears as a fresh, brand-new idea that you had never previously thought of before. The second is remembering an idea, a story, or an experience that you heard from someone else but remembering it as if it was your own. It is a common phenomenon that we experience all the time.

As much as I have tried my best to give credit to all of those from whom I have learned, I am sure that much of what I write here is some form of cryptomnesia. This is not an excuse for plagiarism. It is an acknowledgment that none of this is ultimately "my" wisdom. These stories, lessons, and teachings have been gathered, collected, harvested, passed down, recycled, and composted over generations and generations of our species struggling for liberation. It is wisdom that has come to me from explicit teachings I've been given, implicit lessons that were passed down, conversations I've overheard, and interactions I've witnessed. I've soaked it in from books I've read, movies I've watched, and cultural practices and traditions that have been passed down for thousands of years by my ancestors. It has been in the air I breathe and embedded in my DNA over millennia. It is intergenerational cryptomnesia.

People talk about the idea of intergenerational trauma: that trauma can be passed down from generation to generation through child-rearing practices, cultural traditions, and more. Recent studies have even shown that trauma can alter our genetic makeup, and that it can be passed down to future generations attached to our DNA.[32] If we carry intergenerational trauma, then we also carry intergenerational wisdom. Like the trauma that has been passed down from our ancestors, their wisdom and resiliency is also embedded in our genes and in our DNA.

32. Professor Joy DeGruy's seminal book *Post Traumatic Slave Syndrome*

Being part of the community around Kingian Nonviolence has made me realize the importance of legacy, which in turn has helped me to understand how wisdom is passed down from generations. We stand on the shoulders of all those that came before us. We are all on this journey, this legacy that has been building since the beginning of time. So it would be amiss for me to not honor and offer gratitude to all of our collective ancestors. We are because they were. Ultimately, it is their wisdom that lies on these pages. That is what I mean when I say that there is nothing new in this book.

If we carry intergenerational trauma, then we also carry intergenerational wisdom.

It wasn't always easy for our ancestors, and it hasn't always been easy for me. There have been so many movements I have been a part of where I was convinced that we were on the verge of a worldwide revolution. So many organizations and formations of people that I was convinced were *the one*, the ones that I would work with for the rest of my life to change the world. And each time it didn't happen, I was heartbroken.

I've had so many movement heartbreaks that it would surprise nobody if I became cynical and became scared of committing to this work. I am no longer in touch with many of the people I've mentioned throughout this book. Some have simply drifted away, while others left with a bang. But here I am. The way my path has been laid out—I know nothing else. That said, I am here out of

---

introduced me to the concept of intergenerational trauma. Since the book's release, multiple studies in epigenetics have shown scientific evidence of this. In 2013, neurobiologists Brian Dias and Kerry Ressler published a study in which they made mice fear the smell of cherries by shocking them with electricity every time they were exposed to the scent. They found that the children and grandchildren of these mice—even if they had never been exposed to the smell of cherries themselves—were born with a fear of the smell. Later studies by Rachel Yehuda and Amy Lehrner showed the intergenerational impacts of trauma on descendants of the Holocaust, and Dora L. Costa, Noelle Yetter, and Heather DeSomer's study showed similar impacts on descendants of prisoners of war of the US Civil War.

choice. I choose this path, because as much as I know there will be more heartbreaks to come, this has been the most fulfilling life I know.

A King's Final Orders

The story of Kingian Nonviolence, as it was passed down to me by Dr. Bernard LaFayette Jr., begins on the morning of April 4, 1968, at the Lorraine Motel in Memphis, Tennessee. Dr. King was in town to support the city's sanitation workers in their ongoing labor dispute with the city. Dr. LaFayette was there helping Dr. King organize the Poor People's Campaign, the last campaign that Dr. King would help organize.

As Dr. LaFayette was leaving Dr. King's motel room to head to the airport, Dr. King called out to him.

"You know Bernard, the next movement that we need to start is a movement to institutionalize and internationalize nonviolence."

Dr. LaFayette says that he didn't quite understand what Dr. King meant by that, but he had a flight to catch, and he figured they would finish that conversation the next time. He took off and headed to the airport. Hours later, as Dr. LaFayette was stepping off from his plane in Washington, D.C., a member of the press ran up to him with the news: Dr. King had been shot. They never got to finish that conversation. Dr. LaFayette recalls those words, "to institutionalize and internationalize nonviolence," as the "final marching order" he received from Dr. King. It was the last request Dr. King made to one of his most senior organizers. That has been his life's mission from that moment on.

> "The next movement that we need to start is a movement to institutionalize and internationalize nonviolence."
> —Martin Luther King Jr.

He eventually partnered with his friend David C. Jehnsen, an activist who authored the initial proposal to create the US Institute for Peace, and the two of them spent years drafting the Kingian

Nonviolence Conflict Reconciliation Leaders Manual and its corresponding training curriculum. Together, they have been traveling the world, working to institutionalize and internationalize this knowledge by bringing it to social movements, universities, high schools, law enforcement agencies, and other institutions.

INSTITUTIONALIZATION

Like Doc, I got the "internationalize" part of King's final marching orders: spread the teachings of nonviolence all over the world. But *institutionalize*? What did he mean by that? What does that look like?

In social justice work, we oftentimes talk about how white supremacy, patriarchy, homophobia, transphobia, and other forms of violence and oppression have been institutionalized throughout society. They are embedded into the fabric of our institutions and reinforced every day throughout society without many of us even being aware.

In 2017, I had the opportunity to be a community observer for an event called Urban Shield, a massive trade show for the police. Law enforcement agencies from around the world send delegations to participate in a giant expo of private companies hawking the latest policing and weapons technology. There were SWAT teams to participate in "war games" in order to be trained to respond to terrorism and active shooter scenarios by US and foreign military personnel and private contractors. After years of organizing by community activists, the Stop Urban Shield coalition was given a few observer passes, so the community could see what goes on at these expos and offer feedback.

We talk about the militarization of the police all the time, but I had never seen it in person like I did on that day. Four of us spent twelve hours going from site to site watching military personnel teach war tactics to domestic police agencies. The training scenarios were deeply embedded with racial stereotypes; all of them emphasized shoot-to-kill; and almost all of the scenarios were based on real-life terrorist events that happened overseas, even though the officers being trained were from domestic agencies. There was zero training on how to deescalate a situation. This is just one way that militarization is being institutionalized within US law enforcement agencies. These are real policies and practices that create a certain culture and worldview that translate into real consequences.

My first direct experience with institutionalizing nonviolence came in 2010 through my relationship with Tiffany Childress-Price, a teacher at North Lawndale College Preparatory High School, located just a mile from where Dr. King lived during his days in Chicago. Tiffany and I were certified as Kingian Nonviolence trainers the same summer at the University of Rhode Island. The neighborhood of North Lawndale where Tiffany teaches has struggled with generations of violence, and the school's campaign to bring nonviolence to their two campuses started around the time that Chicago was getting national coverage for particularly high levels of violence. In the first year of their campaign, the school was able to reduce the rate of physical violence at their school by 70 percent at the height of the violence epidemic throughout the city. How did they do it? By institutionalizing nonviolence.

The entire faculty was trained in nonviolence as part of their professional development, and they have refresher courses every other year. A group of student leaders receive a forty-hour training to become youth trainers every summer. These student leaders lead workshops for their peers throughout the year. The entire incoming freshman class receives a presentation on nonviolence by older students. Announcements about nonviolence are made over the PA systems. The school got rid of their metal detectors and security guards and instead invested the savings into their students' education. They track days without any incidents of physical violence, and after so many consecutive days of peace, students are rewarded with ever-increasing prizes such as a DJ in the cafeteria, no-homework days, and a community

BBQ. Nonviolence became as important on campus as math and science. It was embedded within the policies, practices, and culture of the entire school and became part of what the staff and students do day to day.

At East Point Peace Academy, our longest running program is in the San Bruno jail, just outside of San Francisco. Since beginning our work there in April of 2012, thousands of incarcerated men have gone through the Kingian Nonviolence workshop. Many of those workshops have been led by the men in the four cohorts of inside trainers who went through an eight-month program to become certified trainers.

After some time, we decided to focus our work in one particular housing unit called Roads to Recovery. We now teach an advanced course for a select group of men every week and a basic course for the entire unit twice a month. Theresa leads a team of volunteers in a weekly meditation group. In addition, we work with our inside trainers, supporting them to facilitate two-day workshops for the entire unit every quarter. These practices have institutionalized nonviolence in this unit. No one is incarcerated there long without learning the skills of nonviolence.

Unfortunately, a school struggling with violence can't solve it with one workshop on nonviolence or an after-school program where ten kids meet once a month. That's a start, but ultimately, these practices have to be institutionalized to truly be effective. The ancient Greek soldier Archilochus once said, "We don't rise to the level of our expectations; we fall to the level of our training." We may have wonderful expectations about how we're going to relate to each other, such as, "This school year, we're going to create a culture of peace on our campus," or "Next time my partner yells at me, I'm going to remain calm and listen to their concerns," or "We're going to stamp out racial prejudice in our police department." But if you haven't been practicing nonviolence, you are going to go back to your default behaviors. Because of the ways most of us have been conditioned by our institutions, our default responses to conflict tend to escalate the conflict or avoid dealing with it altogether.

To change our defaults, we need to reprogram our responses to conflict, and that takes a while. It takes consistent training to change old habits and conditioning. It takes consistent training for something to become muscle memory. We need systemized and institutionalized structures to support our practice. Imagine if every schoolteacher was given training in restorative justice, conflict de-escalation, mediation, and trauma response.[1] Imagine if our police academies mandated undoing racism and nonviolence workshops for every new recruit. Imagine if our prisons became places of restorative justice and healing, and they provided the resources people need in times of crisis. Imagine if our media institutions supported artists who use their art to heal and help us progress as a society. Imagine if every nonprofit organization actually practiced the value systems they espouse within their own staff.

> **"We don't rise to the level of our expectations; we fall to the level of our training."**
> **—Archilochus**

What aspect of human nature do our institutions nurture? What would it look like if our fundamental assumption about our species was that we are loving creatures who want to live in peaceful relationships with each other and the earth? What would it look like if all of our institutions—from our economic system to our criminal justice systems, from our schools to our media, from the ways we respond to domestic crime and violence to the ways we respond to international conflict—intentionally cultivated the best of who we are?

Violence and division have been institutionalized throughout society. This means that our work is to institutionalize its antidote. As Dr. King inferred in his last conversation with Dr. LaFayette, our work is to embed the practices of nonviolence and conflict

---

1. Or better yet, what if schools had enough funding to have different people who specialize in all of those things in each classroom?

reconciliation as part of the day-to-day operations of our institutions. Imagine if we institutionalize healing in the same way we have institutionalized violence. What kind of a world could we create?

CHAPTER 3

The Water in Nashville

The student lunch counter sit-ins were a movement that swept through the South in the early 1960s, and they were the impetus for the formation of the Civil Rights movement's student arm: SNCC. The sit-ins began on February 1, 1960, in Greensboro, North Carolina, and quickly spread to hundreds of cities and towns.[1] The movement had chapters in hundreds of locations, but there was something special brewing in Nashville, Tennessee.

The leadership of the Nashville chapter of the sit-in movement included Dr. LaFayette, Diane Nash, John Lewis, Marion Barry, C.T. Vivian, and James Bevel—people who would go on to become the backbone of the Civil Rights movement. How is it possible that one chapter of one movement that had hundreds of chapters produced so many important leaders? Spoiler alert: it was the training.

The leadership of the Nashville movement had been rigorously trained in nonviolence by Rev. James Lawson, an African American Methodist minister who had gone to India and studied the nonviolent tactics, strategies, and philosophies of Gandhi. The trainings simulated the types of violence the students might expect by sitting at lunch counters designated for "Whites Only": insults, food being thrown at them, and even physical assaults. Their training lasted for months.

That is one thing I never understood about nonviolence until I met Doc. I used to think that one could attend a four-hour nonviolence training and "get it." So, what would be the purpose

---

1. Much like the Montgomery Bus Boycott, the lunch counter şit-ins were modeled after earlier sit-in campaigns that took place throughout the South, as early as 1939.

of training for all of those months? What would they do other than practice ten thousand ways to turn the other cheek?[2]

NONVIOLENCE AS MARTIAL ART

Since learning about the Nashville movement, I've come to understand nonviolence as a martial art, as a type of kung fu. The word "kung fu" does not actually refer to the Chinese martial art. Derived from the Chinese word *gongfu*, it refers to any skill that can be gained through consistent practice and dedication.

No one goes to a four-hour karate seminar and thinks they've "got it." It takes years of dedicated practice for skills learned in karate training to be useful in real-life combat situations. Bruce Lee once said, "I fear not the man who has practiced ten thousand kicks once, but I fear the man who has practiced one kick ten thousand times." This is because he understood gongfu. A kick needs to be practiced ten-thousand times before it becomes integrated in your body as muscle memory. Then, when you are in a real-life combat situation, it can come out in perfect form, because it has become part of your new default behavior.

Similarly, if you think you can sit calmly at a lunch counter while people throw pies in your face, call you the worst insults imaginable, and physically assault you and your friends without having trained for it, you are deceiving yourself. For most of us, our natural reactions to violence falls into one of three categories: to fight, flight, or freeze. Nonviolence gives us an alternative way of responding: to face. Facing means looking your assailant in the eye, not backing down, not giving into fear, and not reacting in kind. Facing also means genuinely listening to your partner when they are upset, hearing their pain, and taking full accountability for your actions without blaming or getting defensive.

---

2. The idea of "turning the other cheek," which comes from the book of Matthew in the New Testament of the Bible, is one of the most misinterpreted teachings from Jesus. Read Walter Wink's *Jesus and Nonviolence* to understand its full context. This is another book that changed my life.

Facing takes consistent practice, just like any form of martial art. True martial artists practice their art almost every day. They don't go to the dojo only once before a competition. Similarly, nonviolence is something that should be practiced daily, as opposed to going to one nonviolence training only before a major demonstration.

Another reason for using the martial art analogy is because I don't believe that one ever *becomes* nonviolent. Dr. King wasn't nonviolent. Gandhi wasn't nonviolent. You and I are never going to become nonviolent, for the same reason that if you are a practitioner of karate, you never become karate. Meditators don't become meditation. Going to yoga classes doesn't make you yoga. These are not things to become, but practices and lenses through which to view the world and skill sets that we utilize throughout our lives. It is a worldview and a practice, not a destination.

Nonviolence should be viewed similarly. Not as something to become, but a worldview and a skill set in which we are trying to improve in. It is through the consistent practice of the art of nonviolence that we are able to build up our nonviolent muscles so that they may become useful in our daily lives. That is why nonviolence is the martial art of transforming conflict.

SHUGYO

This brings us to another concept borrowed from martial arts. *Shugyo* is a Japanese word often translated as "practice," though it is one of those words that doesn't quite have a perfect English translation. Shugyo is generally not a word that is used if you are practicing basketball or preparing for a high-school play. Shugyo is typically used in the context of martial arts or spiritual practices like long periods of meditation and prayer. Shugyo is never easy and rarely fun. Shugyo is not only about improving in a particular skill but about cultivating character and spiritual development.

I have an ongoing meditation practice, which I view as part of my commitment to nonviolence. I use the practice of meditation not only to calm my mind but to cultivate compassion and to integrate the intellectual understanding of interconnection and interdependence into my body. The practice of meditation has often been secularized in the West, which means it is often taught without the ethical and moral teachings of the historical spiritual teachers who originally taught the practice.

Meditation and mindfulness practices are definitely not only for people who consider themselves religious in some way, but without the ethical checks and balances provided by a religious, spiritual, or cultural foundation, they can become tools of capitalism and other oppressive systems. It's problematic when they are used by corporations to reduce the stress of their workers so they can be better capitalists or by the military so they can produce more efficient killers.

The Buddha passed on the teachings of the Threefold Trainings of *sila* ("morality"), *samadhi* ("concentration"), and *prajna* ("wisdom"). He taught that once we are grounded in morality, then we can use meditation to sharpen our concentration. Through our concentration, we can gain wisdom into the true nature of reality.

When the moral and ethical foundations are removed, meditation can become a shallow version of itself. To some extent this is already happening in the West, with the mindfulness industry turning into what some people call "McMindfulness." Without being grounded in ethics, we could learn to concentrate on our greed, our ego, or other unhealthy aspects of our lives. McMindfulness practices samadhi without sila, and the practice of concentration without morality is unlikely to result in true prajna. Through McMindfulness, we will only gain partial insights, which could ultimately be nothing but an illusion. McMindfulness isn't bad *per se.* Any practice that reduces stress ultimately can be beneficial. But it would not be *shugyo* or spiritual practice.[3] There is a type

3. I would encourage those interested in learning the practice of meditation to look deeply into the value systems of the teacher or center. While popular meditation apps that can be downloaded on your smartphone may be a start, the top apps have been valued at over $250 million, are deeply embedded in

of meditation offered on a donation-only basis by the Vipassana Trust, an all-volunteer nonprofit organization. Students learning the practice attend ten-day retreats that are held in complete silence, with simple meals, no dinner, and a timetable designed to maximize the amount of silent sitting meditation for as many as ten hours per day. Such retreats can be agonizing, painful, boring, and mentally exhausting. When you sit for that long, not only can the physical body experience intense pain, it can also bring up a lot of past emotional and mental anguish that has not been fully healed. Part of the intention of sitting is to face those experiences, look at them directly, not back down, and not react in kind, for the purpose of cultivating love and goodwill. You learn to gaze at yourself with curiosity and loving kindness. It is shugyo, and it is a practice of nonviolence.

Similarly, many people practice yoga primarily as a series of stretches used for physical exercise. There is usually some degree of mindfulness of breathing, calming our mind, and letting go of stress, but yoga is frequently practiced in the West without the spiritual and ethical teachings that were always included in its original form. Doing yoga as a form of exercise is a practice. If you are also studying the ethical foundations of yoga—the *yamas* and *niyamas* (in a word, the dos and don'ts), and meditating on concepts like *ahimsa* (nonviolence) and *satya* (truth), then the practice of yoga becomes shugyo.

This points to another distinction I see between a strategic approach to nonviolence and a principled approach. We can practice tactical nonviolence. You can practice blockades, scaling buildings to drop banners, and shutting down buildings and highways. Those kinds of tactical skills of nonviolence are critical if we are

a capitalist culture, and do not always emphasize the ethical foundations that were traditionally taught alongside the practice of mindfulness and meditation. While not everyone may have access to teachers and centers with an alternative value system, we should at least have some level of awareness and discernment about the ethics and morality that serve as the foundation on which spiritual practices are taught.

ever going to stop the systems of injustice. But when practiced in the absence of the principles, their impact is limited. When we view nonviolent resistance as a part of a process of healing our collective wounds; when we work to cultivate compassion for all beings, including those who perpetuate systems of injustice; when we begin to see that our ultimate goal is not only to change unjust systems but also to change cultures, value systems, and to repair relationships—that is when we begin to enter into the shugyo of nonviolence. Shugyo is not only about learning a tactical skill. It is about engaging in what Gandhi called "self-purification," which involves purifying our own selves of trauma, hatred, and delusion and learning to embody the principles and worldview of nonviolence.

There is some old video footage of trainings conducted by Rev. Lawson for students in Nashville. In one scene, they are sitting in chairs while other students role-play members of the public who have come to harass them by insulting the protesters, ashing cigarettes on their heads, and even physically pushing and hitting them. They may not have called this practice mindfulness, but it is indeed what they were practicing. They are practicing sitting still and staying focused on a central goal while choosing not to be distracted. But it isn't until the next scene in the video that the practice turns into shugyo.

Speaking to the students, Rev. Lawson suggests, "It may have much more meaning to the attacker if, as he strikes you on your cheek, you're looking at him in the eyes." Even in the face of physical abuse, he is suggesting that we look into the eyes of our assailant, to recognize their humanity and to give them an opportunity to reciprocate. Sacrificing our emotional and physical safety, we try to reach the moral conscience of our assailant.

That is shugyo.

CHAPTER 4

On Violence

Before diving into a discussion about the concept of nonviolence, it's important we have some discussion around the concept of "violence." What, really, are we talking about when we talk about violence? Originating from the Latin *violentia* or *violentus,* most dictionaries seem to settle on one key concept in its main definition: the use of physical force for the purpose of causing injury, damage, or destruction. Merriam-Webster defines it as, "the use of physical force so as to injure, abuse, damage, or destroy," while Dictionary.com says, "rough or injurious physical force, action, or treatment." Both definitions are limited and potentially create a dangerous understanding of the word.

"Sticks and stones may break my bones, but words will never hurt me" is one of the biggest lies ever told. We absolutely need to stop teaching this saying to our kids, because words can cause as much damage, sometimes more, than physical actions. Getting punched hurts, but the pain might go away in a day or two. Sometimes the words we hear, especially as young children, can scar us for life.

I remember facilitating a training at a detention school once in Selma, Alabama. In the middle of the discussion, one young man raised his hand and asked, "What do you do when your mother tells you that you were never wanted and that you were a mistake?" Hearing words like that from his own mother will have an impact on that young man that could last decades, if not his entire life.

"You are not worthy." "You are not loved." "You are not intelligent." "You are not good." "You are crazy." "You will never be anything." "You are not enough." Variations of words like these can be as harmful as any physical action, and it is important that we begin to acknowledge that they can have a violent impact. I've known countless incarcerated people who received similar messages from their parents, teachers, and other adults throughout their upbringing. I often wonder how much these messages may have impacted the decisions that they made in life later, which ultimately led to their incarceration.

Sometimes it's the words that we don't say or the actions that we don't take that can be a form of violence. Silence, isolation, neglect, abandonment, ignoring someone, not coming to someone's aid when they need help, or withholding resources from someone in need can also be as hurtful as getting beaten with a stick. So violence is clearly not just the use of physical force, and we need to include nonphysical forms of harm in our understanding of violence.[1] There is a common saying in the world of nonviolence and restorative justice that "hurt people hurt people." Meaning that when people are hurt, when we are carrying around some pain or trauma that we have not found healthy releases for, we lash out and hurt others. I believe that *all* violence is ultimately rooted in this. That means that even physical acts of violence are rooted

---

1. On the other hand, I love what psychologist Jonathan Haidt has to say about "microaggressions," a term coined by Harvard professor Chester Pierce. In an article for *Psychology Today*, Derald Wing Sue, author of the book *Microaggressions in Everyday Life*, defines microaggressions as, "everyday verbal, nonverbal, and environmental slights, snubs, or insults, whether intentional or unintentional, which communicate hostile, derogatory, or negative messages to target persons based solely upon their marginalized group membership." Common examples include asking an Asian person, "Where are you *really* from?" when they may be as American as any white person, or asking someone "What *are* you?" when inquiring about their racial or ethnic background. Haidt suggests that these incidents do exist, that they cause harm, that we should have a term to describe them, and that we should train people not to do them. He also suggests that calling them acts of "aggression" is not helpful because it rarely is. Calling it aggression can give the impression that the conflict is more escalated than it actually is. They may have some basis in ignorance or may be unskillful ways of communication, but they may ultimately be an attempt at making a connection with someone. Creating a culture that sees violence everywhere actually perpetuates hypervigilance, which in turn perpetuates trauma. We need to acknowledge real violence in places where we don't always acknowledge it, but we also need to be discerning in that process.

in the emotional. There is not a single person in this world who hasn't experienced nonphysical violence. None of us are exempt from it, and all of us know what it feels like to be hurt. Once we name that nonphysical forms of harm can be violent, then we quickly see that violence is something that impacts all of us, and we all have a responsibility to address it.

Another crucial reason to expand the definition of violence is that nonphysical forms of violence impact society at a much greater level than physical violence. According to statistics from the Centers for Disease Control and Prevention, there are almost three times as many suicides as there are homicides every year in the United States. If we think violence is just a physical act from one person to another, we're missing the point.

Thinking of violence as only a physical act can also become an easy way for people to escape the responsibility of causing harm. "I'm not a violent person because I don't hit people." Instead of pointing the finger and saying that the problem is "over there," one aspect of nonviolence is to own the ways in which we perpetuate harm to ourselves, our loved ones, our community, and society. Once we own our violence, we can put our energy into working to transform ourselves. As practitioners of nonviolence, we are working to combat all forms of violence.

SYSTEMS OF VIOLENCE

It's important to note that interpersonal violence happens within the context of systemic violence. In fact, in the institutions that we live under and the history that we carry, violence is so prevalent that it's hard to separate *any* act of violence in our society from systemic violence. Driving around Oakland, sometimes I can become numb to seeing so many homeless people on the streets. But every once in a while, I see someone on a corner asking for money with their family, young children in tow. And that breaks my heart every time.

Poverty and homelessness are systemic forms of violence. The trauma of young children who experience these forms of violence may manifest later in their lives as violence that they may perpetuate on others. This violence may manifest as individual acts, but they are a result of the larger forms of systemic violence they had to endure. Poverty didn't just happen for no reason, and it is not perpetuated because people are lazy.[2] Systemic violence can have a different impact than isolated incidents of interpersonal violence. The nature of systemic violence is that it can feel inescapable and omnipresent. It repeats over and over and over again, day after day after day. If you are homeless, you are reminded of that every single day. If you live in an impoverished neighborhood, you witness violence every single day. If you are from a marginalized community, you are reminded that you are an "other" constantly. If you live in a war-torn country, your trauma is being triggered all the time. The impact of that constant, repeated exposure to violence impacts not only your body but your soul.

Civil rights leader Andrew Young once said, "You can get hit by a baseball bat playing baseball, but segregation destroys the inside of your mind and your soul. And it doesn't heal that easily." When your mind or soul is destroyed, you are much more likely to harm yourself or lash out and hurt another person. As we will continue to talk about throughout this book, the institutions that govern our lives have a much deeper impact than we realize. It is impossible to consider peace, justice, and nonviolence without an intimate understanding of the way in which our institutions perpetuate violence and a deep commitment to undoing harm on the systemic level.[3]

---

2. For more on this, I highly recommend Ta-Nehisi Coates's fantastic article, "The Case for Reparations," which appeared in the June 2014 issue of *The Atlantic*. It can be found online here: https://theatln.tc/2j2mgr4.

3. There are plenty of books, movies, articles, and YouTube videos breaking down systemic violence out there. Going further would require me to write an entirely separate book, so I will stop here, though examples are spread throughout the book.

DEFINITIONS OF VIOLENCE

So what, at its core, is violence?

The World Health Organization (WHO) defines violence as, "The intentional use of physical force or power, threatened or actual, against oneself, another person, or against a group or community, which either results in or has a high likelihood of resulting in injury, death, psychological harm, maldevelopment, or deprivation." In some ways, that's a good definition. It may be useful in the realm of international negotiations. But in another way, this definition is highly problematic.

When I was being trained to teach Kingian Nonviolence, I heard a statement that has significantly influenced my presentation style. "If you cannot explain a concept to an eight-year-old child, then you don't understand it well enough." I am a fan of Taoist philosophy. One of the central tenets of Taoism is that everything *is*. Period. The more we try to define what that "is" is, the further we are getting from the central truth: that all of reality simply just is.[4] I feel like that's one of the problems with the WHO's definition of violence. They overcomplicate it.

This happens a lot in social change work. Some activists have a tendency to over-intellectualize. We use all the big words in our vocabulary, and at some point we've lost half of our audience. Maybe I'm over-sensitive to this because of my lack of formal education, but using highly intellectual terms and academic jargon can make the actual message inaccessible, and this inaccessibility and exclusion can be considered a subtle form of violence.[5] Intellectual and academic language also have a tendency to lose the humanity of the message, which is dangerous. If we're trying to make changes in the world, it's important that we learn to speak about issues in ways that cut through the intellect and have a human impact.

---

4. Says the person writing a three-hundred-page book on what nonviolence is....
5. One example of this is how hard it is to understand and navigate criminal law—something that disproportionately impacts communities that typically have less access to formal education.

There is power in simplicity. There is wisdom in being able to understand an issue or a conflict so well that you are able to drill it down to its very core and articulate it in a few short words. When we over-intellectualize something, we lose its essence. In Kingian Nonviolence, we define violence as "physical or emotional harm." It captures everything the WHO is trying to say, and more. However, over time I've come across two definitions I like even more than the Kingian definition.

Jonathan told me that one time he was facilitating a youth workshop, and a young girl said, simply, that "violence is painful." Our minds and intellect may be able to find holes in that definition. I'm sure there are things that are painful that may not be considered violent. At the same time, when a young girl says, "violence is painful," everyone in the room understands exactly what she's taking about. Everyone knows what it's like to be in pain. It cuts through the intellect and speaks directly to the heart of an issue.

The second definition that I have come to appreciate comes from Rosenberg, who said that "violence is the tragic expression of unmet needs." As human beings, we all have the same universal needs. Rosenberg teaches that all actions are an attempt to meet those needs, and sometimes, we choose poor strategies to get those needs met.

We may have a need to be heard, so we scream at a loved one. We may have a need to feel powerful or in control, so we may turn to abusing someone with less power. Those may not be the most effective strategies, but they're still an attempt to get a universal need met. One reason we sometimes choose ineffective strategies is

"Violence is the tragic expression of unmet needs."
—Marshall Rosenberg

because the strategies available to us may be limited by circumstance. Two people may have the same need for peace after a hard day at work. One person may have access to a yoga class, a therapist, or a walk in the woods by their house, while the other person may not have access to any of these things because of their economic circumstances. Another reason we may choose poor and ineffective strategies is that we are not even connected to what our needs actually are.

I once had a conversation with a woman who was mentoring a young incarcerated man. She said that this young man told her, "I *need* to hurt that motherfucker." Wanting to hurt someone is not a need, but a strategy to meet a need. I asked her to consider what this young man's core needs may have been. Perhaps it was a need to feel powerful. Or to be heard. Or for justice and accountability. Once we connect with our needs, we can figure out the best, most effective, and healthiest strategy to meet them.[6] It is important to be aware of the complexity of violence, the different systems and policies that cause violence, the institutions that perpetuate oppression, and the statistics about the disproportionate ways that violence impacts certain communities. But structures, politics, and systems are about the human causes of violence. Pain and harm are the impacts of violence, and to build effective movements for change, we need to speak to them.

---

6. I recommend people study Nonviolent Communication for more on this. In particular, Rosenberg's book *Nonviolent Communication: A Language of Life* is a great start.

CHAPTER 5

On Nonviolence

The Japanese word *kotodama* translates to something along the lines of, "spirit of the word." Many people believe that the words we voice have a divine spirit to them, and voicing something can have an impact in the material world. In mystical Judaism, Buddhism, Hinduism, and many other wisdom traditions, there are practices of repetitively chanting mantras and sutras out loud, with the belief that the sound vibration carried by the syllables has an effect on our reality. I view this concept slightly differently. I believe that words are nothing more than sounds we make with our vocal cords, and it is *the spirit that we put into the word* that gives it its true nature, its true meaning, and its true kotodama.

Nipponzan Myohoji has a practice of chanting "Na Mu Myo Ho Ren Ge Kyo" over and over again. And again. And again. And again and again and again. Over and over. In the monasteries, we would chant for four hours each day. During our monthly fasting ceremonies, we would chant up to fourteen hours per day. I once chanted for fourteen hours with only one break and no food or water—voluntarily. During the Pilgrimage of the Middle Passage, we chanted every minute we were walking. Of course, at some point, after countless hours of chanting, some inquisitive mind would ultimately ask the question, "Hey, what are we chanting?"

Different monastic practitioners respond to that question differently. But my favorite explanation came one morning from Utsumi-Shonin, the head monk of the Atlanta temple and the Great Smoky Mountains Peace Pagoda. He explained that his teacher, Nichidatsu Fujii, or "Guruji," the founder of Nipponzan Myohoji, taught him not to give people the literal definition of the chant. He explained, "When we tell people the meaning of the chant, they focus too much on the literal meaning of the words and stop putting their own prayers into it. The literal meaning doesn't matter. It's the prayer we put into each chant that matters." So that's how I understand kotodama. It's the spirit that we put into each word that gives it true meaning.

This can be very useful for a term like "nonviolence." Too often, people emphasize the etymology of the word or its dictionary definition that they miss the spirit that so many of us intend when we speak it. Nonviolence is such a frequently misunderstood word that I often consider taking it out of my vocabulary all together. If there is only one thing I want readers to take away from this book, it is this: *The idea that nonviolence is about "not being violent" is one of the most common and dangerous misunderstandings that exist.*

This is why, in Kingian Nonviolence, we make a distinction between non-violence spelled *with* a hyphen, and nonviolence spelled *without* a hyphen. "Non-violence" is essentially two words: "without" and "violence." When spelled this way, it is an adjective that only describes the absence of violence. As long as I am "not being violent," I am practicing non-violence.

The idea that nonviolence is about 'not being violent' is one of the most common and dangerous misunderstandings that exists.

I live in a beautiful neighborhood. With about an equal mix of Black, Latino, and Asian residents, it is one of the most diverse neighborhoods in Oakland. I sometimes hear six or seven languages being spoken on my block alone. It also happens to be a neighborhood with more than its fair share of challenges. For whatever reason, the specific corner I live on seems to attract a lot of conflict. From shootings to illegal dumping, human trafficking, and a seemingly disproportionate number of car accidents, I have witnessed a lot of madness out of my kitchen window.[1] One day, I was taking a nap in my apartment when I was woken up by a commotion below my

---

1. If any Oakland city officials are reading this, a stop sign on East Fifteenth at Thirteenth Avenue would be greatly appreciated. Thank you.

window; a man and a woman were yelling at each other. I tried to go back to sleep, but the fight kept getting louder and getting worse. Finally, I decided to get out of bed and look outside, and I saw a woman on the ground being beaten, crying and screaming for help. I jumped up, put on my shoes, and ran downstairs. By the time I arrived, about fifteen of my neighbors had also come outside, but they were just watching this woman getting beat, doing nothing to help. I managed to break up the fight and get the two to walk away from each other, one fuming with anger and the other in tears.

My neighbors who were just watching this woman get beat were practicing "non *hyphen* violence." They weren't throwing punches or kicks. They were explicitly being "not violent." In fact, you could argue that I was more violent than they were, since I used a limited amount of physical force to pull the two apart. So, you see how, from a Kingian perspective, what a difference that little hyphen makes. You see how big of a misunderstanding it can create if we think that nonviolence is simply about the absence of violence. If we define nonviolence as "not violent," then we can hide behind the veil of nonviolence while still condoning violence and perpetuating or even inflicting harm. Our commitment to "nonviolence" could become an act of violence.

It's easy to be a bystander. It's easy to stay silent and look on when violence is happening right in front of us. As kids, we used to see it on school playgrounds when a fight would break out, and an entire crowd would gather around to watch. This is the dynamic that we see play out in society every day.

We see rising homelessness, and we turn the other way. We see unarmed Black folks being killed by police, and we see society blaming the victim. We hear about high suicide rates amongst LGBT youth, and we do little or nothing about it. We read reports on the climate crisis but leave it to the next generation to deal with. We watch our communities and the earth being assaulted every day, and we just gather around and watch.

None of my business. Nothing to see here.

Nonviolence is not about what *not* to do. It is about what you *are going to do* about the violence and injustice we see in our own hearts, our homes, our neighborhoods, and society at large. It is about taking a proactive stand against violence and injustice. Nonviolence is about *action*, not *inaction*.

NEGATIVE PEACE

This misunderstanding of nonviolence leads to a dangerous misunderstanding of peace. Similar to gross misunderstandings of nonviolence, calling for a misunderstood peace in society can be an act of violence. On February 3, 1956, after a court battle that lasted almost three years, a woman named Autherine Lucy became the first Black student to attend classes at the University of Alabama in Tusca-loosa. Within days of her arrival, riots broke out on campus. People threw stones at the university president's home. Crosses were burned. A mob of more than a thousand people surrounded the car she was traveling in, and rioters climbed on top of it and began jumping up and down.

> **Nonviolence is not about what *not* to do. It is about what you *are going to do*.**

In response to this violence, the University of Alabama suspended, and ultimately expelled, Lucy from campus. They claimed that her presence was causing a threat to the safety of the school.[2] The following day, because Lucy was no longer allowed on campus, the riots stopped. The local newspaper ran a headline that read, "Things are quiet in Tuscaloosa today. There is peace on the campus of the University of Alabama."

There is *peace*. What kind of peace was the paper talking about? Peace for whom? And at what cost?

On March 18, just one month later, Dr. King gave a sermon in

---

2. This was a year after the *Brown v. Board of Education of Topeka* Supreme Court decision that ruled segregated schools unconstitutional, so the University of Alabama had no grounds to expel Lucy based on her race.

response to this incident titled, "When Peace Becomes Obnoxious."[3] In the sermon, Dr. King said the peace the newspapers described was not a real peace. He said that this is "the type of peace that all men of goodwill hate. It is the type of peace that is obnoxious. It is the type of peace that stinks in the nostrils of the Almighty God." Strong words from the man who would go on to win the Nobel Peace Prize. When Dr. King spoke of a "peace boiled down to stagnant complacency" and "deadening passivity," he was talking about what peace educator Johan Galtung calls "negative peace," a peace that describes the absence of tension that comes at the expense of justice. Dr. King went on to say that, "peace is not merely the absence of tension, but the presence of justice."

Oftentimes in our society, we think of peace as calm, quiet, and serene. We conjure up images of watching the sunset on a tropical beach, meditating in the forest by a creek, incense, scented candles, and kumbaya around a campfire.[4] That can be as problematic as thinking that nonviolence is about not being violent. I guarantee you that the moment after the atomic bomb was dropped on Hiroshima in 1945, things were really quiet. So did we create peace? If someone is screaming in my face, and I stop them by knocking them unconscious, did I just create peace?

As ridiculous as that sounds, this is how our society tries to

> **"Peace is not merely the absence of tension, but the presence of justice."**
> —Martin Luther King Jr.

---

3. This is one of my all-time favorite sermons by Dr. King. I highly recommend you read it. It is available online, and it's really short, so you have no excuse. "I Have a Dream" is a great speech, but there is a reason why it is the only Dr. King speech that most people know; it was one of his safest speeches. We are not taught in our schools how radical and militant Dr. King's politics were. Sermons like this, or the little-known speech "The Crisis in America's Cities" shows the side of Dr. King that this country has largely forgotten (or ... cough, cough ... hidden from our communities).

4. "Kumbaya" has become a term used to discredit pacifists and nonviolent activists for simply wanting to sing campfires and "get along," but it is in reality an African spiritual created by the Gullah Geechee people, descendants of slaves, who now live in South Carolina and have an incredibly powerful story of survival. It was a call to God to help people out of oppression.

create peace, because we have such a gross misunderstanding of the concept. This misunderstanding is what allows us to justify going to war to create peace. If we just kill all the terrorists, we'll have peace. Winning a war means killing as many of "them" as it takes for them to give in and sign a peace treaty. Negative peace.

This misunderstanding justifies the militarization of the police. If we just lock up all the protesters, then our streets will be quiet, and we can have some peace. Dr. King acknowledged that if Black people simply accepted second-class citizenship, then the streets would be less tense because the protests wouldn't be happening. Negative peace. It justifies mass incarceration. If we just lock up all the bad people, we'll have peace in our neighborhoods. Negative peace.

Back in 2011, the city attorney of Oakland was pushing for gang injunctions, a controversial civil order that would give more power to the police to harass and arrest "suspected gang members"—code for young men of color. I remember saying to the city council at the time that if all we wanted was to decrease violence at all costs, there is a strategy that is guaranteed to work: lock up every single young person in Oakland, which would dramatically decrease the violence in our city. But if we want to create peace that requires a whole different strategy. That requires an investment in the city's youth. That requires an acknowledgment of the history of systemic violence that breeds poverty, which in turn breeds violence. That requires a commitment to healing the harm that so many young people in Oakland have suffered. That requires justice. And that is a lot of work (though arguably less work than it takes to endure perpetual violence and injustice and to keep repressing harm though incarceration).

Negative peace is prevalent in many of our relationships, homes, workplaces, faith communities, and institutions of higher learning. This is often the type of negative peace created and maintained by a ubiquitous, unspoken understanding that surfacing conflict is not welcome. My home country of Japan deals with this type of negative peace on a national level. As a culture, we tend to be conflict-averse. We are taught that the honorable thing is to hold it in, keep our heads down and endure. It is considered rude to bring up difficult topics that could create tension because we would be placing a burden on others. It's impolite. We'd be taking up too much space. So we endure.

Japan may be one of the safest nations on earth in terms of violent crime, and from the outside looking in, it looks like a peaceful culture. But we also have one of the highest suicide rates in the world. *Gaman* is another concept that doesn't quite have a literal translation in English, but it is considered an honorable trait to endure suffering with patience, perseverance, and dignity. And it can be. To learn to endure life's challenges with dignity can absolutely be a positive trait, but when it results in a nation of people trying to simply endure trauma, isolation, and living a life without purpose—when people are taught not to speak out about injustice and oppression and to "stay in their place"—that becomes repression and a form of violence. It is negative peace.

I attended a conference once where someone described this phenomenon as the "tyranny of civility." We're told in corporate workplaces not to speak out about sexual harassment because it would "create conflict." We're told in our churches not to question the use of church funds because "it's improper." We're told in our schools not to raise the issue of professors' ignorance of their power and privilege because "it's not our place." So we go on pretending there's no problem and holding it all in. Enduring. Negative peace, negative peace, negative peace.

We see this everywhere in our society today. Racism? Not a problem anymore; the only people still talking about racism are the racists! Patriarchy? Look at all the women leading major corporations now! Poverty? The economy has never been better! Look at the stock market!

It is easier in the short term to sweep issues under the rug and settle for a cheap yet ultimately unsustainable negative peace. It is an entirely different conversation to proactively work against violence and build toward a positive peace that includes justice for all. It requires us to lift the veil off injustice and work to repair the harm.

DISTURBING COMPLACENCY

So what does that work look like? When we associate peace with only the absence of tension, we actually move farther away from the positive peace that Dr. King called for. In his famous "Letter from a Birmingham Jail," Dr. King wrote, "My citing the creation of tension as part of the work of the nonviolent resister may sound rather shocking. But I must confess that I am not afraid of the word 'tension.' I have earnestly opposed violent tension, but there is a type of constructive, nonviolent tension which is necessary for growth."

In 2015, in response to the police killing of Freddie Gray, the city of Baltimore erupted into an uprising. This included some members of the Baltimore community engaging in acts of violence. Buildings were burned. Car windows were smashed. Former Baltimore Ravens star Ray Lewis implored the protesters to "stop the violence."

As a nonviolence trainer, I don't necessarily think that burning buildings is the most effective tactic to creating lasting change. And at the same time, I was disappointed at Lewis's statement. There is great irony in his call for protesters to "stop the violence." Because that is exactly what the protesters were trying to do. The uprising in Baltimore wasn't only about the killing of Freddie Gray. It was a response to five hundred years of violence against people of African descent in this country. People were out in the streets because they were the ones sick of the violence perpetrated in their communities for so long.

Dr. King once said, "A riot is the language of the unheard." Riots are ultimately a cry for peace from communities who have never had it. To condemn oppressed people for lashing out against centuries of violence is to ignore the larger context of violence they are lashing out against. It is the inevitable response from a community whose pain had gone unacknowledged and unheard for centuries.

Calls for Black Lives Matter protesters to be peaceful following the latest police killing can be a form of repression and therefore a form of violence. It is a call for peace that acts as a euphemism for "stop complaining," "stop being so mad," or "stay in your place." The work of creating peace is a messy process filled with conflict and tension. Peace is messy. Justice is loud. If we expect that creating peace in a society as violent as the United States will be a neat, calm, and quiet process, we will be in for a rude awakening.

Peace-building by definition acknowledges the presence of harm in the first place. Otherwise there is no need to build peace. Taking on violence is not easy, and it will not be a clean process. It is about undoing harm, performing an operation so that we can heal the wound. There is no such thing as a clean operating room. The bigger the harm, the messier the operation will be.

Real peace-building requires us to learn how to have the conversations we don't want to have with our families and with society. It may require us to hold interventions, shut down highways, or perform other acts of resistance. When we do those things, we are not creating the conflict. We are simply surfacing the conflict that already exists so that it can finally be addressed.

Dr. King was arrested twenty-nine times in his short life. Many of those times, he was charged with "disturbing the peace." Think about that for a moment. Let that sink in. Go ahead, I'll give you a minute.

Dr. Martin Luther King Jr., civil rights leader, Nobel Peace Prize Laureate, a man now used as a moral compass for this nation, was charged by the United States government for disturbing the peace. This still happens today to many activists. When we use nonviolence to confront violence and injustice, we are not disturbing the peace, we are disturbing complacency. We are disturbing the normalization of violence. We are disturbing negative peace.

When massive homeless encampments become normalized, we need to disturb that. When we accept a 50 percent dropout rate from urban high schools, we need to disturb that.[5] When we invest in a prison system that produces an 83 percent recidivism rate, we need to disturb that.[6] When corporate interests are destroying our planet and endangering the livelihoods of future generations, we need to disturb that.

When we use nonviolence to confront violence and injustice, we are not disturbing the peace, we are disturbing complacency. We are disturbing the normalization of violence.

The charge of "disturbing the peace" should be stricken from the criminal codes of this country until we finally learn to live in real, positive peace. We cannot disturb something that doesn't exist in the first place. When we engage in the hard work of nonviolence and social change, we are not disturbing peace. We are fighting for it.

5. A 2009 report by America's Promise Alliance shows that only 54 percent of all young people in the country's fifty largest cities graduate high school on time. How is this not a national crisis? How is it possible that our nation accepts this as normal?

6. The Bureau of Justice Statistics released an updated report in May of 2013 that tracked more than four hundred thousand people released from state prisons over a nine-year period. They found that 68 percent of them were rearrested within three years, 79 percent within six years, and a shocking 83 percent within nine years. Yet this is the system that we continue to fund to the tune of tens of billions of dollars per year.

CHAPTER 6

On Conflict

Quick, what's the first word or image that come to mind when you think of conflict?

When I ask this question in workshops, most people say things like yelling, arguing, fighting, or violence: things with negative connotations. From the perspective of nonviolence, we believe that all conflicts are neutral, and it is how we respond to those conflicts that results in a good or bad outcome. We believe that things like yelling and fighting are not conflict. Rather, these are things that happen when a conflict is mismanaged. You can respond to a conflict in your life in a way that leads to an argument or physical altercation, or you can respond to it in a way that ends up in a lesson learned, a strengthened relationship, or reconciliation. Those things are just as likely an outcome to conflict if we know how to manage conflict well.

At a recent workshop, Chris talked about how the news continues to perpetuate the myth that conflict equals violence when they refer to war. When the media talks about the "Syrian Conflict," for example, they are not referring to the root causes of the Syrian civil war. They are referring to the tragic and violent responses to the conflicts that nation is facing.

Realizing and naming the fact that you are in a conflict can actually lead to opportunity. For example, if we realize that we have differences in values from someone, it can be an opportunity to learn to see things from a new perspective. Discovering we have limited resources can be an opportunity to redistribute resources in a more equitable way, build a new system of sharing resources, or look at ways to build sustainability. Discovering that we have very different goals than someone else can be an opportunity to learn to collaborate across differences in a way that everyone's goals are achieved.

In early 2015, comedian W. Kamau Bell responded to a conflict in a way that led to a positive outcome. Bell's wife, who is white, was eating lunch with some friends at a local eatery in Berkeley, California. They were sitting at an outside table when Bell, who is African American, approached them from the street. Bell was chatting with his wife and her friends when he heard loud knocking coming from inside the restaurant. An employee from the restaurant had assumed that Bell was a homeless man harassing a group of customers. Bell wrote later in a blog post that the employee glared at Bell as she, "Jerks her head to her left aggressively, and I see her mouth say something to the effect of ... 'SCRAM.'"

He goes on, "Seriously. That is what happened. OK. Maybe it wasn't exactly, 'SCRAM!' Maybe it was, 'GIT!' Or maybe it was, 'GO!' Whatever it was, it was certainly directed at me. And it was certainly the kind of direction you should only give to a dog."

Bell could have responded in many different ways. Rather than yelling or escalating the situation, he went home and penned the blog piece about it.[1] The piece went viral, creating a huge conversation about the forms of racism that exist in liberal Berkeley. Bell rode the momentum created by his piece and organized a community-wide town forum on race—featuring a panel made up of himself, the owner of the cafe, an ACLU attorney, and the president of the Berkeley High School Black Student Union. The event was held in a school gymnasium and was attended by several hundred people. This conversation ultimately led to the owner of the cafe working with Bell and the racial justice organization Race Forward to create an implicit racial bias training for the retail and hospitality industries. The café owner committed to putting his entire staff through this training and offering it to other local businesses in his area. It was one small step in institutionalizing undoing racism.

---

1. Check it out here: www.wkamaubell.com/blog/2015/01/happy-birthday-have-some-racism-from-elmwood-cafe.

In October 2009, I worked with an initiative that brought together African American activists from rural Mississippi, Indigenous leaders from remote reservations in the Southwest, and Latino organizers from farm-working communities in the Pacific Northwest, among others. Bringing so many groups together meant that we often had to work through cross-cultural differences. A conflict emerged in our check-ins on the first day. A member of the organization's board got frustrated that we were taking a long time in our check-ins when we had such a packed agenda.

After some time processing, a Black Methodist minister from a rural Southern community made this observation: "In my community, if you take more than a couple of minutes to check in or introduce yourself, it's considered rude because you're taking up other people's time. But I now realize that in some Indigenous cultures, if you *don't* take enough time to check in, *that* can be considered rude because you're not sharing enough about yourself with others. What I perceived as disrespect was in fact another culture's way of showing respect. How beautiful it is that we have so many diverse ways to build connection and honor each other."

In both this case and Bell's experience, the emergence of the conflict was uncomfortable and rooted in ignorance. Conflict is never easy or comfortable, but the emergence of conflict or ignorance offers an opportunity. The outcome of both conflicts was a lesson for all involved. Because the parties in both situations were able to constructively respond to the conflicts rather than escalating them, a positive result came about.

So how do we respond well? In the heat of the conflict, it is hard not to get emotional. Once emotions get triggered, it's hard to see things objectively. This is why it is helpful to study the nature of conflict and understand how it operates objectively. You don't improve as a martial artist by getting into street fights all the time. You improve by practicing in the safety of a dojo, outside of the heated emotions involved in a real-life combat situation. You practice your moves repetitively, over and over and over again, so that those skills become integrated and embodied as muscle memory, and when you are in a real conflict, you're not thinking about it. Your body naturally reacts, because it has become your new default. Part of our practice in nonviolence, part of our shugyo, is to learn to identify the types of conflict we find ourselves in.

Four Major Types of Conflict

Within the framework of Kingian Nonviolence, we study four major types of conflict. Understanding what type of conflict you are engaged in gives you information about how to move through it. While this is certainly not meant to be an exhaustive list of types of conflict, it is a helpful framework to be able to analyze conflict. Let's look at each of these four.

Pathway Conflict: Same overall goals, different ways of reaching them. This is a very common type of conflict that is easy to visualize. Pat and Alex want to go to the store, but Pat wants to walk, and Alex wants to ride the bike. Or Pat wants to take the scenic route, and Alex wants to take the fast route.

The conflict may escalate, and they may get into an argument. Emotions might get so heated that they may begin to feel that their path to get to the goal becomes even more important than the goal itself. They lose sight of the fact that they are on the same team, trying to get to the same place.

Pathway conflicts surface all the time in activist groups, especially in coalition work. Different groups may be fighting for the same overall goal, but may have very different perspectives on how to get there. Should we try to shut down the city council meeting or work back channels to try to find allies within the council? Should we accept corporate donations or refuse to accept money from certain institutions? In a Pathway Conflict, the most important thing you can do is to remember that you're trying to get to the same place.

Mutually Exclusive Conflict: Different goals, choosing to function together. Sometimes we assume that we are on the same team as someone; we assume that we have the same goals, but in reality, we may have different goals, and it is important that they are named.

Pat and Alex may assume that they both want to go to the store, but maybe Pat really just wants to go for a walk, and the store isn't as important. If that's the case, it may be easier for Alex to give up on the bike and walk to the store so both their goals can be achieved.

We sometimes mistakenly think that different goals are mutually exclusive—meaning one goal has to be ignored to meet the other. In reality, there are often ways of working together so that even with different goals, we can both actually get closer to our goals than if we'd worked independently. We just have to articulate the mutual benefit we are gaining by working together.

Years ago, the prison abolitionist organization Critical Resistance was organizing a campaign to stop the construction of a new prison in Delano, California. One of their partners was a local environmental organization that wanted to protect the land that the prison was going to be built on top of. They each had different goals, but they were able to work together in a way that resulted in both meeting their goals.

Distributive Conflict: Not enough resources to go around. Pretty straightforward, right? However, it's important to acknowledge that most distributive conflicts, especially at a social level, actually stem from the *perception* that there are not enough resources to go around.

Schools in low-income neighborhoods not having enough resources to go around is a real source of conflict. But if the US government spent less on going to war, perhaps there would be enough to go around to all of the schools.

In a distributive conflict, what you want to look at are the ways that the resources are currently being distributed to see if there is a more equitable distribution that would solve the problem. An important question here is for the parties involved to ask themselves, "What is enough?"

Values Conflict: Different values, different visions. This is the most common type of conflict that exists. Wars over religion. Abortion. Gun ownership. Health care.

There is an element of a values conflict present in all conflicts. If Pat didn't value walking to the store, there wouldn't be a conflict. So, all conflict has some basis in what we value.

But the opposite is also true: in all value conflicts, there exists at least one of the other types of conflict. This is important, because value conflicts tend to be the most emotionally charged. When we feel like our values are being challenged, it can be hard to stay calm.

Gun control is often viewed as a values conflict. Different value systems around the right to own guns and the government's ability to control gun ownership. It's an emotionally charged debate.

But if you ask a proponent of gun control why they support gun control, they might tell you, "I want to make sure my family is safe." And if you ask an opponent of gun control why they oppose gun control, they may tell you, "I want to make sure my family is safe."

So, in addition to being a values conflict, it is also a pathway conflict: Same goals, different path. Framing the conflict as a pathway conflict may be less emotionally charged, and it may be easier to move through the conflict by having real dialogue.

By the time I got rid of my last car, it was literally falling apart. It was being held together by tape, string, screws, epoxy, and whatever else I could get my hands on to keep it together. Every once in a while, I would be driving on the highway, and I would hear a new sound, a sign that something was wrong (again). Because I am not a mechanic, I didn't know what was wrong, and I wouldn't know how to respond. I would have to take it to a mechanic who could diagnose it for me. "Your car is making that sound because the timing belt is off." Now that I had the diagnosis, I would know how to respond.

Naming the type of conflicts we are in is like being able to diagnose the conflict. It pinpoints and articulates exactly what the problem is. Diagnosing the conflict can help you frame the conflict, giving you some choices about how to engage in the conflict in a way that makes reconciliation more likely. A few years ago, I was having a conversation with someone about prisons. Based on my observations and life experience, I believe prisons cause more harm to society than they do to help.[2] This person believed we need to incarcerate more people.

---

2. That topic is a whole different book, but if you are struggling with this statement, I would highly recommend *The New Jim Crow* by Michelle Alexander or *Are Prisons Obsolete?* by Angela Davis.

Initially, I had assumed that we were in a pathway conflict. I assumed we both wanted safe communities but had different ideas of how to achieve that. I was engaging with her within the framework of a pathway conflict and explaining how I believe restorative justice does a better job of creating safety. But as we kept talking, I found out that she had lost a friend to violence. Of course she wanted safe communities, but in that moment, what was more important to her was a sense of justice and accountability. We were in a mutually exclusive conflict. I wanted safety, she wanted justice.[3] Continuing to argue that restorative justice does a better job of creating safe communities was not getting me anywhere, because community safety was not what was most important to her in that moment.

After spending some time acknowledging her loss, I could have moved the conflict into a pathway conflict by sharing that justice and accountability are also very important for me and explaining to her why restorative justice practices create more accountability than our current system. Or, I could have kept it in the realm of a mutually exclusive conflict but changed how I was going about the conversation and acknowledged her need for accountability and justice, named my goal of having safe communities, and explained how restorative justice could accomplish both.

These types of conflicts aren't like buckets, where every conflict neatly fits into one or the other. In reality, there are almost always several different things going on. The intent is to try to identify the type that is showing up the most and to respond based on that diagnosis. If it doesn't work, try the next diagnosis. It is about taking a breath, analyzing and understanding the situation, then trying to come up with the most effective response.

THE HISTORY OF CONFLICT

In addition to teaching that conflict in itself is neutral, we also teach that *all conflict has history*. We often only see the moment

3. Lots more on what we mean by "justice" later in the book.

that a conflict erupts into violence; we take a snapshot of that moment and try to understand what is happening. What we do not see is the entire history of how that conflict escalated to that point. Without understanding that, we cannot truly understand the conflict.

Sometimes the history of the conflict is just between the people involved. Maybe Pat and Alex have walked to the store the last ten times, and Alex really feels like they should ride their bikes this time. Sometimes the history could be that Pat had a bad morning and is taking it out on Alex. Or maybe Alex has some unhealed trauma from childhood, and something that Pat said triggered that trauma, and that history is surfacing in their current conflict. Sometimes the history is generations in the making.

All conflict has history.

The Black Lives Matter movement exploded in Ferguson, Missouri, after the police killing of Michael Brown. Some people watched with surprise. "Why are people so upset?" some asked. "It's tragic, but it's not worth rioting over."

What happened in Ferguson wasn't about the shooting of Mike Brown. It was about a five-hundred-year legacy of Mike Browns. From slavery to Jim Crow to mass incarceration, the people of Ferguson were responding to centuries of systemic racism and violence. Ferguson was a pressure cooker with generations of pain. If we don't unpack that legacy, then we won't understand the conflict. If we don't understand the history of systemic oppression of African slaves and their descendants in this country, then we will never fully comprehend the Black Lives Matter movement. Understanding the intensity levels of conflict is one way to begin to unpack complex histories of trauma and pain.

Three Levels of Conflict

In addition to the four major types of conflict, Kingian Nonviolence offers three intensity levels of conflict as well, which offer another way of looking at conflict to help analyze and unpack it.

Normal Level: A normal level of conflict happens as a result of daily life pressures—traffic, bills, or minor disagreements about where to go to dinner. They are an unavoidable part of our lives, and none of us get through one day without experiencing some normal conflict.

At this level, you can often take a deep breath and get through your day. If a friend is experiencing normal levels of conflict, you can give them a hug or suggest they take a deep breath, and they'll be fine. You can easily prevent the conflict from escalating any further.

But what happens when you forget to set your alarm, wake up late, rush out of bed, stub your toe, open your fridge to find no milk for your cereal, get to your car and find a parking ticket, get to work late, and your boss yells at you? When normal conflicts add up, they escalate to the next level....

Pervasive Level: This is where you can feel the tension in the air, where it feels like one wrong comment could lead to a fight. This is the level that you can begin to see, hear, and feel the conflict beginning to escalate. Those warning signs are critical to notice. People begin to raise their voices or stop talking. People start to call each other names. In interpersonal or group conflict situations, they use words like "You *always* do this," or "You *never* do that." Body postures change. You can feel your blood warming.

I heard Dr. LaFayette say once that if you look out your window and you see rainclouds in the morning, that's a warning sign that it might rain. You would prepare yourself by grabbing an umbrella or a raincoat. But in our society, we often see warning signs that a conflict is escalating and do nothing about it until there's a thunderstorm.

Rather than waiting until someone gets hurt and then trying to figure out what to do, nonviolence is about learning to identify the warning signs and intervening as soon as possible. Normal conflict is much easier to deal with than a pervasive conflict, and if we don't intervene in conflict at the pervasive level, it can easily explode into the next level....

Overt Level: This is where conflict comes into full bloom. An overt conflict doesn't necessarily have to be physical. But at this level, real harm is being done. The overt level of conflict is the transition point between conflict and violence.

The best thing you can do now is to manage the conflict. Stopping the immediate harm becomes your priority, even if it requires a limited amount of physical force. In an interpersonal conflict, we may need to separate the two parties. In an international conflict, we may need to enforce a ceasefire. We need to let things cool down so that you can begin dialogue again.

In a social conflict, we may need nonviolent direct action such as shutting down a highway to protest an injustice. In each case we are trying to manage the conflict by stopping the immediate harm and deescalating things so we can get back to a dialogue.

Remember my duct-taped car from the last section? Well, for a long time, it had an oil leak. It wasn't that big of an issue, I just needed to keep an eye on it. Every once in a while, the "check oil" light would turn on. This would be a *normal level* of conflict. All it required was for me to pull over and feed some oil to my engine. No big deal.

If I ignored that warning sign, I would eventually see smoke coming out of my hood. *Pervasive level.* Now, pulling over and putting oil in my car was not enough. Because I had ignored the original warning sign, I had to let my car sit and cool down before I could add oil and hit the road again. If I ignored the smoke and still kept driving, it could have escalated to an *overt level* of conflict, and my transmission might have blown. Then I would have been dealing with a major ordeal.

I mentioned that at the normal level you can tell someone to take a deep breath. Have you ever told someone at a pervasive to overt level of conflict to take a deep breath? It might get you punched in the face. Different levels of conflict require different responses, which is why it is critical we understand the level of conflict we are engaging in.

Filling out a petition may not be the appropriate response to the latest police killing of an unarmed Black person, especially when you understand the five-hundred-year history of systemic racism underlying that individual shooting. Occupying land and shutting down highways may be an appropriate response to the construction of the latest pipeline being built through sacred Indigenous land after a five-hundred-year history of stealing Indigenous lands.

A petition may be appropriate for a normal or pervasive level of conflict, but when we look beyond the immediate manifestation and consider the entire history of a conflict, we may see that the conflict is actually very overt, and our nonviolent responses have to be appropriate. As a conflict escalates, our nonviolent response has to escalate to match its intensity. The higher the level, the more training and expertise is required in our response. Anyone can put oil into an engine. It takes a trained mechanic to fix a transmission system.

NORMALIZING CONFLICT

Some time ago, I met a brilliant man serving a life sentence in San Quentin State Prison. With his permission, I want to share a bit of his life story.

Years ago, Rafael was at a baseball game with his friends. He told me he was having a great day. His favorite team had just won the game. He and his friends were having a great time, laughing and joking around, enjoying a beautiful day. After the game was over, he and his friends were sitting in his car in the parking lot when a man walked past his car and brushed up against it as he walked by. Rafael ended up getting out of his car and stabbing and killing this man. I asked him what happened. How did he go from having a great day to killing a complete stranger over such a minor incident?

He shared with me that two weeks prior to that day, he had been in a fight and shot somebody. The person he had shot had survived. So Rafael knew that the person he had shot was coming after him, and he had been on edge those entire two weeks. This was just the most recent source of stress in his life. He had witnessed violence in his home from a young age and suffered from poverty all of his life.

After a lifetime of violence, that high level of tension had become so normal to him that he thought that he was having a great day—a normal day with only normal levels of conflict—when in reality he was experiencing a highly pervasive level, ready to boil over at any given moment. Take a water bottle. You can fill that bottle to a point where all it takes is one tiny drop of water to make it overflow. A stranger brushing up against his car was that last drop in Rafael's bottle.

Part of the work of nonviolence is about finding ways to heal, release that pressure, and heal from our traumas—constantly checking in with ourselves to see how full our bottle is and pouring out water when we need to. We know conflict is inevitable, and we know the more space we have in our bottle, the more space we have to absorb new conflicts without it overflowing.

Another part of nonviolence is understanding how systemic forms of oppression play into our analysis of the levels of conflict. Members of communities who have lived under generations of systemic racism and poverty never even get to experience a true normal level of conflict. Some people and some communities are living in a constant state of pervasive or overt conflicts, always ready to overflow. This is not because of some lack of capacity on their part, but because systemic forces have never given their communities time to breathe.

A saying from Islam teaches us that "a moment of patience in a moment of anger prevents a thousand moments of regret." It is oftentimes decisions that we make in split seconds that drastically alter the course of our lives. A second of patience may have led to a drastically different outcome in Rafael's life. Unfortunately, not all of us have the privilege to access the resources that may give us that moment of patience. The more violence we have been surrounded by in daily life, the fuller our bottle is, and the more likely we are to run out of patience. The more privilege we have, not only are we less likely to have experienced as much violence to begin with, but the more we may have access to resources like therapy, a supportive family environment, time to relax, access to nature, and other ways to destress and empty our bottle.

For some communities, a pervasive or even overt level of conflict have become normalized. I remember in 2010, I was with a group of trainers at North Lawndale College Preparatory Charter High School in Chicago. We were starting a five-day training to certify a group of student leaders as trainers in Kingian Nonviolence. The program began on a Monday, and the city of Chicago witnessed fifty shootings in the weekend that led up to it. We began by discussing this heightened level of violence, when one of the students told us, "Well it's a hot summer weekend. That's normal in Chicago."

A year prior, we had been at the same high school, facilitating the same training for a different cohort of students. Midway through the training, one of the young women in our group received a text message that her best friend had just been shot and was in the hospital. We put the training on hold and tried our best to create space for this young woman.

Tiffany Childress-Price, a teacher at that school, voiced that the level of violence her students witness is "not normal." She went on to say that there are "neighborhoods in Chicago where young people getting shot is not part of the daily reality."

That's when another young woman stood up and began to challenge us. "That's not true," she said. "This is how it is everywhere. This is how it's always been." For this one young woman, this level of violence was all she had ever known. She couldn't even imagine that this wasn't the case everywhere. This level of violence had become the norm to her.

When we talk about a normal level of conflict, we are not talking about what has become normalized in so many communities. We are talking about a low-intensity level of conflict. Racism has become normalized. Poverty has become normalized. Patriarchy has become normalized. Ecological destruction has become normalized. So many things have become normalized in our society, and part of the work of nonviolence is to never normalize violence and injustice.

UNUSUAL, YET GENUINE

Some people believe that when a conflict escalates to the overt level, the only option we have is violence. It is not. There are countless examples of successful nonviolent responses to the most overt forms of violence in interpersonal, intercommunal, and international situations. A nonviolent response usually requires more training and/or more creativity. In the heat of an overt conflict, a violent response is oftentimes easier to think about. It requires less planning and less training.

Lori, a dear friend and fellow Kingian Nonviolence trainer, once told me a story of how she was able to nonviolently de-escalate an overt conflict. Lori is an incredible musician with an angelic voice. One day, she was coming home from work and saw a fight break out. One man was on the ground getting beaten by another. So what is a musician to do? She ran inside her house, grabbed her guitar, ran back outside, went right up to the two men and started singing a gentle tune. As she tells the story, the one who was standing looked up at her mid-punch with a confused look. I imagine the thought running through his mind must have been along the lines of, "What the hell is this crazy woman doing singing in my face?" With a confused and puzzled look, he stopped fighting and walked away.

Justin, another Kingian trainer in the South Side of Chicago, tells a similar story in which he came home one night to find a group of men fighting in a schoolyard across the street from his house. He immediately ran toward them, climbed the fence, and ran full speed toward the group of men. I imagine they must have thought that Justin was running over the join the fray or at least to use physical force to break up the fight. But instead, he stopped just short of the group, and started clapping and singing "This Little Light of Mine" at the top of his lungs. Again, the confused group stopped fighting and dispersed.

Part of what made Justin and Lori's responses effective was that they were coming from a genuine place. Dr. LaFayette often says that, "An unusual yet genuine act has the potential to arrest the conscience of your assailant." Responding to a fight by singing is certainly an "unusual act." But it was also genuine, because Justin and Lori had been cultivating that kind of universal love for years through their practices of nonviolence. That is why it is so critical that we train in the art of nonviolence. If it is your first time lifting weights, you do not start by putting 500 pounds on your barbell. You start with 50, work your way up to 75, then 100, 150, and eventually with enough training you may get to lift 500 pounds.

In 1960, David Hartsough, an activist who would go on to have more than 125 arrests for his nonviolent resistance, was participating in a lunch counter sit-in at the People's Drug Store in Arlington, Virginia. He was sitting on the counter, reading his Bible and meditating over Jesus's instructions to "love your enemies," when he turned around and saw a white man holding a knife to his heart. The man told David, "You nigger lover, get out of this store in two seconds, or I'm going to stab this through your heart."

I'll let David explain what happened next, from his book *Waging Peace: Global Adventures of a Lifelong Activist*:

> Loving my enemy was suddenly more than just a discussion in Sunday school or a confrontation among schoolboys over ice balls. For a fleeting moment I doubted that Jesus meant to include a man so hateful among those who deserved to be loved. I had just seconds to respond to him, and I was grateful for those many hours of role-playing and practice the previous two days. I turned around and tried my best to smile. Looking him in the eye, I said to him, "Friend, do what you believe is right, and I will still try to love you." Both his jaw and his hand dropped. Miraculously, he turned away and walked out of the store.

What David did was the equivalent of lifting 500 pounds. It was not his first time. He was able to do it because he had already committed himself to a life of nonviolence and had been training for that moment.

David's choice might have gotten him killed, but a violent response might have as well. David goes on to write, "If I had tried to fight back, I probably would have been stabbed." If he had simply given into fear, he would have been surrendering to violence and allowing segregation to continue. In that moment, a nonviolent response was "not only the right thing but also the most effective thing."

In the heat of an overt conflict, "an unusual yet genuine act" can shake someone up enough to open up a brief moment of vulnerability. And it is in that moment that we can reach their humanity. It's in that moment that they may show a crack in their armor, and we can reach the conscience of an assailant.

RELATIONSHIP, SKILL, AND STRUCTURE

I once heard someone say, "Conflict is the spirit of the relationship asking itself to deepen." It is through conflict that relationships are strengthened, and we begin to see each other in our authenticity. When handled right, conflict is a sacred gift. But it has to be handled right.

When managing conflict, having tense discussions, or working to heal old wounds, I like to use a Venn diagram I first saw used by NVC teacher Miki Kashtan (which I then adapted a bit) to list three conditions that can help make conflict generative:

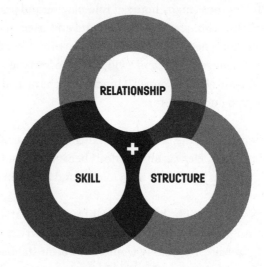

Three conditions for a creative conflict: relationship, skill, and structure.

My belief is that at least two of these three things need to be in place for a difficult conversation to go well. With a skilled facilitator, a tense discussion among a group of people who enjoy strong, trusting relationships has a good chance of resulting in a positive outcome. If no one in the group has much experience facilitating, then instituting some form of structure—such as using a talking stick, a well-thought-out agenda, or some other facilitation tools— can replace a skilled facilitator.[1] One time, my mother asked me to facilitate a conversation within our family. Our family experienced a lot of challenges growing up, and because of the conflict-averse nature of Japanese culture, we rarely talk about it. Knowing the work that I do, she wanted me to help open up some difficult conversations and move us toward healing.

Conflict is the spirit of the relationship asking itself to deepen.

I freaked out. I trusted the relationships we all have with each other as family members, and I was pretty confident in my ability as a facilitator. But I knew that if we were going to start to talk about wounds that exist in our family dynamics, my own traumas would rise to the surface, and my skills as a facilitator would go out the window. I had to make sure there was a strong structure in place, so that we would not be relying on my facilitation. I introduced the idea of a talking circle and a talking piece.[2]

I had written down a few prompts, such as "What's one thing you want to tell each person in the family?" and "What's one thing

1. Eastern Mennonite University's Little Books of Justice and Peacebuilding series has two books that offer some useful approaches: *Cool Tools for Hot Topics* and *Dialogue for Difficult Subjects*.

2. A talking piece is an object that gets passed around in a circle, signifying whose turn it is to speak. While there are many ways to facilitate a talking circle, traditionally only the person with the talking piece is allowed to speak, and there is no cross-talk. This creates a sense of safety for the speaker. Pat St. Onge, an Indigenous elder, once told me that a talking piece is called a "talking" piece, but it is really about listening. It is a reminder to the people not holding it to pay full attention to the person with the piece, which could be a stone, a stick, a sacred object, or something with no particular significance.

that no one else in the family knows about you?" I explained that we would pass the talking piece around, and we would each answer one question at a time, with no cross talk. That structure allowed me to be fully engaged in the discussion, allow whatever emotions came up for me, and not to worry about facilitating the conversation.

There is obviously no cookie-cutter approach to conflict, but the Relationship, Skill, Structure diagram can help you gauge what is in place and what is missing, thereby helping you figure out how to adjust. Over the years, I've participated in forming and managing countless groups, organizations, coalitions, and networks. I've come to the conclusion that structures, policies, systems, and bureaucracies are often an attempt to compensate for a lack of trust and relationships between people.

Systems and structures can be helpful and supportive, and there will always be times when we need to rely on them. But ultimately our goal should be to increase and strengthen our relationships as well as our skills in managing conflicts so that we can rely less on systems and more on one another. We should only call on systems and structures when necessary, as opposed to relying on them as the default. If we trust each other and have some basic skills, we should be able to manage conflict without a mediator, without calling the police, and without creating more bureaucracy to manage it.

> **Structures, policies, systems, and bureaucracies are often an attempt to compensate for a lack of trust and relationships.**

CHAPTER 7

The Colonization of Our Minds

In the introduction to this book, I talked about how Dr. King considered the German philosopher Hegel one of his biggest influences, despite Hegel's racist worldview. Dr. King's ability to take what benefited him and to leave the rest behind is a critical aspect of the nonviolent worldview. If we can't even entertain the possibility that our opponent's view has value or some small nugget of truth, how can we begin to find a resolution? Exploring others' viewpoints to understand where they are coming from is a vital component that is often missing from today's political conversations, resulting in increased polarization and little hope of reconciliation.

Nonviolence takes a dialectic approach to conflict, which means that we seek out truth by understanding that one side of a conflict never has a monopoly on truth. We understand that by listening to alternate perspectives—not to find holes in opposing arguments and criticize them, but with a genuine attempt to understand and synthesize aspects of the opposing truth to ours—we strengthen our own perspectives. We get closer to Truth with a capital T.

When I first met David C. Jehnsen, the coauthor of the Kingian Nonviolence curriculum, he told me that this dialectic worldview is one of the most important elements of the curriculum. I didn't see it then. I saw the value of trying to synthesize two opposing beliefs, but it just didn't seem that deep to me. Over time, I began to see what David meant. I now see the importance of a dialectic worldview *everywhere*. Our inability to see nuance, our inability to see beyond a right/wrong binary, and our inability to look for the truth in the other side of a conflict is one of the biggest contributing factors to division at every level.

Edmundo Norte, the dean of Intercultural and International Studies at De Anza College in California, once said, "The black/white, right/wrong, one-way or the other worldview is the most pervasive way that our minds have been colonized by the state." If we look back to any of our Indigenous worldviews, we understood that things are rarely, if ever, black and white. Our world is nuanced, and most things exist on a spectrum. Yet in a society that is oftentimes dominated by an Abrahamic worldview that pits "good" against "evil," we are unable to see the nuance.

When I'm in an argument with someone, I usually know I'm right. If I'm correct, then the other person must be wrong, right? If the other person is wrong, what's the point of even listening to them? There's nothing I can gain from understanding a perspective that is wrong. I've seen this pattern play out countless times. Because we disagree about some things a person says, we assume that we have nothing in common. We stop listening to try to understand and instead only listen to identify the holes in their arguments in order to strengthen and justify our own position. It's the opposite of confirmation bias.[1] We are living in a culture of opposition bias.

Many of us operate like this: *Because I'm a liberal, I have nothing to learn from a conservative. Because I'm pro-choice, I have nothing in common with someone who is pro-life. Because I support gun control, someone who doesn't has no idea what they're talking about.* I've felt this polarization get worse in the past few years. In left-wing politics, there seems to be a prevailing worldview that people who don't agree with every social justice principle are racist, sexist, classist, and basically just the worst type of human being. You're either with us or you're a racist, and there's no in between.

People on the right seem to think others who don't agree with their worldview are over-sensitive communists or anti-patriotic

---

1. Confirmation bias is the tendency to look for, interpret, or favor only the information that supports your already held belief, ignoring any facts that may challenge that.

elitist morons who just want to sit on a moral high horse and complain about everything. You're either with us, or you're an SJW snowflake, and there's no in between.[2] Part of the work of nonviolence is to expand the in-between space, sit in the nuance, and sit in the contradiction.

One practice I have adopted is to listen to conservative podcasts and read right-wing papers and books by authors I may have significant disagreements with. As I listen, my focus is on trying to find what I do agree with or to understand *why* they believe what they believe. This way, when I find myself in conversation with someone who has different views, I can help us to find common ground—the starting place for creative resolution.

I consider this practice like sparring sessions in a gym. It's not real fighting, but it gives me practice for real-life conflict situations. Listening to someone I disagree with on a podcast prepares me to have conversations in person with a greater level of understanding and empathy than I might otherwise. It has been enlightening to realize I don't disagree with everything a conservative talk-show host has to say. It has been humbling to listen to their criticisms of progressive worldviews and policy proposals and realize I agree with some of what they say.

Troy Williams, a formerly incarcerated leader and restorative justice facilitator, once told me: "The person on the other side might be 99 percent wrong. But what's the 1 percent of what they're saying that you can understand and agree with? Understanding that 1 percent will strengthen your own perspective."

SOMETIMES THEY'RE JUST WRONG

What if there is no 1 percent? What if someone is just flat-out wrong? Even in that case, it's still important to understand where

2. "SJW" is shorthand for Social Justice Warrior, a term used by those on the right to criticize people on the left that they deem too sensitive. How sad that the idea of being a warrior for social justice is now a derogatory term. "Snowflake" is another term used by those on the right to make fun of leftists who they deem to be easily triggered by anything they consider offensive.

that person is coming from. Understanding another person's perspective in a conflict does not mean you condone it. It does not mean you agree with their conclusions. The purpose is to gather more information about the conflict so you can see the full picture. Without understanding how the other side is viewing the conflict, you are responding to the conflict with only 50 percent of the story (yours).

There are plenty of opinions I hear in conservative podcasts that I simply disagree with. But when I listen for the perspective from which those opinions are coming, I hear genuine concerns and fears and genuine attempts to understand our world to figure out what's best for society. Many people on the left believe that people who voted for Trump are either racist or stupid and don't know any better. That sort of oversimplification does not allow us to understand the nuance and the reality of the situation. If we do not try to understand the complexity of a conflict, we will not have the information necessary to resolve it.

Understanding another person's perspective in a conflict does not mean you condone it.

When I was organizing around the shooting of Oscar Grant, I found myself in a meeting with one of the deputy chiefs of the Oakland Police Department, someone who I believe genuinely wants to work in partnership with community to find real resolutions. During the meeting, he told me about an old Supreme Court case from 1989 called *Graham v. Connor*. Long story short, this Supreme Court decision set the national standard in how incidents of police shootings are investigated.[3] The investigation takes a snapshot of the moment that force was used and asks,

---

3. I regret not having the time and space to go deeper into the *Graham v. Connor* case. This ruling is critical in understanding police violence today and is the reason why so many officers are never even charged after gross incidents of violence. Particularly for anyone interested in the Movement for Black Lives, but really anyone, I highly recommend looking further into this. I would suggest starting by listening to the Radiolab podcast, "More Perfect: Mr. Graham and the Reasonable Man," available online.

"In that exact moment, would a reasonable officer have acted in the same manner?" In other words, according to this investigation methodology, if an officer says he or she was scared in that exact moment, regardless of the circumstances that led up to that moment, it is considered a "justified shooting."

It doesn't matter if the officer ended up shooting a twelve-year-old child like Tamir Rice. It doesn't matter if the person shot was running away, like Walter Scott. It doesn't matter if the person killed had his hands in the air, as was reported with Michael Brown. It doesn't matter if police were found to have unnecessarily escalated the situation and that the person shot was being held face down on the ground, like Oscar Grant. From the perspective of the investigation, none of that matters.

From the perspective of law enforcement, all that matters is whether or not the officer was reasonably scared in the moment the shot was fired. This is a perspective that I adamantly disagree with. I believe it is dangerous and way too shallow a standard in an era where police killings happen at a rate of more than 2.5 per day, an unfathomable number.[4] After finding out more about the history of *Graham v. Connor*, it made sense to me why all of these shootings are considered justified by a court of law. I disagree with it, but I understand it. Now that I understand it, I also understand that one thing the movement needs to push for is to change the investigation methodology. So often we have hoped that if we scream "justice" loudly enough, things will magically change. But what we need is to understand the issue well enough to develop concrete demands for changes in policy, procedure, and the law. In this case, understanding the perspective of law enforcement helped me to understand the issue much better.

When we ask whether or not a shooting was justified, the community and the police are using the word "justified" in two

---

4. *The Washington Post* has been tracking police killings in the United States since 2015. That year, there were 955 people killed by police in the United States. There were 963 people killed in 2016 and 987 in 2017.

different ways. We are using the same finger but pointing at two different things. The community is asking the question from the perspective of the victim: Was the shooting necessary? Was it right, or was it wrong? Did the victim deserve to get shot? Law enforcement officials are asking the question from the perspective of the officer: Was it justified that the officer might have been scared in that moment? The question about whether or not the victim "deserved it" doesn't enter the equation.

The ability to understand and share the feelings of another is the definition of empathy, a word used frequently in nonviolence. Empathy can sometimes be confused as a weak and passive thing, when in reality it can often require tremendous humility to try and understand another's perspective so that we can have a better sense of what's happening. The kind of empathy that enables someone to understand another person's story and perspective isn't just about being nice or condoning actions we don't agree with. It's about being strategic and smart.

CONTRADICTING TRUTHS

Sometimes, contradicting perspectives can both be true at the same time. This can be confusing if we see the world as black and white. But truth and perspective are not a zero-sum game. My truth does not negate yours, even if our truths don't match up.

Here's an example. I believe that the focus on individual responsibility in violent crime is problematic. Yes, people choose what they do, as we are all beings with free will.[5] But the choices we make are limited by our circumstances. A person may choose to sell drugs or rob a liquor store, but if the choice is between that or watching your children go to bed hungry, what kind of a choice is that? If a person engages in an act of violence, but violence has

---

5. This, of course is also debatable. Many Eastern worldviews would hold that we are all nothing but a series of causes and conditions, playing out karmas and *sankharas* that were set in motion long before we came into being. Some scientists, including neuroscientist Sam Harris, also argue that free will is an illusion.

been the only example that has ever been set in their lives for dealing with conflict, is that really a choice? In cases of extreme poverty, I believe that socioeconomic factors play a much more significant role than individual choice in the prevalence of crime.

Understanding the larger factors that contribute to cycles of violence is part of how people begin to free themselves from its grip. When incarcerated people realize they are not in prison because they are "bad" people, incapable of making good decisions, but rather "good" people who have been in bad circumstances, they can begin to imagine making new choices. On the other hand, I have found that when a person who has caused harm fully owns their role in it and holds themselves 100 percent accountable without making any excuses, they can begin to heal. A person's ability to say, "I did that, I made that decision, it's on me and nothing else," is a critical component to their own healing journey. Both of those realities—the role of socioeconomic and historical factors in crime and the role of personal responsibility—are seemingly at odds, but both are 100 percent true and necessary to recognize for healing to take place.

Truth and perspective are not a zero-sum game.

As another example, I've been part of campaigns to defund police departments. I am generally opposed to domestic police agencies investing in things like drones and armored personnel carriers when those millions of dollars could be spent on things like education and health care. I believe those investments will ultimately make our communities safer than investing in weapons and strategies that suppress and only perpetuate violence.

However, I once had a conversation with a police officer who described a situation in which they were attempting to enter a building while a shooter was firing shots at them from a second story window. He described how they were able to safely enter the building and subdue the shooter only because of the armored vehicle. I remember him telling me that it's easy for people to say that these vehicles are an unnecessary use of city funds when their lives aren't dependent on it. I still believe 100 percent that we should be divesting from law enforcement and investing in community resources, but I can't argue that an armored vehicle could make the difference between life and death. I acknowledge that for those officers, this perspective is 100 percent true.

Another example is the case of the militarized training of law enforcement officials, which many people oppose. Militarized trainings involve boot camps where a strict hierarchy is heavily enforced. Newer recruits are placed through rigorous and sometimes painful trainings with little sleep and rest. Officers are told when to wake up (typically early), when and what to eat, and are generally stripped of choice and free will (other than to quit the program). The intent of such training is to break you down so they can build you back up again.

Many people consider these types of trainings violent and traumatic and not helpful. However the same people who see these boot camps that way may also regard my time in the monastery with respect, when in fact this last paragraph describes my time in monastery to a T. Many Buddhist monasteries operate under a strict hierarchy, and if you think there is anything easy about monastic life, I challenge you to try it. It can be incredibly rigid and demanding, and you are stripped of much choice. And yet, that is where I found liberation.

It is 100 percent true that having choice taken away by a rigid structure can be violent, and it is also 100 percent true that the discipline of that rigid structure can be liberating. These are two opposing truths that can somehow coexist. So many unproductive arguments could be avoided if we simply stop digging in our heels and trying to prove that our truth and our perspective are the only truth and the only right perspective.

PART TWO
THE WILL

The Six Principles of Nonviolence

The Six Principles of Nonviolence
1. Nonviolence is a way of life for courageous people.
2. The Beloved Community is the framework for the future.
3. Attack forces of evil, not persons doing evil.
4. Accept suffering for the sake of the cause to achieve the goal.
5. Avoid internal violence of the spirit as well as external physical violence.
6. The universe is on the side of justice.

The six principles, which we will explore in these next chapters, were first articulated by Dr. King in his famous essay, "Pilgrimage to Nonviolence."[1] The essay first appeared in the April 1960 edition of *The Christian Century* magazine as part of a series of essays by critical thinkers called "How My Mind Has Changed" and later appeared as a chapter in King's first book, *Stride Toward Freedom*. It is perhaps the best articulation of his philosophy of nonviolence. Dr. LaFayette and Jehnsen took the words laid out by King in this essay and codified them into what we now call the Six Principles of Kingian Nonviolence. The six principles are oftentimes referred to as "the will" of nonviolence. They are the spirit that drive this work forward, and they are, in totality, the core of the philosophy of Kingian Nonviolence Conflict Reconciliation.

The Oxford dictionary defines a principle as "a fundamental truth or proposition that serves as the foundation for a system of belief or behavior or for a chain of reasoning." To me, a principle is

---

1. The next six chapters, to be exact. What a shocker.

a universal truth. As described in the first of the six principles, all of the principles are intended to serve as a foundation for beliefs and behaviors we try to bring into every interaction—to every aspect of our lives. They are not things that we practice over here but forget about over there. They are not propositions that we apply in certain cases and not in others. If we agree with them, then we treat them as universal truths, applicable always.

These six principles come as a package. To practice one without practicing all of them would be an incomplete practice. You can learn all the different ways to throw a punch, but if you don't learn the kicks also, you're not learning the full array of skills of kickboxing.

These six principles of nonviolence are a package. To practice one without practicing all of them would be an incomplete practice.

It is important to see the principles as an interrelated whole because a question raised in one principle may be answered in another. Something missing in one principle may be found in the next. No one sentence or concept can fully capture the complexity of our world, but the six principles of nonviolence in totality add up to a complete philosophy.

If you come to a two-day introductory workshop in Kingian Nonviolence, we spend about four hours exploring these six sentences. I've been studying them for ten years at this point, and I am still understanding them in new, deeper ways. So if parts of them don't make immediate sense to you, I encourage you to stay open and curious and continue to grapple with them as I have.

CHAPTER 9

Principle One: Nonviolence Is a Way of Life for Courageous People

"Nonviolence is for punks."

"Nonviolence is weak."

"I'm not gonna be nonviolent and back down."

"I'm not gonna just sit there and let someone abuse me."

These are all common things I hear in my work, and they are all rooted in a misunderstanding of nonviolence. The misunderstanding lies in the difference between "non-violence" and "nonviolence."

The reality is that a commitment to taking a stand against violence, fighting injustice, and working to address harm takes an incredible amount of courage. Nonviolence is about *doing something.* Taking action to fight for justice and Beloved Community is an act of courage. This is not to say that people who use violence are cowards. As much as I may disagree with someone's use of violence, or as much as I may disagree with their reasons for engaging in acts of violence, I can still understand and respect the courage it takes to fight for something. Anyone who risks their lives, their personal safety, or their reputation is practicing courage.

Yet, one could argue that acting with nonviolence takes even *more* courage than acting with violence. Imagine you were going into a situation where you knew you might face some kind of physical violence—would you feel safer knowing you had a weapon on you, and you could fight back, or knowing that you were unarmed and committed to accepting any blow without retaliating?

Nonviolence takes great courage when understood in the proper context. It takes courage to walk away from a fight. I hear that a lot, especially in my work with incarcerated men. In this context, it makes sense. Walking away from a fight in a hypermasculine prison culture could make one look weak and vulnerable. You could become a target.

Going against what is expected to take a stand for what you believe, despite what others may think or what the consequences may be, takes incredible courage. In fact, as much as you are walking *away* from one thing, you are walking *toward* something else. You are walking toward a commitment to nonviolence, toward a better future, and toward Beloved Community.

But context matters. In some contexts, walking away from a fight could be the exact opposite of courage. If you are walking away from a conflict because you're scared to fight, and don't know what else to do, that could be called cowardice. If you refuse to stand up to injustice, that is not nonviolence. Nonviolence is not about refusing to engage in violence out of fear or a lack of capacity to use violence. It is about acknowledging that violence is an option but choosing a tactic that you believe is more powerful or more aligned with your values.

Nonviolence is a proactive approach to confronting and transforming conflict. It requires action. Refusing to fight out of fear is inaction. Committing to doing something to transform violence is action. In some ways, you could even make the argument that a person who breaks a store window in a protest for justice is more in alignment with the true understanding of nonviolence than a person who sits at home, does nothing to confront injustice, and criticizes the protester for breaking the window.

This is not to condone the breaking of windows. I believe that property destruction, especially in the United States, is typically a highly ineffective strategy, but at least the window-breaker is doing something to confront injustice.[1] At least that person has the will and courage to take to the streets, demand change, and

1. There are exceptions that I have seen. There is more on the topic of property destruction in general in the appendix.

risk arrest and possible injury for a cause that they believe in. It takes no courage to sit on your couch at home and criticize how others choose to fight for change.

Mahatma Gandhi, one of the most well-known practitioners of nonviolence, once famously said, "I do believe that, where there is only a choice between cowardice and violence, I would advise violence." Gandhi made many comments throughout his life that hammered home this point:

> Whilst I may not actually help anyone retaliate, I must not let a coward seek shelter behind nonviolence so-called. Not knowing the stuff of which nonviolence is made, many have honestly believed that running away from danger every time was a virtue compared to offering resistance, especially when it was fraught with danger to one's life....
>
> My creed of nonviolence is an extremely active force. It has no room for cowardice or even weakness. There is hope for a violent man to be some day nonviolent, but there is none for a coward. I have, therefore, said more than once... that, if we do not know how to defend ourselves, our women and our places of worship by the force of suffering, i.e., nonviolence, we must, if we are men, be at least able to defend all these by fighting.
>
> Self-defense is the only honourable course where there is unreadiness for self-immolation.[2] Leaving aside the gendered nature of his language, it was clear to Gandhi that nonviolence was not about inaction and not about letting someone continue to abuse you without doing anything about it.[3] It was not about being nice and polite in the face

---

2. This excerpt is taken from *The Mind of Mahatma Gandhi*, edited by Ramachandra Krishna Prabhu and U. R. Rao, and *What Gandhi Says: About Nonviolence, Resistance and Courage* by Norman G. Ficklestein.

3. I don't wish to invalidate the significance of patriarchal thinking, which is so deeply entrenched in many of the teachings of great leaders like Gandhi and King; taken at face value, their writing would suggest that only men existed in

of injustice. For Gandhi, violence was clearly more coura-geous than inaction. And yet, he viewed nonviolence as the highest form of courage. For Gandhi, nonviolence under-stood in the proper context was, "the summit of bravery" and "infinitely superior to violence."

COURAGE OF VULNERABILITY

Even after years of studying and teaching Kingian Nonviolence, every once in a while I hear someone talk about a principle or concept in a way that opens up a whole new level of understand-ing for me. One day, I was in a workshop inside the Correctional Training Facility (CTF), also known as Soledad State Prison. All of our workshops inside this prison are led by our inmate train-ers. One of our trainers, Roy Duran, was breaking down Principle One: "Nonviolence is a way of life for courageous people" for the workshop participants, his incarcerated peers.

Suddenly, Roy went into full-on prophetic mode and blew everyone away with the most powerful explanation of this prin-ciple I have ever heard in my life. With his permission, I'm going to offer the words he shared with us:

> As a young boy, I was sensitive, empathic, and loving. However, through virtually all the agencies of socializa-tion, I was taught that my behavior was not in line with the rules of who I was supposed to be as "a man." I was supposed to be tough, strong, and violent, or at least convince people that I was willing to be. I learned that the rules also informed me of who I was not supposed to be: sensitive and vulner-ably honest about my emotions.
>
> As a consequence of accepting the indoctrination of

the world, or that women were only objects to be protected. While that kind of gendered language was used almost universally during their time (including by women), we also need to name that toxic patriarchy is at the root of so much of the violence in our world—it is, in fact, perhaps one of the single biggest contributors. More on this in chapter sixteen.

the ideology of toxic masculinity, I became drawn to big, strong, powerful, and violent role models. Mike Tyson, Jean-Claude Van Damme, and Tony Montana from *Scarface* were people that I wanted to emulate. I was convinced that rash, reckless, and violent behavior was me being "a man" and "courageous." In retrospect I can see that I wanted to be safe, secure, and have an identity and purpose that I would be confident in. I took the easiest route I could find in my neighborhood, and I became a drug dealer and gang member. In my distorted view of reality, I had a sense of pride and loyalty, and I achieved criminal success.

I was charged, tried, and convicted of murder. After receiving my life sentence, I was shook to my core by the tidal wave of consequences from my self-centered, violent behavior. A week after I was sentenced, my dad committed suicide. A month later, my grandfather died from a heart attack. My mom's health was failing due to stress, and my kids were living in an unstable hell worse than any abuse I ever experienced. I took away my own ability to hold my own daughter.... I could only imagine what the family members of the man I murdered were going through.

It was later that I learned what it really means to be courageous. I love etymology, the origin of words, because I have found that words in their original language often have a deeper meaning than the translation of the word. For example, "courage" comes from the Latin *cor*, meaning "heart." I learned that in its earliest forms, the word meant "to speak one's mind by telling all one's heart."

Courage means that I have the internal fortitude to honestly speak from my heart and to act in congruence with the content of my heart. I realized later that it didn't take any courage for me to commit murder. That was an act that was based on fear. I was afraid of being judged, of being seen as weak, of not being accepted, of letting people see my emotions, of letting people see the real me.

I ultimately learned that being my truest self is what takes the most courage. To me, courage means that I'm going to be true to myself even if everyone around me is telling me that what's wrong is right. I am willing to suffer if that is what life offers.

Courage showed me how to open up and talk about the things I'm most ashamed of, being vulnerable. Speaking about our true emotions, being vulnerable and showing all of our heart, showing all of who we are is what takes the most courage. I'm my most authentic self when I'm speaking my mind and revealing my heart.

Courage showed me how to open up. I attend groups inside, and I share things that could get me killed if I said them in the wrong places.[4] But I feel most alive in these groups. I'm my most authentic self. Courage is about speaking truth. Dr. King died for it. I just hope I can live for it. If the price is death, at least I'll know I died for truth. For now, I'll just live for it.

Right now I am fighting the good fight of nonviolence in the middle of a gang war in prison. The fear of the unknown is real and so is my commitment to love.

People were left in tears. I found myself wishing badly that it were easier to bring recording devices into prison, because it felt like a moment that deserved to captured forever for posterity, for the benefit of humanity.

This "ordinary courage" that Brown talks about, and that Roy practices on a daily basis, is an understated form of courage and an understated aspect of nonviolence. Over time, I've learned

---

4. This is a comment I've heard from several men in several different prisons. The work of opening up, being vulnerable, speaking of the things they are most ashamed of, and speaking honestly about their experiences could make them a target inside. Knowing that, these men still choose to speak. If that's not courage, I don't know what is.

that so much of nonviolence is about learning to be seen in our vulnerability.

Years ago, I attended a "Jam" organized by my friend Shilpa Jain's organization YES. Jams are hard to describe, but they are gatherings of mostly young adults exploring issues of identity, change, and transformation. During the opening circle, I remember telling people that crying is not something I do much of, and I jokingly challenged Shilpa to make me cry. Of course, I was the first man in the group to completely break down.

> "Courage means that I have the internal fortitude to honestly speak from my heart and to act in congruence with the content of my heart."
> —Roy Duran

During a fishbowl discussion, I shared a story that I had never shared in public.[5] I had no idea how much shame and trauma I still had wrapped up in that story until I spoke about it.[6] The words fell out of my mouth and dropped into the middle of the circle with the weight of an anvil. I thought it was a story that I had gotten over. I hadn't. At all. I lost it. I broke down in tears. It was the first time in my adult life that I cried like that in public.

Much of my work inside prisons is about helping to create space to open up about the stuff that we least want to talk about, such as our most painful wounds or the things of which we are most ashamed. Brené Brown teaches that "shame derives its power from being unspeakable." We lock up and repress all of the things that we are ashamed of, so it lies dormant, harnessing power over us in ways that we do not understand.

I had no idea I was holding so much shame for all of those years until I spoke it out loud for the first time. That shame was at the root of so much of the violence and harm in my life. It was responsible

---

5. A facilitation tool where a small group of participants sit in a circle and have a discussion while everyone else sits in a larger circle around them listening.
6. I'm going to refrain from going into what that actual story was, since it's not only my story, but involves multiple people.

for my insecurities, my inability to have authentic connections with others, and the emotional harm I caused the people closest to me. I have learned over time that speaking directly about those things is the only way to unburden myself from those forms of violence. Speaking about our shame and being vulnerable in that way is an act of nonviolence. It is an action aimed to address harm, and healing this harm is an act of nonviolence.

Specifically, I have become a firm believer in sharing our vulnerability in community settings: circles, community mental health models, and communities working on self-transformation. We are harmed in relationships, so we need to heal in relationships. We are harmed in community, so we need to heal in community.

Being vulnerable in front of people can take incredible courage. Especially those of us who have been socialized as men have a lifetime of messaging that tells us, "boys don't cry." One of the first times I was inside CTF, Barrios Unidos's founder Nane Alejandrez was speaking to a group of about two hundred incarcerated men when he started to shed tears from the podium.

He acknowledged that in an environment like a prison, it may not be possible for someone to cry. He said that was part of the reason why he was crying in front of everyone, because when one person is vulnerable, that could be healing for those who witness it. "You don't know who is not capable of shedding their own tears. You don't know who else you're crying for." His willingness to sacrifice his own tears, to be vulnerable as a way to serve others was a courageous act of nonviolence. It was fierce vulnerability.

We are harmed in relationships, so we need to heal in relationships. We are harmed in community, so we need to heal in community.

A WAY OF LIFE

In addition to addressing the courage of nonviolence, this first principle also talks about a lifelong commitment. Nonviolence *is a way of life* for courageous people. Nonviolence is not a switch that you turn on when you go to a protest and turn off when you are back home. It is not something you ignore when you are in your meetings organizing the protest and sign a pledge to only when you hit the streets. It is not something you practice in your workplace and then disregard in your personal relationships. Nonviolence, at its best, is something that we aim to practice in every interaction, in every moment of our lives. It is a way of life.

In mindfulness meditation, we sit (or walk) in silence, continually bringing our awareness back to our breath. There is a popular misunderstanding about meditation that we simply sit and do nothing. On the contrary, meditation is a practice of incredible discipline. For as long as you are meditating, you are constantly focusing and refocusing your mind on your breath. Every time you realize that your mind has wandered off, you gently bring your attention back to your breath..So while one may seem to be sitting absolutely still from the outside looking in, there may be an active and dynamic process of mindfulness and concentration occurring below the surface.

My friend Bill Bank, one of the first Kingian Nonviolence trainers certified in Oakland and a long-time meditator, once described meditation to me as the practice of "having awareness that your mind has wandered off and bringing your attention back to your breath. And repeating that a billion times." Every time you refocus your attention onto your breath, you are training yourself to be fully aware, to be mindful of the present moment.

We spend most of our lives worrying about the future or fretting over the past, and so rarely are we focused on this exact moment. We spend most of our day running on autopilot, performing one task while planning the next. The practice of meditation cultivates our mindfulness of the present moment. If we are only mindful when we are in sitting meditation, we are missing the point. The goal is to cultivate the muscle of mindfulness so that we can take that into every moment of our lives. For me to be mindful in this exact moment, I start to feel the keys of my laptop against my fingernails and listen to the sound of the blender in the cafe where I am working. This is an example of practicing mindfulness as a way of life.

We do not *become* meditation through the practice of meditation, but we can become more mindful, calm, or present in life by cultivating those characteristics through the practice. Similarly, we will never *become* nonviolence, but how do we cultivate courage, love, and understanding in every interaction we have? What does it mean to adopt nonviolence as a way of life? Nonviolence as a way of life is not about perfection. No one becomes purely nonviolent, so it is not about living a life where we never cause harm. That is as impossible as living a life in which our minds never wander. Even the greatest meditators in the world have wandering minds.

Practicing nonviolence is about trying to live it as a way of life, trying to embody it, and trying to exercise those muscles every day. It is about trying to utilize the muscles that we have cultivated in our interactions, in our attempts to create change at a personal or social level. It is an aspiration. With the first principle, Kingian Nonviolence firmly plants a flag on the side of a principled approach to nonviolence, as opposed to a simply tactical commitment. It is not just effective strategy for political change. It is a moral imperative for social transformation.

We commit to practicing nonviolence in every interaction in every moment, as best we can, because our goal is so much broader than passing a new law or winning a political campaign. Our goal is to repair harm, reconcile relationships, and move ever so slightly closer to Beloved Community.

Principle Two: The Beloved Community Is the Framework for the Future

We've chanted them at rallies, read them in talking points, and included them in our list of demands.

"We demand justice for *all* people."

"*All* life is sacred."

"Liberation for *all* beings."

But when we say "all," do we really mean all? My experience tells me that we rarely actually mean it. Usually what we mean to say is that we are fighting for justice for all of *our* people. The people we like. The people on our side. And too often, justice for *our* people comes at the expense of *those* people. When we are able to defeat those people, then our people will have justice.

In nonviolence, when we talk about building a world where all people can achieve justice and fulfill our potential as human beings, we really mean all people. That is Dr. King's vision of "Beloved Community," where all people can live in peace. Beloved Community is an acknowledgment that the only way for a peace to ever be sustainable, the only way that our people can always be safe, is if all people are free.

One of the hardest concepts to fully commit to is the idea that there is no one outside of Beloved Community. No one. Not the person that dresses differently than us, not the person who has hurt us the most, not the person who believes in a different God, or the person with different political beliefs. Even fans of the Los Angeles Lakers must be included in Beloved Community, and that's a tall order.[1]

---

1. As a die-hard fan of the Boston Celtics, this is hard for me to accept. But I'm working on it. It's an ongoing practice.

We know we're far from being in that place, which is why this serves as the framework for the future. It's the vision that we are working toward. Many people come to our workshops and suggest there are small examples of Beloved Community that exist today. Their family and their friends. Their spiritual community. The people they organize with. Their colleagues. While it is important to recognize and appreciate real community, I also want to push back on that and challenge us to think deeper. What did Dr. King mean when he spoke of Beloved Community?

Building Beloved Community is not about loving the people who are easy to love. It is about cultivating love for those that are difficult to love. *Those people* over there. The *others*. Those who root for the Los Angeles Lakers. The people who voted for *that guy*. The people who work in the very systems that are destroying our communities. The corrupt corporate CEO. The foreign dictator responsible for countless deaths.

If you are not struggling to love people, if you are not trying to build understanding with those you disagree with, then you are not really doing the work of building Beloved Community. The work of building Beloved Community is understanding that we're not trying to win *over* people, but to *win people over*. Historically, winning a war has meant defeating the opponent. There is a clear winner and a clear loser. The victory is *over* your opponent. But in nonviolence, there is no real victory until everyone is on the same side.

Building Beloved Community is not about loving the people who are easy to love. It is about cultivating love for those that are difficult to love.

Dr. King once wrote, "The aftermath of nonviolence is the creation of Beloved Community, while the aftermath of violence is tragic bitterness." While violence may be effective in temporarily keeping us safe from harm, it can never create relationships. Violence can never heal the harm that has been done. Violence can never bring about reconciliation. Violence can never create

Beloved Community. Only love can do that.

A LOVE THAT BUILDS COMMUNITY

All this talk of love …

I wasn't always comfortable with it. In some contexts, I am still uncomfortable with it. What has been helpful for me is to realize that when we use the word love, we are talking about many different things. Understanding and discerning what we are talking about is important in the context of nonviolence.

I've come to realize that one of the main reasons why I used to struggle to talk about love is because I come from a culture where our understanding of love is very limited. The word for love in Japanese, pronounced *ai*, has a very limited context. It only refers to romantic love. So in our language, we don't tell our friends or family members that we "love" them. The word simply does not exist, and because the word doesn't exist, it is hard to articulate, hard to understand, and hard to conceptualize. In addition, Japanese is a culture that simply does not express feelings of love very often, especially verbally. It is expressed in the most subtle ways, and it can be easy to miss.

Working with Asian and Pacific Islanders who come from immigrant households, I have noticed that this is a particular pain that many of us carry. We grew up in an American culture where the word "love" is thrown around so often that it sometimes loses its meaning ("I love burritos!"), but then we go home to a culture where it is never expressed. It can be painful to learn at school that families are supposed to express love verbally in a particular way and go home to not experience that. It can be painful to not have the word to express love to your own mother in a way that seems to come so naturally to your friends.

On the other hand, the English language has a broad context for the word love. I can love my mother. I can love my partner. I can love my friends. I can love my dog Wasa.[2] I can love a

2. Wasa is the most loving creature in the known universe. The name is short

burrito from El Farolito. It's the same word. It's the same sound we make with our vocal cords, but the concept we are communicating varies. That is why it can be helpful to understand different types of love. The Greek language has at least five different words for the concept of love. Knowing this can help us with this discernment.

Eros is the root of the word "erotic" and is commonly understood as romantic love—Cupid's love. Historically, the word eros referred to a divine love. Dr. King wrote that "in Platonic philosophy, eros meant the yearning of the soul for the realm of the divine." Many ancient practices use this type of love to commune with the divine and see eros as a practice that exists in the spiritual realm. In our overly sexualized culture, words like erotic have come to be purely associated with sex, but historically, eros love was more than purely sexual. Anyone who has been in love understands that.

Mania is manic love, or lust. It is the love I have for the burritos from El Farolito. It is the love that drove me to watch sixteen games of the eighteen-game losing streak the Boston Celtics had in 2007. It is mania love that is often misinterpreted as eros love because of our society's objectification of sexuality. You can lust after sex, but you are not necessarily loving the person with whom you are engaging in it with. There is nothing wrong with mania love, and it can be as genuine as any other type of love. It is just an important discernment to make.

Then there is *philia*, a love that refers to the brotherly, sisterly, friendly love that you develop for your companions. Philadelphia, known as the "city of brotherly love," is named for this type of love. This is a different type of love than what you feel for your intimate partner, but it's a strong bond, nonetheless. It is the type of love cultivated through shared experiences, common values, and interests, and it's almost always reciprocal. I love you because you love me.

---

for Wasabi, though her name is spelled Wasa B. There was no Wasa A.

Philia is also different than *storge*, the love that you have for family (blood or otherwise). Storge is familial love. Your family members may not share your interests or even some of your most important values, but there is a love that is hard to break regardless. You may not see each other for years or decades, but it is likely you will always feel that connection. Friends may grow apart, but family bonds endure over time.

When we talk about love in the context of nonviolence however, we are talking about what the Greeks refer to as *agape*. Agape love is unconditional love for all of humanity, for all life on earth and for all that exists in the cosmos. It is what Dr. King called "disinterested love," because you have no interest in whether the object of your agape loves you back or not. Agape is the type of love that is capable of building Beloved Community.

You do not have agape love for someone because of all of the experiences that you have been through together. You do not have agape love for someone because of the things they do for you. You do not love them for the ways that they make you feel. You love them simply because they exist. You love them because you acknowledge a sanctity that exists deep in the souls of all people. When you experience agape love, you see past people's faults, and you see their humanity. You see them at their best even when they themselves don't see or express it.

German writer Johann Wolfgang von Goethe once said, "Treat people as if they were what they ought to be, and you help them to become what they are capable of being." That's agape love. It's about helping people fulfill their potential. Social activist Dorothy Day said, "I really only love God as much as I love the person I love the least." That's agape. It's about understanding that "God's love" is about cultivating love for those who are the hardest to love.

We already love the people that are close to us. That's why we consider them to be part of *our* community. Agape love requires us to love those that are not close to us, because we acknowledge that they are part of Beloved Community. I'm not much of a God person, but agape is often referred to as godly love in the Christian context. And who is unworthy of God's love? Is there anyone that God's love is incapable of reaching?

A workshop participant once said that, as a Christian, he agreed with the understanding of agape love as God's love. He went on to say that if agape is God's love, and if Beloved Community is a place filled with agape, then it's not our responsibility alone to generate that love. It may be impossible to think of loving the person who has hurt you most. Beloved Community, he explained, is not about you having to generate that love. It's a place where that love already exists, and your job is simply to step into it.

> "I really only love God as much as I love the person I love the least."
> —Dorothy Day

To really understand nonviolence, it is important to acknowledge the existence of agape love and its distinction from the other types of love. When people talk about "loving your enemy," we are not suggesting that you try to cultivate the same loving feelings that you have for your friends. That would make no sense, and it may not be possible.

We don't have to hang out with our worst enemies in the way we hang out with our friends. We don't have to invite them over for the holidays.[3] We might not choose to spend any time with them at all, but we do have to acknowledge their humanity. We do have to understand that they are not that different from us, and we do have to work toward a world where we can all achieve our full potential. If someone is hurting you or actively participating in injustice, chances are they have not achieved their potential as a human being, and we can try to cultivate compassion for that.

Agape love is love with power. It is love that is tough. It can be tough to cultivate and tough to receive, but it is also tough to defeat. Agape love requires that we love everyone in Beloved

---

3. My friend Sierra sometimes says that Beloved Community is a *big* place, and we can have love for people, and they can live *all the way over there* in Beloved Community.

Community, which means not giving up on anyone and holding everyone accountable to the values underlying Beloved Community. If you truly love someone and see them as sacred, you would not allow them to continue to cause harm. You would hold that person accountable, for *their* sake. Agape requires that we hold all individuals accountable and remind every person of our relationship to Beloved Community. Beloved Community acknowledges that we are all connected and dependent on each other.

INTERDEPENDENCE

"We are caught in an inescapable network of mutuality, tied in a single garment of destiny. Whatever affects one directly, affects all indirectly."

Sounds kinda Buddhist-y, doesn't it? But these words were written by a Southern Baptist preacher named Martin Luther King Jr. He wrote these words in a letter addressed to seven other Christian ministers and a Jewish rabbi in Birmingham, Alabama, because this is an idea that exists in all spiritual traditions. Many Buddhist teachers remind us that the Buddha didn't teach Buddhism. He taught universal truths that emerge in all cultures throughout the world. The Dharma, or the teachings of the historical Buddha, is not a religion, but an articulation of those universal laws of nature.

Vietnamese Zen Buddhist teacher Thich Nhat Hanh refers to the idea of interdependence as "interbeing." He writes:

> If you are a poet, you will see clearly that there is a cloud floating in this sheet of paper. Without a cloud, there will be no rain; without rain, the trees cannot grow; and without trees, we cannot make paper. The cloud is essential for the paper to exist. If the cloud is not here, the sheet of paper cannot be here either. So we can say that the cloud and the paper inter-are.

But this concept of interdependence is far from unique to one part of the world. In reality, the idea that "we are caught in an inescapable network of mutuality" seems to emerge in all cultures.

The word *ubuntu*, from the southern African Nguni language, refers to the idea that "I am because you are." Archbishop Desmond Tutu once said that a person with ubuntu "has a proper self-assurance that comes from knowing that he or she belongs in a greater whole and is diminished when others are humiliated or diminished, when others are tortured or oppressed."

In the Jewish tradition, the Hebrew word *echad*, meaning "one," often refers to the oneness of God. But its interpretation as "one" in the mathematical sense is not quite accurate. The word echad refers more to the oneness of all beings. It is the oneness that binds all beings together. I've also seen echad translated as "bound together" or "compound unity."

The West African Adinkra symbol for *Ese Ne Tekrema* means "teeth and tongue" and represents how teeth and tongue play different roles in your mouth but must rely on each other to be complete. *Kapwa* is a central concept in Filipino psychology and can be translated as "togetherness," "shared self," or "being with others." Author, poet, and retired multicultural studies professor Leny Strobel describes kapwa as "the tendency to see the world with all its beings as a holistic system where things operate interdependently."

The Diné/Navajo word *hózhó* refers to the interdependence and balance between one's clan, their birthplace, nature, and beauty. Everything in the physical and spiritual realm is related to hózhó, and "to be in hózhó" is to be at one with all that is around you. *In Lak'ech Ala K'in* is a Mayan concept and greeting that means "I am you, and you are me," or "You are my other self."

In a sermon given during Christmas of 1967, Dr. King expanded on the concept of interdependence even further:

Did you ever stop to think that you can't leave for your job in the morning without being dependent on most of the world? You get up in the morning and go to the bathroom and reach over for the sponge, and that's handed to you by a Pacific Islander. You reach for a bar of soap, and that's given to you at the hands of a Frenchman. And then you go into the kitchen to drink your coffee for the morning, and that's poured into your cup by a South American. And maybe you want tea: that's poured into your cup by a Chinese. Or maybe you're desirous of having cocoa for breakfast, and that's poured into your cup by a West African. And then you reach over for your toast, and that's given to you at the hands of an English-speaking farmer, not to mention the baker.

And before you finish eating breakfast in the morning, you've depended on more than half the world. This is the way our universe is structured; this is its interrelated quality. We aren't going to have peace on Earth until we recognize this basic fact of the interrelated structure of all reality.

My life has been forever altered by everyone I have interacted with and learned from. Indirectly, I have been impacted by everyone who ever interacted with *that* person. And on and on we go.

For example, Dr. LaFayette has deeply affected my life in a direct way. All of the lessons I have learned from him, all of the wisdom he has handed down, and all of the opportunities he has opened up for me have forever altered my life. To a large extent, he had that wisdom to hand down to me in the first place because of the things he learned during the trainings he received when he was nineteen from Rev. Lawson and from the time he spent organizing alongside Dr. King. Dr. King was in turn heavily influenced by his relationship with people like Howard Thurman and Bayard Rustin. So, in an indirect way, my life has been impacted by all of those people as well.

Similarly, my life has been informed by my former stepfather, a Native man who introduced me to Indigenous ceremony, which is still an important aspect of my life today. He also introduced a lot of chaos and trauma into our home. When I look back at my childhood and think of him, I see a hurt and broken man. I see someone who carried his own heavy burden of pain, for which he could not find a healthy release, so he unleashed it on us. I think of all of those who must have hurt him and contributed to him becoming the type of person he became. All of those people, whose names I will never know, have impacted me.

I have only ever met a handful of people from the Democratic Republic of the Congo. But I sit here typing these words on my MacBook, a piece of technology that contains minerals like coltan. The mining of coltan contributes greatly to human rights abuses that have taken countless lives in countries like the DRC. My technology purchases contribute directly to the suffering of innumerable people. All of our experiences, traumas, and life lessons are influenced by countless people we will never know. If our traumas are interconnected and interdependent, then so must be our healing and liberation.

A teaching that comes from the Aboriginal people of Australia says, "If you have come here to help me, you are wasting your time. But if you have come here because your liberation is bound up with mine, then let us work together."[4] It's a beautiful concept and a quote that has become quite popular in many social justice circles. White people shouldn't be working to defeat white supremacy in order to save people of color. They should be doing it because white supremacy destroys the souls of white people. Male-identified people shouldn't be working to undo patriarchy because they want to protect women. We should be

---

4. The Aboriginal activist Lilla Watson is often credited for this quote. However, I read an interview with her where she asked that any credit for this quote be given to her people since it is their wisdom. After some consideration, I have decided to credit her people in the main pages but also acknowledge her name in this footnote.

doing it because we understand that patriarchy rips apart a core part of our own humanity.

Solidarity isn't about developing a condescending or patronizing savior complex. It is about being in relationship to people because we understand that our liberation is ultimately dependent on their liberation and vice versa. This means that our liberation is not only bound up with the liberation of Indigenous communities, Black communities, or other marginalized communities, but it is also bound up with, say, the liberation of Donald Trump.[5] People like Trump don't simply fall out of the "network of mutuality," nor does the universe weave separate webs of interdependence based on political affiliation.

The best way to protect those that we love is to love those that may hurt them.

Interdependence, interbeing, Beloved Community, agape love. These are, to me, universal principles, universal truths I choose to live by. This means they do not waver or change depending on the context. We either hold them to be true or we don't, or else it would not be a principle.

To be liberated, we need to work for the liberation of Trump, and anyone else we may have disregarded in a similar way. Because in this interconnected, interdependent world that we live in, the healing and liberation of Donald Trump would affect all of us greatly.

We need to work for Trump's liberation not only for his own sake, but because the safety of the people we love depend on it. The best way to protect those that we love is to love those that may hurt them.

STUMBLING BLOCKS

I was wondering how long I'd get in this book before it was time to mention Donald Trump. I'm actually pretty proud of how far we

---

5. As I write this, Trump is the sitting president of the United States. Depending on when you read this, there may be some other politician or world leader you may focus on for the purposes of this discussion.

got. But in a conversation about nonviolence and social change in today's world, I suppose a discussion about him is inevitable.[6] Let's start with this: Trump is a broken man who is acting out of his brokenness. When I look at him, I see a man so far removed from his own sense of humanity, a man so far from achieving his full potential as a human being that I can have compassion for his condition.

In the summer of 2017, I was at the University of Rhode Island at their annual summer institute helping to train fifty new trainers in Kingian Nonviolence from a dozen different countries. During the training, I shared a powerful moment with Jason, one of the participants. We were sitting on a bench outside as he told me about a realization he had had during a group conversation. He said that for the first time, he saw Trump as a sad, nine-year-old kid who never got the validation that every child needs. He still sees Trump as that child—a child with a huge hole in his heart that he is constantly trying to fill with external validation. *The largest crowd to ever show up at an inauguration. The most successful president of all time. The biggest campaign rallies ever.*

Listening, I felt like the size of the gaping hole in Trump's heart is so large that his private Boeing 757 jet could fly through it. Recognizing Trump's brokenness allowed Jason to truly experience empathy for him for the first time. It's critical that this empathy, that agape love, is the foundation for our work of social change. In the current state that he is in, Trump is acting as a stumbling block on our way to Beloved Community. His actions are having an immediate impact that is harming communities,

---

6. For context, at the time that I am writing this, Trump has become public enemy number one amongst people on the political left in the United States and worldwide. He has become the personification of evil in many people's eyes and one of the main challenges in people's commitments to nonviolence. Before the 2016 presidential elections, Hitler was the name that would come up in our workshops as a challenge to nonviolence. "Yeah, this nonviolence stuff is great, but what about Hitler?" (More on Hitler in the appendix. This is a footnote to a footnote.) Now, it's not Hitler but Trump whom people name as a way to try to find a loophole around committing to nonviolence.

and his policies and the cultural norms that he is setting can set us back years if not decades.

We need to stop the immediate harm first. This conflict has reached the overt level, and we need to triage before we can begin the healing process. A commitment to Beloved Community does not mean that we have to always play nice. Nonviolence cannot be a naive and unrealistic approach to social change. I am not suggesting we throw flowers at Trump and hope he changes his ways. We need to resist his actions. We need to block his policies.

This brings us to an important lesson I heard once from Max Airborne, a community Dharma teacher and activist from the Bay Area. During a Dharma talk at the East Bay Meditation Center one evening, I heard them say that Beloved Community is like the North Star. On our long path toward it, we may at some point come up against an obstacle blocking our path. And we may need to turn around and backtrack a bit, but only so that we can round the corner, walk around the obstacle, and find ourselves walking due north again.

Trump and others like him are currently acting as an obstacle on our path to Beloved Community. Our main priority in this moment may not be to focus on Trump's own healing. Our main priority may have to be to block as much of the harm that is coming from his administration as possible. That will mean resisting his policies, blocking his actions, and even removing him from office. That means that the actions we take will cause him distress, and it may seem like we are moving away from a world that holds him as a member of Beloved Community. But even as we engage in this work, we can do it in a way that holds Trump's humanity and dignity in place, because at the end of the day our goal is to circle back around and head due north. So there are stumbling blocks along the way, but even when we need to backtrack temporarily, our goal is to always move toward Beloved Community once again.

THE CHALLENGE OF DIVERSITY

Beloved Community requires diversity, and diversity itself can be a stumbling block. Diversity is hard. And when I say "diversity," I mean *real* diversity, not the surface-level diversity that checks off the box for having enough people of color in the room. Diversity is not just about who is in the room but about how we share space and power and relate to each other across cultural gaps. What are the assumptions in the room? What type of language is being used?[7] What are the cultural norms around time, space, and leadership? How are agendas being created and meetings facilitated?

Over the years, I've found myself in many "people of color only" spaces. People of color meditation. People of color yoga. People of color organizing spaces. I've also found myself in other caucused spaces, like Japanese-only spaces, Asian and Pacific Islander spaces, immigrant spaces, men's circles, etc.

There is great value in these containers. Sometimes we need to be with people who share a common identity or affinity with us. Sometimes this is for practical reasons, safety reasons, or strategic reasons. For people who do not have a lot of experience being marginalized, for those who may not understand the stress of constantly being "the other" in the room, it may be hard to realize the importance of these spaces.

Before finding the East Bay Meditation Center, I used to have a judgment that silent meditation was "something white people did."[8] How ironic, since my own people have been meditating for more than a thousand years. And yet, because of how exclusionary white meditation communities in the United States can be, and

---

7. Just because two people are speaking in English, it does not mean they are speaking the same language. Not only could there be different understandings of the same word, but misunderstandings could happen based on different relationships with tone, volume, silence, humor, etc.

8. Nipponzan Myohoji does not practice silent meditation. They drum and chant during practice periods, so while I had spent time in monastic life, the practice of silent meditation was foreign to me.

how isolating it can feel to be the "only one" who is different in a room, I had developed this judgment and stayed away from this important practice for years. It was only when I attended EBMC's People of Color Sangha that I saw people who looked like me engaged with this practice.[9] And it was only then that I felt safe to begin to explore meditation for myself.

There is also great benefit for caucused spaces for those with privilege. I have been part of many men's groups, men's retreats, and other spaces designated for male-identified people only. These spaces allow us to explore how issues like patriarchy have affected men and how we perpetuate it. We can work with each other, support each other, and hold each other accountable as we learn to combat it. While we will ultimately find healing together, it is important that men not always burden women and gender nonbinary people with work that we must do as men. There is simply some shit that we need to talk about with each other.

However, I have also seen containers like these become semi-permanent obstacles to Beloved Community. I have seen too many people become too comfortable in these spaces, get too used to being in spaces perceived as "safe," and become so used to only seeing people with a shared identity that the mere presence of anyone different can become a trigger. The intent of caucused spaces should always be to heal so that we can be in Beloved Community, which includes everyone of *all* identities. It's one thing to be in these spaces and share some inside jokes about those in the privileged class of any identity. It's another thing when we find ourselves only in these self-selected spaces that those jokes unconsciously begin to turn into animosity or resentment for that entire identity group.

One of the many benefits of the San Francisco Bay Area, where I live, is its incredible diversity. Diversity in cultures, languages, food, and landscapes. The politics around racial

9. Sangha is a Pali (the ancient language spoken by the Buddha) word meaning a community of spiritual practice.

identity, gender identity, class analysis, and other issues are so far ahead of many places in the country—more nuanced and more alive—that many people of marginalized identities move here to find safety in numbers, which can be liberating. Ironically, some people move to the Bay Area for its diversity and then find themselves self-segregating to the point that they don't actually experience that diversity other than in superficial ways. People of color-only spaces, queer-only spaces, vegan-only spaces, leftist-only spaces. Sometimes these spaces are explicitly self-selecting, other times they become so implicitly. Either way, we can find ourselves moving away from the promise of Beloved Community.

Fields like social science, psychology, and neuroscience tell us that the more homogenous a group is, the more members begin to see others as "outsiders," and therefore as a potential threat. That sort of tribalism is a great threat to Beloved Community. Psychologist Jay Van Bavel once conducted an experiment in which he had a group of college students watch an image of a doll's face slowly transform into that of a real person's face. He asked the students to hit a button the moment they felt like the doll became a person. Most of the students hit the button about halfway through the transformation.

But then he ran the test again and introduced a new variable. He told the students the name of the college that the person in the photo attends. He found that if he told the students that the person went to the same college they did, the students would identify the person as human more quickly. When he told the students that the person in the photograph attends a rival college, they would wait longer before identifying them as human.

The more we surround ourselves with people who look and talk like us, the more our tribalism kicks in, and we begin to see the world in two—an "in-group" made up of "our" people and an "out-group" made up of "those" people. The more we begin to see any group as "those" people, the easier it becomes to dehumanize them and see them as outside of Beloved Community.

It is critical that we work to understand our own identity and how it has shaped us, as well as working to understand where we sit in the spectrum of power and privilege based on that identity. But there is great danger in engaging in identity politics to the point that it fractures Beloved Community.

**"When my brothers try to draw a circle to exclude me, I shall draw a larger circle to include them."
—Pauli Murray**

Pauli Murray, a civil rights activist and a pioneer in gender equality, once said, "When my brothers try to draw a circle to exclude me, I shall draw a larger circle to include them."[10] It is this ever-expanding attempt to create larger and larger circles that gets us closer to Beloved Community.

Beloved Community includes the privileged and the marginalized, the oppressor and the oppressed. The prisoner and the prison guard.[11] The rich and the poor. People of all genders and sexual orientations. In order for us to begin moving toward that world, we need to stop attacking *any* people as if they are the problem.

---

10. Murray is another unsung s/hero of the movement that more people should study. Murray was an activist before terms like "transgender" were commonplace and described themselves as having an "inverted sex instinct." While Murray never even had the option to identify as transgender, they were a pioneer for what would later become the trans movement.
11. Of course, when we truly live in Beloved Community, I hope we don't have prisons or economic classes to begin with....

Principle Three: Attack Forces of Evil, Not Persons Doing Evil

Hate the sin, love the sinner. Hard on problems, soft on people. Don't hate the player, hate the game.[1] There are many different ways to articulate this principle, but they all speak to the same core concept in nonviolence: people are never the enemy, injustice is. The very idea that we can continue to use force, fear, and intimidation to enforce our will over another person to get what we want is the problem. The belief that attacking individual people and overpowering them to try and solve our issues in any sustainable way is the problem.

People are not our enemy. Violence is our enemy. Injustice is our enemy. Any worldview that stands against life, love, and community is the enemy.

When we stop seeing people as our enemy, the framework for how we bring about transformation in our relationships and in society changes drastically. When we see that reconciliation of relationships and movement toward Beloved Community is our ultimate goal, we see that the ways we try to make change must be aligned with this principle.

I have a theory: when we understand people's stories, then all of their actions, including all of the ways in which they hurt people, make sense. It doesn't justify their behavior; it doesn't condone their actions, but when we can see *why* they did what they did, we can begin to empathize. I have heard countless stories from countless people, many of whom have committed gross acts of violence, and so far this theory has held up 100 percent of the time.

People are never the enemy; injustice is.

1. Seriously, there are teachings of nonviolence everywhere we look.

I was having dinner once with Janis Pruitt-Hamm, a veteran activist with the Fellowship of Reconciliation and a retired marriage counselor. She told me that there is one important question that everyone needs to ask themselves to build a strong foundation for a relationship. That question is, "How do my partner's traumas come out, and can I live with that?" I believe that applies not just in romantic relationships but in all human relationships.

Every human being has trauma—some unresolved pain and conflict that unknowingly influences how we relate to the people in our lives. When our actions harm others, it is most often the result of our lashing out in reaction to our own pain, our own insecurities, and our own harms. When I look back at my own life and think of all of the people who have hurt me, I not only see the pain that I experienced, but I can easily see the pain that drove those people to those actions. When I think back at the times that I have hurt others, I can see the pain and the insecurities that drove me to my actions.

> When we understand people's stories, then all of their actions, including all of the ways in which they hurt people, make sense.

Human beings are not the problem. It is the actions that we take, which are dependent on the experiences that we've gone through in life, which in turn are so intrinsically influenced by our culture and the larger systems over which we have no control. The structures and mechanisms that perpetuate harm are what we need to fight. In order to change them, we need to understand individual people's stories and the systems that influence them.

THE ROTTEN BARREL

Every time there is an incident of corruption in a large institution, whether it be a government agency or a corporation, we are told that this was an isolated incident, that this was a case of a bad apple in an otherwise good barrel. But what if it's not the apple? What if the barrel itself is rotten? You can throw away as many rotten apples as you can find, but until you replace the barrel itself, it will continue to spoil good apples. That's what seems to be the case in so many of the institutions in our society today. They seem to turn "good," normal people into "bad apples."

Take policing. There is no doubt in my mind that most people who choose a career in law enforcement enter with good intentions. I have no doubt that most people believe from the bottom of their hearts that they are on the good side trying to keep society safe. Very few people enter law enforcement with the conscious intention of using their powers to abuse people and oppress communities.[2] I do believe that there are people who enter law enforcement because they have insecurities and want to be in a position where they feel powerful, and that can easily lead to abuses of that power. But I have observed that even those people—for the most part—truly believe they are on the good side, using their powers to protect society. Yet, police violence, corruption, and abuses of power are prevalent at every level of law enforcement. What is it about the profession of law enforcement, particularly in the United States, that creates such a hostile environment?

In August of 1971, Stanford psychology professor Philip Zimbardo embarked on the now infamous Stanford Prison Experiment.[3] After converting the basement floor of a building at Stanford University into a makeshift "prison," he hired twenty-four young men to take part in what was originally designed to be a two-week role-play experiment. He began by running background tests on all twenty-four of his subjects, ensuring that none of them had a violent background and were considered psychologically stable and healthy. He randomly assigned half of them roles as prisoners and the other half as prison guards, gave each

---

2. I do believe that unconscious racial bias does influence how people view crime in communities of color, which impacts how those communities are policed. But again, I do not believe those are conscious thoughts in the forefront of people's minds as they enter law enforcement.

3. Zimbardo's TED Talk about this and other experiments, as well as its parallels to the Iraqi Abu Ghraib prison scandal, is highly recommended and can be viewed at https://youtu.be/OsFEV35tWsg. His book *The Lucifer Effect* is also a great source.

group appropriate uniforms, oriented the guards with some basic parameters (no physical abuse or deprivation of food and water but constantly reinforce the power dynamic between inmate and guard) and let them have at it.

Within hours, Zimbardo and his team began to witness good kids engage in horrific abuses of their fellow students, not much different from the types of abuses we saw happen in real life during the Abu Ghraib prison scandal in Iraq. The young men playing the role of prisoners began having psychological breakdowns within thirty-six hours. Five of them ended up having complete emotional breakdowns and had to leave the experiment. The entire study had to be cancelled six days later.

Zimbardo would go on to say that this was ultimately about putting good people into bad environments and seeing what wins. The study showed that environment and context can take away a person's individual and logical ability to make choices for themselves. The culture took over. The barrel began to rot the apples.

As a volunteer in several of California's correctional institutions, I have to attend an annual volunteer orientation training for each prison I visit. Theses trainings generally consist of long PowerPoint presentations explaining obscure prison regulations. They are almost as exciting as the day-long traffic schools I've had the pleasure of attending. Almost.

Many of these trainings consist of hearing the same repetitive messages over and over again using different language and different angles. Don't trust these men. Don't do them any favors. They will lie to you. They will cheat you. They are dangerous and will try to take advantage of you at every turn. They are only attending your programs because it will look good on their record. That is all in a three-hour orientation. I can only imagine what it must be like to attend a six-month long academy to become a correctional officer, how much an experience like that may affect your worldview and attitudes toward incarcerated people, especially if you go in without a strong opinion of your own to begin with.

My friend Carmen Perez, a lifelong advocate for criminal justice reform, used to work as a probation officer, mentoring young incarcerated people who were caught up in the system. I remember one day she told me that she used to come home in tears all the time during her training because of the worldview that the instructors were trying to impose on her. That her safety was of the utmost concern and that the young people with whom she worked—young people who look like her and her siblings—were nothing more than a threat.

Carmen entered that career with a long history of activism and a passion for serving low-income communities, but such backgrounds are rare among rookie probation officers. What if she had taken the job simply because she needed a paycheck? What if she had gone in never having met anyone who was incarcerated and had no personal connection with any of the people she would be supervising? What if she couldn't relate to their struggles, and her only perception of prisons had come from watching media that overdramatize prisons and exaggerate the violence within them? What if Carmen had taken the job to cover over her own insecurities by having power over other people? Would this be a system that would reinforce those insecurities and give her an avenue to abuse her newfound power and control?

In the worst cases, this type of influence can easily lead to abuse and murder. We continue to see this dynamic play out over and over and over again. Take the case of Jeronimo Yanez, a twenty-eight-year-old police officer in St. Anthony, Minnesota. On July 6, 2016, Officer Yanez and his partner pulled over a 1997 Oldsmobile because, according to them, "The two occupants just look like people that were involved in a robbery."[4] The two occupants were Philando Castile, a thirty-two-year-old African American man, and his girlfriend, Diamond Reynolds. Reynold's four-year-old daughter Dae'Anna was sitting in the backseat. They were on their

---

4. This quote was taken from transcripts of police radio transmissions obtained by various media outlets.

way back from the grocery store when they were pulled over. There was no panic. This was an all-too-normal occurrence for Castile. Just another day Driving while Black.[5] Less than one minute into the interaction, Yanez fired seven rounds at Castile, hitting him five times. He would die twenty minutes later. Reynolds began filming the incident shortly after Castile was shot and streamed it live on Facebook. Years after watching that video for the first time, there are two voices that I can't get out of my head. The first is the voice of young Dae'Anna, consoling her mother after they had both witnessed the murder of Castile. "It's okay Mommy. It's okay, I'm right here with you...."

But there is another voice from earlier in the video that still haunts me, and that is the voice of officer Yanez. His is not the voice of a ruthless killer. It is the desperate fear of a young man who made a deadly decision in the heat of a conflict and is just realizing the gravity of that decision. When looking into this incident, I found out that Yanez had attended two seminars put on by a private company called Calibre Press in the two years preceding the shooting. The seminars, each two days long, are titled "The Bulletproof Warrior" and "Street Survival." Critics claim that these seminars instill a sense that officers are constantly in danger. They show graphic images of officers killed in the line of duty, with the message that if you hesitate for even a second to pull the trigger, you could end up as one more fatal example at the next seminar.

This does not excuse Yanez's actions. But to me, the story begins to make sense. Officer Yanez and many like him are being trained to be afraid and trigger happy. Layer that on top of the history of race in this country, the tense relationships between law enforcement and the African American community, and stereotypes of young Black men in the media. In the absence of concerted efforts

---

5. Multiple news outlets have reported that prior to this fatal incident, Castile had been pulled over by the police fifty-two times for minor traffic violations. Assuming he got his license when he was seventeen, that amounts to getting pulled over every 3.5 months of his entire adult life.

to change the way police are trained, it's no wonder why these shootings continue to happen.

Or take the case of Eric Casebolt, an officer in McKinney, Texas. In 2015, residents of an upper-middle-class neighborhood in McKinney called the police to complain about a pool party involving dozens of teenagers, many of them Black. When Casebolt showed up on the scene, all hell broke loose as he started yelling obscenities at the teens and ordering them around while pointing his baton at them. At one point, Casebolt grabbed a fifteen-year-old girl by her braids and threw her down on the ground and pulled out his gun and aimed it at another group of teenagers.

While nothing justifies his actions, again when you understand more of the backstory, it begins to make sense. The pool party was the third call that Casebolt received that day. His first call was to the scene of a suicide, where he had to console the widow of a man who had just killed himself by shooting himself in his head in front of his own children. Right after having to take photographs of the man's body, Casebolt was called to another incident where he had to talk a girl down from killing herself in front of her family by jumping off a ledge. Those two incidents took an emotional toll, as they should. No one would want our police officers to be so disconnected from human emotion that witnessing such tragedies would have no impact on them. However, instead of being given counseling or time to take care of himself, Casebolt went right on to his next call of the day.

Who is really at fault here? Officer Casebolt, for letting his humanity get the best of him, or the institution of policing, which didn't care enough about Casebolt's mental health to even give him the rest of the day off? Do we blame Casebolt for acting outrageously after witnessing two tragedies, or do we blame the system of policing that instructs employees to "suck it up" and move on to the next case?

The system of policing is an institution that hurts all parties. I am not naive enough to think that we do not need some system of individuals who are highly trained to intervene in situations of escalated conflict. But the system we have today does not serve anyone long-term, and it needs to be changed. Attacking any one individual will not lead to any long-term change.

I have talked to officers who have shot and killed people in their work. One officer told me with his voice shaking that nothing is ever the same once you take someone's life. I could feel the tears welling up in his eyes on the other side of his dark sunglasses. Another person had a son who had to retire from the force after shooting and killing somebody. Despite the rhetoric that I sometimes hear from my peers, no one "enjoys" taking the life of another human being. If some individuals have been so dehumanized and desensitized that they are not able to recognize the damage to their own soul after taking another's life, it is only because a system has beaten the humanity out of them.

Despite what some people think, there are good apples in an otherwise rotting barrel. In one volunteer training I took in a California prison several years ago, a prison guard began his presentation by saying that he believes in "a world without prisons." He went on to say that while that is the world he wants to live in, in the meantime we have people who are causing harm, and went on to say how much he appreciated those of us who came to run programs in the prison.

East Point's programs on the inside would not be possible if not for the countless individuals who go out of their way to help us get into the prison system. There are people within the system who work as hard as any prison reform activists I know to be in service to incarcerated people. In some instances, these same people may be in positions where they use their power over the inmates in oppressive and violent ways. Nobody is either all good or all bad. This is the case in policing, government, the military, corporations, schools, and every institution throughout society.

As a person of Japanese descent, when I think about the history of World War II, I tend to think less about the bombings of Hiroshima and Nagasaki or about the internment of Japanese Americans here in the United States and more about the atrocities that my own people committed throughout the Pacific. I think about the legacy of the Rape of Nanking, one of the grossest acts of violence throughout the history of that war. I think about the "comfort women," women who were forced into sexual slavery by the thousands.

I think about how Japanese people—my people—are often known for being so "polite," and how this polite culture turned men into monsters capable of the worst human rights violations imaginable. I think about how malleable human nature is. I think about how easy it is for us to think, "I could never do those things," but how history shows us over and over again how people can do horrific things given the wrong circumstances, given the wrong influences, given the "forces of evil."

Poverty. War. Patriarchy. A violent criminal justice system. A corrupt capitalist corporate culture. A broken education system. These are the things that are our enemies, not the people who are caught up in them.

ACCOUNTABILITY AS AN ACT OF LOVE

None of this is to say that there isn't plenty of room for personal accountability. Not just room for it, but a necessity for it. If we are going to build Beloved Community, personal accountability for harm must be a part of that process. If you truly love someone, you would hold them accountable for the harm that they are causing. When people are acting out with violence, they are not at their best, and you would hold them accountable for the ways in which they are not showing up with full authenticity. You would work to bring out the best in that person. At its best, accountability is an act of love.

Casebolt and Yanez both should have been fired immediately, and they should never be able to work in any position of power again, never mind as police officers. But beyond that, what does accountability mean? The word "accountable" comes from the Old French word *acontable,* meaning, "answerable" or "liable to be called to account." Merriam-Webster defines it as, "an obligation or willingness to accept responsibility or to account for one's actions." It defines accountable as, "capable of being explained."

Years ago, my friend Maegan and I, along with two incarcerated trainers, were interviewing people for a restorative justice group we were about to start in San Quentin State Prison with the organization Insight Prison Project. When asked why they were interested in participating in the group, one of the men answered, "I want to understand how I got to a place where I was able to take a person's life." Decades after he committed his crime, he still could not understand how his life got to the point where he was able to take the life of a complete stranger. Without having the insights that could help him connect his own traumas to his crime, how could he hold himself truly accountable? He could not explain himself how it had happened. His crime was not "capable of being explained."

At its best, accountability is an act of love.

Having worked with people who have experienced violence, one thing I've found is that one of the most common questions they have is "Why?" Why did you do this? Why me? Why? And if he can't explain why, if he can't understand why he did it himself, how can he ever hold himself accountable?

On the other hand, I've seen the incredible healing potential of someone who experienced great harm hearing the "why" from someone who has done their work and has had the insights that allow them to explain it truthfully. Hearing the why and understanding the story of the person who caused them harm can be an important aspect of healing for the person who experienced it, and it can play a big step toward forgiveness.

We think we are holding people accountable because they are serving a life sentence in prison. We too often equate accountability with punishment. But accountability isn't something you can shove down someone's throat. It has to come from within.

I believe that the process toward true accountability can only begin when the person who caused the harm can understand what brought them to the point in their lives where they did what they did and understand, own, and feel genuine remorse for the impact that their actions had on everyone that they touched. That remorse and ownership is a prerequisite for genuine accountability.

If I hurt somebody, then I lose a part of my humanity in that process. In order for me to heal that wound in myself, I need to understand the impact of my actions and feel the remorse. That remorse, as painful as it might be to feel, is like medicine—a necessary component in my own healing. Creating space for me to understand that is an act of loving accountability. It reminds me of the law of interdependence—that I cannot harm another without it somehow affecting me.

If we are attacking the person who caused the harm, it usually puts them on the defensive and actually does the opposite of what I just described. If we are busy accusing the person who caused the harm of being evil, of being monsters, of being criminals and murderers, there is a natural tendency for that person to build up a wall and defend themselves from those attacks. And in doing that, they are moving farther away from sitting with the harm that they caused and feeling remorse.

This brings up a major problem with our criminal justice system. When you threaten someone with a long prison sentence, you put the "defendant" in a position to do exactly that—to defend themselves and try to prove their innocence. The game is set up in a way that produces the exact opposite of accountability. You can't in reality "hold someone accountable." You can only hold space and support someone cultivating their own sense of accountability.

We live in a "call-out" culture, where we point fingers and blame others in the name of holding them accountable. We crucify people for a perceived lack of "woke-ness." If anyone says anything that can be perceived as racist, sexist, homophobic, or problematic in any way, we label them as such and attack them and their character. I get it. Calling someone out for their perceived ignorance or attacking them for the harm that they may have caused you can be cathartic. If we simply want to shame someone and make them feel awful, that's one thing. But if we want accountability, we may want to try a different tactic. Because you can't shame someone into transformation.

When people talk about "holding someone accountable," the key word should not be accountable, but holding. What does it mean to hold someone? When people talk about holding people accountable, does that person feel held, or do they feel attacked and judged? Are they feeling opened up, or are they getting defensive?

You can't shame someone into transformation.

Bonnie Wills, a community elder and restorative justice facilitator once said that "our power lies in our defenselessness." It's the point when we feel like we have nothing we need to defend, when we can own all of our actions without an ounce of defensiveness that we are at our most authentic, our most powerful. That sort of courageous vulnerability becomes nearly impossible for someone if they are being attacked.

In many of the restorative justice circles that I've been in, we don't always start by talking about the harm that the person caused. We start by exploring the harms that the perpetrator has been through, the traumas that they are holding, and the pain that in many cases has never been seen, heard, and validated. Having your pain invalidated can be one of the most hurtful experiences you can go through. For people labeled as "criminals," they are defined by their worst actions, and there is no space given to the pain they carry, which may have contributed to the choices that they made.[6]

The black/white analysis of perpetrator and victim belies the

6. Years ago, I had the privilege to work with Insight-Out Prison Project's GRIP Program. Founded by Jacques Verduin, a pioneer in prison programming, GRIP is a year-long restorative justice group that stands for Guiding Rage into Power.

complexities of harm and violence. If "hurt people hurt people," we need to validate the original hurt to open up the possibility of making people whole again. Seeing people only as the perpetrator of harm only recognizes a part of who they are. As long as we only see the worst side of a person, they will always build up a wall against forced accountability.

Other times, it may be helpful to start a process of cultivating accountability by naming the harm that a person caused. Sometimes naming and showing the harm can be a wake-up call to the person who caused it, and it can help them understand the impact of their actions. There are no cookie-cutter approaches to this work. But the goal is not to attack the person and make them feel like a horrible human being for what they did. The point is to help them understand the impact, feel remorse, and begin the process of making amends. They have to *want* to make amends for the accountability to be genuine.

We need to create spaces for transformation. If someone is to be completely vulnerable, without an ounce of defensiveness, if we want someone to fully own the impact of their actions, then there needs to be some level of trust that the person can accept responsibility for that harm and not be cast out from society. There needs to be some level of trust that their humanity and dignity will stay intact through the process of accountability. They need to know that there will be a place for them to land on the other side. They need to trust that they are still part of Beloved Community.

It is only when one's own pain has been acknowledged, when they are seen as a whole person, and when they trust that they will still be part of the web of humanity that one can truly let their

Each GRIP group views itself as a close-knit tribe, and the one that I met was called "Tribe 928." The 928 represents the 928 years that the thirty-three men in the group had collectively served.

When the group started, they went around the room and added up all the years that they had served. They also went around and added up the amount of time that it took each of them to commit their offenses. The total was fourteen minutes. Fourteen minutes of their lives resulted in 928 years of incarceration. Fourteen minutes. If each of us were labeled for the worst thirty seconds of our lives....

guard down enough to fully sit in the remorse for the harm that they caused. Many people in social justice spaces understand these principles in theory. Yet when it comes to real harm that directly impacts us, these principles often get thrown out the window. Activists are critical of the criminal justice system for its lack of understanding of these principles, yet when a member of law enforcement commits an act of harm, the response is more often than not to call for punishment and incarceration.

We need to constantly remind ourselves of what our long-term goal is. If our goal is simply to punish someone for the sake of punishment, if our goal is to banish someone from the web of humanity, if our goal is to simply let the person know how horrible they are and shame them for their actions, then responding to harm with more harm is perfectly effective. But if our goal is accountability and the healing of relationships, we need to create space for people to be held.

Even in more minor incidents, we need to keep our goal in mind when working toward accountability. I was facilitating a workshop one day, and a guest speaker and I had an interaction in front of the group that got a bit tense. It wasn't anything major, but I felt that the way he talked to me was condescending, and I could tell that others in the room felt it.

My natural tendency is to be conflict-avoidant, but as this happened during a nonviolence workshop that I was facilitating, I decided to practice what I preach, and I approached him after the workshop. I told him in no uncertain terms that I felt that he had been condescending, but I also told him that I was not coming from a place of anger, and my intent wasn't to attack or to shame him. I told him that I had great respect for his work, and I had no doubt that he felt the same for me. My approaching him was not an attack on his character as much as a desire for him to be more aware of his language and presentation style. My intention was for his growth. My hope was that my desire to hold him accountable was an act of service to him.[7] Principle three is one of the most critical practices in a worldview of nonviolence. It does not mean that we don't hold individuals accountable; we just need to see that accountability is an act of love, not an act of punishment. It is about inviting people to be their best, most authentic selves.

THE ROLE OF ANGER

This principle also does not say that there is not a role for anger. The idea that nonviolence is about "teaching people not to be angry" is another common misconception. Dr. King was one of the most pissed-off people of his time. He was angry about racism, poverty, war, and materialism. There is plenty in this world that we need to be angry about.

Yet anger can be dangerous also. It is like fire. It can manifest as a forest fire, dangerous and out of control, burning down everything in its path. But it can also manifest in the form of charcoal. Harnessed. Sustained. Focused. It can be used strategically to cook food or to keep you warm. Similarly, anger in the form of rage can be dangerous and out of control, burning down everything in its path. But I believe that there is a type of anger that is deeply disciplined, sustained, and in control.

Dr. King oftentimes spoke of "righteous indignation."[8] It's the type of anger that is sparked when we witness human dignity being threatened. It is a type of anger that can be cultivated and

---

7. While I'm confident that he did not feel attacked by my confronting him, I also did not get the sense that he really heard me or that my message really landed for him. I could have continued the conversation with the hope that he would ultimately hear me, but after about twenty minutes I decided that I had done my part. I did not have an ongoing relationship with him and felt that I had expended enough of my emotional labor. Despite not feeling deeply heard, it still felt good—both that I approached him in a way that felt in integrity with my beliefs and that I had the awareness to end the conversation when it felt right to me. I was able to leave without feeling any resentment toward him.

8. This is different than the self-righteousness that we oftentimes see in activism.

channeled in the right direction: to protect life against the forces of injustice. Rage toward individuals can be harmful and dangerous. It can hurt both parties, it can widen divisions between people and communities and move us further away from Beloved Community. But indignation toward systems of violence and their impact can help liberate all people who are caught up in those systems.

Another way to look at it is to use anger as a spark, rather than the fuel. A participant at a workshop once said that the goal "isn't to react from anger but to use it to fuel a loving response." Anger can be helpful if it motivates and cultivates a thoughtful response but not if it controls you and causes unskillful reactions. I also want to note that none of this is about casting any judgment for outward expressions of pure rage from people who have been genuinely hurt or historically marginalized. Expressions of rage are a perfectly natural response to violence and injustice.

I've also seen some people in nonviolent spaces be incredibly judgmental about people who express rage. I think we need to create more spaces for people to express and release their rage. I believe that expression can be a necessary step in the process of healing. The point I am trying to make, however, is that expressions of pure rage put people in a vulnerable and potentially unsafe place, which is not always conducive to helping to heal relationships between two people who are in conflict.

Sometimes when a forest fire gets out of control, the best thing to do is to create barriers around it and simply let it burn out in a safe container. Sometimes we actually need to spark controlled burns to protect forests from future fires or to stop the spread of a large wildfire. If you're going to grill some food with charcoal, you first need to spark a flame and let it burn for a while. Once the flames wind down, you are left with a pile of cooler charcoal that's good for sustained cooking. If we are in a place of blind rage, we need to honor that reality and find spaces to release it. Once we do, we may find that beneath that rage is a cooler, sustained coal of indignation. That is what we take with us into action.

CHAPTER 12

Principle Four: Accept Suffering without Retaliation for the Sake of the Cause to Achieve the Goal

While facilitating workshops, I've often found this principle to be the trickiest to talk about and the one that people are most likely to push back on. I've heard questions like, "Is this suggesting that marginalized people should suffer even more?" or "How does this apply to communities who have already suffered so much?" or "This is fucked up." Other people simply reword it for themselves to try to get to the spirit of Dr. King's teachings. One reworded synthesis could be, "self-chosen sacrifice can be redemptive and help transform conflict."

This principle does not say, "accept suffering" period. It says, "accept suffering without retaliation *for the sake of the cause to achieve the goal.*" It refers to self-chosen suffering, and it has to be for a goal. Passively accepting abuse or oppression is not practicing this principle. This principle rests on a core assumption that standing up to violence and injustice will put you in a position of risk. Nonviolence means courageously sticking your head out. You are likely to face anger and defensiveness or even retaliatory violence.

Nonviolence oftentimes gets put up against an impossible double standard. Some argue against nonviolence by saying, "nonviolence won't work because if people use it to stand up against their oppressor, they might get hurt." Embedded in that criticism is an assumption that if you stand up against oppression using violence, you are not going to get hurt. The act of standing up to oppression and injustice puts us at risk, regardless of whether we are doing so violently or nonviolently. That is not a risk unique to nonviolence. If anything, nonviolent movements are likely to have fewer casualties overall than violent ones, for obvious reasons.

This principle is about *choosing* to accept the risk that comes with putting ourselves in danger. If we stand up to oppression, chances are, we will have to suffer along the way. Accepting suffering at the onset gives us a different relation to those inevitable struggles and challenges. It gives us choices about how we experience the inevitable. If we go into this work thinking that it will be easy, then when we experience suffering, we may resist it. The more we resist the suffering, the more we will internalize and resent it. Combating violence from external forces while cultivating internal violence from within our own hearts is fighting on too many fronts at once.

Accepting that suffering by choosing and volunteering for it gives us a different relationship to it. Instead of fighting it and resenting it, it can become redemptive. Whether we are recruits for the Navy SEALs going into "Hell Week"[1] or meditators going into a Vipassana retreat,[2] we know there is going to be suffering involved. We accept that suffering, because we know it serves a purpose and we will be stronger for it. We live in a culture that is so averse to suffering that we do everything we can to find ourselves surrounded by comfort. But there is no growth in comfort. It is through tension that we grow.

There is no growth in comfort.

Talking to many leaders from the Civil Rights era, I found there was also a recognition that people were already suffering anyway. Living under Jim Crow was oppressive. So, if people were suffering anyway, *not* out of choice and *not* for the sake of freedom, why not turn that dynamic around? By choosing to accept suffering

---

1. An infamous week of rigorous training where recruits are put through a grueling schedule testing the limits of their physical and emotional capacities. My meditation teacher Mushim once told me about this and asked, "If people are willing to put themselves through that much pain and that much training to learn to kill people, what are we willing to do to train people for peace?"
2. Ten hours a day of silent sitting meditation for ten consecutive days. It sucks. In the most beautiful way. I'm trying to make it at least an annual practice for me.

and doing so in public, Civil Rights activists were able to use that suffering to push the movement forward.

NARRATIVE AS A WEAPON

On Sunday, March 7, 1965, just over six hundred voting rights activists marched across Selma's Edmund Pettus Bridge. On the other side, they were met by a row of state troopers. Earlier that morning, in preparation for this planned march, Sheriff Jim Clark had called for all white males above the age of twenty-one to come to the county courthouse to be deputized as state troopers—with no training.

Rev. Hosea Williams, an SCLC leader who was leading the march along with John Lewis, approached the line of officers to negotiate. He was immediately pushed back as the row of troopers advanced towards the crowd, swinging batons and launching tear gas. Mounted troopers rushed into the crowd on horseback, beating anyone in their path. More than sixty people were injured during what became known as "Bloody Sunday." Not one of the marchers fought back.

Images of nonviolent marchers—including elderly people, women, and youth—getting beaten bloody by police went out to the national newswires. Those images painted a clear picture of who was on the right side of justice. When a movement is able to maintain nonviolence and maintain the moral ground in the face of state repression, it exposes the violence and the hypocrisy of the state. That narrative is an important weapon in nonviolence. That narrative woke up the conscience of a nation. Two days later, 2,500 people descended on Selma in support of the movement. Two weeks later, close to eight thousand people gathered in Selma to begin the long trek to Montgomery, Alabama. That historic march contributed greatly to the passing of the Voting Rights Act of 1965.[3] During the Occupy Wall Street movement, there were several key

---

3. On June 25, 2013, the Supreme Court ruled in *Shelby County v. Holder* that two key provisions within the Voting Rights Act were unconstitutional, decimating voter protections. The struggle continues.

incidents that increased the movement's momentum. One of the first moments was on September 24, 2011, when two young women at the Occupy encampment were pepper sprayed by the police. A short video of these women screaming in pain went viral, and the movement grew.

A month later on the other side of the country, a young Iraq war veteran named Scott Olsen was out in the streets demonstrating with Occupy Oakland when police shot him in the head with a lead-filled beanbag, fracturing his skull and causing permanent brain damage. This sparked the Occupy Oakland general strike a week later, perhaps the largest mobilization during the entire Occupy movement.

When a movement is able to maintain nonviolence and maintain the moral ground in the face of state repression, it exposes the violence and the hypocrisy of the state.

A month after that, students at the University of California, Davis, were sitting nonviolently in a blockade as UC Davis police officer Lt. John Pike stood over them and calmly sprayed the students with a can of pepper spray the size of a fire extinguisher. The video went viral, and memes of officer Pike remain one of the most iconic images of the movement. These moments helped to build Occupy. But if any of those people had fought back, it would have backfired.

From the fall of 2011 to late spring of 2012, the Occupy movement was my whole life; it was all I did, all I thought about. I was in Occupy-related meetings almost every night. I was part of almost every major mobilization during Occupy Oakland. I saw its rise and fall and watched its swells and declines in momentum. From what I witnessed, every time there was property destruction, every time the media had an opportunity to paint the movement as violent, the number of people who participated in our next mobilization decreased. Every. Single. Time.

I have seen this dynamic play out multiple times throughout the course of several movements. When nonviolent activists are attacked and are able to accept that suffering, the movement grows. When people use violent tactics to fight back, the movement shrinks.

This speaks again to the importance of training. If you've never been hit, and you enter a professional boxing match, you're probably not going to react very well when you get punched in the face for the first time. Engaging in those hard sparring sessions in the gym will prepare you and increase your capacity to accept blows. The training sessions that many leaders of the Civil Rights movement went through were intense. They knew the risks they were taking, and the intensity levels of their trainings matched that level of risk. Their ability to accept suffering was incredibly courageous and admirable, but it was possible because they prepared for it. Looking back at the lunch counter sit-ins, Dr. LaFayette shared in the documentary *A Force More Powerful* that "our capacity and willingness to suffer outweighed any power they had."

Rev. Lawson says in the same film, "Violence has a very simple dynamic; I make you suffer more than I suffer. I make you suffer until you cry uncle and you surrender." But if you are willing to accept that suffering from the beginning, if you have already made that sacrifice and prepared yourself physically, mentally, and emotionally for it, then it gives you power over violence. The choice one makes to accept violence for a cause takes away much of its power.

> The choice one makes to accept violence for a cause takes away its power.

MIRROR NEURONS

Someone once said that nonviolence was about "making the oppressor see the injustice of their ways through your suffering."[4] As human beings, seeing someone else suffer does something to us. It is a basic human trait. Neuroscience has shown that all of

---

4. I used to credit Gandhi for this quote, but I have since been unable to locate the exact quote. It may have been Gandhi; it may have been someone else. Another case of cryptomnesia.

our brains have mirror neurons—a brain cell that fires when we feel an emotion or when we witness someone else feel an emotion. They are our "empathy neurons," hardwired into our brains as a kind of neural basis for compassion.

The practice of nonviolence is sometimes about sacrificing our own suffering to reach someone's moral conscience as a way to turn them around. It's a way to try to reach the deepest part of who they are; the person behind the mask, underneath the uniform, or on other side of the badge. And maybe we won't reach them, but we might reach the people who are observing that dynamic play out.

I remember when I was young and getting into trouble a lot; as long as my mom would scream at me, it was very easy for me to ignore her. Being yelled at triggered my defense mechanisms, and it was my amygdala—the less developed, fight or flight part of the brain—that would engage. It was always the moment that she started to cry that broke me. The walls I'd built would come crumbling down, and I would instantly understand the impact my actions were having on her.

When we experience injustice or harm, we often express rage. That rage might be legitimate and righteous, but it is an ineffective method of communication. It puts the other person on the defensive, and they are less likely to hear you. Articulating our suffering, demonstrating the impact of harmful actions, and showing our vulnerability are much more effective ways to turn someone around.

But it is hard work. No one ever said that the work of nonviolence is easy. The work of transforming conflict into reconciliation is difficult; it is physical, emotional, and spiritual labor. But because our goal of Beloved Community is too important, we choose to accept the suffering that comes with it. While this principle is essential to nonviolence, we also need to be careful about our own limitations and boundaries. Without boundaries, our suffering can begin to internalize and manifest as internal violence of the spirit, at which point we are no longer practicing nonviolence.

CHAPTER 13

Principle Five: Avoid Internal Violence of the Spirit as Well as External Physical Violence

One time I gave a lecture on nonviolence as part of Barrios Unidos's lecture series in Soledad State Prison. After I spoke, Nane, BU's founder and executive director, opened the mic up to the audience. A young man walked up to the mic. He said he had only come to the lecture because he was bored and figured it would be better than just sitting in his cell.

"I'm twenty-two years old," he said. "I've been in prison for four years. My entire life, I've never felt like I was going to be anything more than a criminal and a thug. I've never heard anyone tell me that I can be something more, and after hearing those words from you, I feel like I want to make a change." This young man is now home, doing great, working and supporting his family.

I think about that moment all the time. I think about how deep internal violence of the spirit cuts. For someone to believe that they could never be anything more than a "criminal and a thug" is an act of deep internal violence. It's a message he heard from external sources (media, bad educators, others who believed the same, etc.), but at some point he internalized them, and they became acts of internal violence he was doing to himself.

I also think about the fact that *that's all it took*. For one person to tell him he was worthy. For one person to tell him that he has value and that he is more than his worst act.[1] In twenty-two years of his life, society had failed in providing this young man that one simple thing. Sometimes, the work of nonviolence is complicated

---

1. That is what prisons do. You become the sum total of the worst act you've ever committed, and that goes on to define who you are. A single act, often committed at the lowest point of your life.

and requires us to build strategies to fight large systems of injustice. Other times, the work of nonviolence is as simple as telling someone they are worthy.

"Internalized oppression" is when messages from oppressive systems and worldviews about our inferiority take root inside our own minds until we start believing in our inferiority. This term did not exist in Dr. King's era, but it is part of what he was talking about. *I'm never gonna be anything more than a criminal and a thug.* Internal violence. In addition to harmful beliefs, internal violence also manifests as negative self-talk.

"I'm not good enough."

"I'm not pretty enough."

"I'm always going to be alone."

"I'm never going to be successful."

It manifests as emotions like despair and hopelessness.

"Things are never going to get better."

"The world is only getting worse."

"We will never be able to create change."

These things are usually rooted in unhealed trauma. So the work of nonviolence isn't only about combating the violence "out there." It is equally about doing the work of healing "in here," so that we can release the spirit of violence that we have embodied in our own hearts.

DRINKING POISON

"Hating someone is like drinking poison and expecting the other person to die."

It's one of my favorite quotes, though I have never been able to track down its origins. It speaks powerfully to another important interpretation of this principle: that hatred, anger, and resentment are forms of internal violence we do to ourselves.

We've all tasted that poison. We've all had moments, days, or entire periods in our lives when we were caught up in hating and resenting someone. And that hate and resentment did nothing to the person toward whom it was being targeted. That person is probably having a wonderful day somewhere not even thinking about us, while we are not able to move forward in life because our hearts are so weighed down.

"I have decided to stick with love.... Hate is too great a burden to bear." We all know what Dr. King meant when he uttered those words. We all know intimately how heavy a burden hatred is in our hearts.

In 1995, Tariq Khamisa, a twenty-year-old student and the only son of Azim Khamisa, was senselessly shot and killed while delivering pizzas. The young man who pulled the trigger, fourteen-year-old Tony Hicks, was the first fourteen year old to stand trial as an adult in California.

Azim Khamisa now tours the country with Ples Felix, Tony Hicks's grandfather, talking about the importance of forgiveness.[2] He often reminds people that, "Forgiveness is something you do for yourself." The person you forgive may not want or accept your forgiveness. They may not even know that you have forgiven them. Forgiveness is something we do to unburden ourselves from the weight of resentment so that we can move forward.

Forgiveness is not easy work. I remember sitting in retreat one day at Deer Park, a Buddhist monastery in the lineage of Thich Nhat Hanh. We were having a discussion in a small group led by Sister Kaira Jewel.[3] One participant shared how hard it is for him to forgive people who are overtly racist and hateful. With the patience and compassion gleaned from decades of practice, Sister Jewel acknowledged this man's frustration while sharing, "We must learn to have compassion for people's ignorance."

I have tried to remember that teaching each time I am hurt by

> **"Forgiveness is something you do for yourself."**
> **—Azim Khamisa**

---

2. Check out their amazing work at the Tariq Khamisa Foundation at www.tkf.org.
3. She has since left monastic life but continues to teach dharma and meditation. Check her teachings out at www.kairajewel.com.

someone's actions. Violence is *always* rooted in ignorance. It may

> **"We must learn to have compassion for people's ignorance."**
> —Kaira Jewel

be ignorance about another person's culture, ignorance about their own pain and how it is being expressed in their lives, or ignorance about how to move through their own trauma. Understanding this has helped me live in a consistent attitude of forgiveness.

True accountability from someone who has harmed us may be helpful, but it is not a requirement for our own healing. Our ability to let go of resentment is not dependent on anybody else. The spirit of nonviolence depends on our ability to uplift our own spirits and to care enough about ourselves to be able to let hatred go.

This is necessary in movement spaces as well. I have been part of too many movements fueled by toxic amounts of anger and resentment. The toxicity seeps into our relationships and into the spirit of the movement. When hundreds and thousands of people are brought together by a common bond of hatred, how can we possibly imagine such a movement to be a liberating space?

THE HEALTH OF MOVEMENTS

"People be asking me all the time, 'Yo Mos, what's getting ready to happen with Hip Hop?' I tell 'em, you know what's gonna happen with Hip Hop? Whatever's happening with us. If we smoked out, Hip Hop's gonna be smoked out. If we doing alright, Hip Hop's gonna be doing alright. People talking about Hip Hop like it's some giant living in the hillside, coming down to visit the townspeople. We are Hip Hop. Me, you, everybody. We are Hip Hop. So Hip Hop is going where we going. So next time you ask yourself where Hip Hop is going, ask yourself, where am I going? How am I doing? And you get a clear idea."

Those were some of the opening words from Mos Def's classic album, *Black on Both Sides*.[4] It reminds me of a quote from Gandhi, who once said, "Nobility of soul consists in realizing that you are yourself India. In your emancipation is the emancipation of India." Social movements are like living organisms, made up of thousands of individual cells—us. Our levels of internal violence impact the health of the overall movement. Because we have all experienced trauma, it's no wonder our movement spaces can sometimes feel so toxic.

Movements working against large systems of oppression must first understand the dynamics of that oppression. We cannot undo something that we don't understand. So, we study the history of systemic oppression, its impact on our communities today, the pain of our ancestors, and how that pain has been carried forward through the generations.

At some point, it can feel like that's all we ever talk about. It can feel like all we know about ourselves are the ways in which we are oppressed and oppress others. We become such experts at our own oppression that we start to forget that we are anything more than that. We forget how powerful we are. We forget how resilient we are. We forget how resilient our ancestors were. We may talk about it, but we embody our oppression while only giving lip service to our resiliency.

The work of healing is tricky. It is akin to performing surgery. Once we begin to open up old wounds, a skilled surgeon needs to be there to perform the surgery and patch it up again, so we are not walking around with open wounds waiting to get infected. I fear that is what is happening too often with activism right now. We have intellectual conversations about oppression and trauma, which can open up deep wounds. Because we don't take the work of trauma healing seriously, many of us are now walking around with those wounds wide open.

---

4. Now known as Yasiin Bey.

When our identities become fixated on our trauma, we can easily be thrown off keel by any number of things. We become hypervigilant, a sign of someone living with trauma. We begin looking around every corner for the next trigger or the next thing that may traumatize us. We forget to breathe. Our wounds get infected. Healing is about moving through trauma, but we oftentimes open up the wounds and get stuck. The work of healing can involve talking about our deepest pain or about the things we have the most shame around. It can feel cathartic to talk about those things.

I was having a conversation once with Mushim over dinner, and she said that in the Bay Area, there are many "healing" spaces where people are encouraged to talk about their pain. It can feel good to talk about it and be seen by our community. But if that space isn't held well, if there isn't a skilled facilitator, we can become "indulgent in our pain" and get stuck.

I've even seen this happen in the streets during protests and demonstrations when people's pain comes pouring out. While there is obviously a need for that pain to be expressed, a demonstration in front of police wearing riot gear is not a place conducive to healing. We do not perform surgeries in the middle of a highway. We perform them in safe spaces, with skilled healers and teams of assistants who dig around and fix what needs to get fixed, patch up the wounds, and allow them to scar.

"Preach from your scars, not from your wounds."
—Rev. Nadia Bolz-Weber

Lutheran minister Rev. Nadia Bolz-Weber teaches us to "Preach from your scars, not from your wounds." Avoiding internal violence of the spirit means dealing with our traumas and moving through them so they become scars. Scars are strong, and they give us character. They connect us with our pain, but they protect it like a shield. *That* is what we need to take into battle.

VIOLENCE HURTS EVERYONE

In my work with people who have caused great harm to others, I have found that there is another side to the idea that, "hurt people hurt people." That is, hurt people hurt people, and hurting people hurts.[5] We cannot cause harm to another human being without harming ourselves in some way. Degrading life does something to degrade our own sense of dignity and humanity. Seeing ourselves as somehow separate from the person you are harming, seeing ourselves as being outside of the web of interdependence takes away from who we truly are. Enacting violence on another person hurts that person, but it is also an act of internal violence that we are doing to ourselves. I believe this to be a universal law of nature. It is very common for a person to be buried under so many layers of trauma that they cannot even connect or feel their pain for causing harm onto someone else. It may feel like we can harm someone without it having any negative impact on ourselves.

I have heard many stories from incarcerated men who have taken another person's life and felt no sympathy for their victim in that moment. But once we begin to unpack their story and give space for the pain and trauma that they themselves have been carrying, it becomes clear that they are also holding a great deal of pain and shame for the violence they have perpetuated. The external violence was rooted in internal violence, and their violent actions only helped to exacerbate their internal pain even more.

Anthony Johnson was part of the first cohort of incarcerated men to become certified as a Kingian Nonviolence trainer in San Bruno jail. One day, he told me about his first memory of an interaction with law enforcement. He was a young child, and it was shortly before Christmas. The police raided his house, looking for his stepfather who was a suspected drug dealer. Presuming that

---

5. Some people also say, "Hurt people hurt people, and healed people heal people." I like to add, "Hurt people hurt people, and hurting people hurts. Healed people heal people, and healing people heals."

he was hiding drugs in the presents beneath the tree, the police ripped open every single hand-wrapped box. It's easy to empathize with young Anthony, but what of the police officers? What would it do to your soul to raid a family home with guns drawn, rip open Christmas presents in front of a crying child, and carry away a father in front of his family?

Maybe the officers didn't feel it. Maybe they viewed Anthony as collateral damage and blamed his stepfather. If that were the case, this only means that the officers were so removed from their own sense of humanity that they couldn't feel empathy for young Anthony or connect to their own pain for having to perform such a "duty." I cannot bring myself to believe that any sane person can perform such an act without it negatively impacting their soul.

Many people have suggested it is problematic for me to ask anyone, especially marginalized peoples, to have empathy for their oppressors. I get that. As a relatively privileged person, it's easier

Compassion is not a zero-sum game.

for me to say these things. But compassion is not a zero-sum game. Having compassion, empathy, and understanding for the officers who raided Anthony's home doesn't take away from the compassion and empathy I have for Anthony.

I once read a quote from an elder in the Civil Rights movement, who said, "The Civil Rights movement was a battle for the bodies of Black folks and the souls of white folks." This was an acknowledgment that being a white supremacist destroys your soul. It is not healthy to have so much hatred in your heart, to believe in what Dr. King called, "a false sense of superiority," or to believe that you are somehow separate from the interconnected web of humanity.

Being on the receiving end of violence and oppression causes pain, but being on the giving end of violence and oppression results in internal pain of the spirit. It sometimes feels to me like the difference between being an oppressor and being the oppressed, being the perpetrator of crime versus being the victim is really just a matter of degree and perspective. Violence is a disease that hurts everyone, and nonviolence acts as its medicine.

TEARS AS MEDICINE

I have come to learn that tears are among the most powerful human tools for healing, and various systems, the system of patriarchy in particular, have ripped this medicine away from many men. An older man named Marcus once shared his story with me. When Marcus was a small child, his mother passed away, and he started to cry. His own father told him to go hang out with the girls if he was going to act like one. And he didn't cry for forty years after that. He now realizes that the repression of his feelings contributed greatly to the murder he committed later in his life. I have heard countless stories like Marcus's.

While my own story isn't nearly as extreme, I also struggle with accessing my tears. I attended a retreat once where we got into a deep conversation about the wounds inflicted by patriarchy. During a lunchtime conversation, a woman leading the group quoted bell hooks talking about how patriarchy hurts men, something I'd never really thought about. I felt a wave of emotion come over me, but I knew I would never let myself cry in front of a group during an informal lunch-time conversation.

I left. The conversations we had been having over the previous couple of days were bringing up some raw emotions, and I knew I had to let them out. I walked into the woods by myself, found a quiet place where I could be alone, and for the first time in my entire life, I *tried* to cry. The moment I sat down, tears came pouring out of me like thunder.

And then, after about thirty seconds, I stopped. I found myself thinking about how Kevin Durant was going to fit in with the Warriors.[6] But I knew I had more to feel, so I forced myself to

---

6. This was the summer of 2016 when the Golden State Warriors, one of the best basketball teams in the world, had just signed Kevin Durant, one of the best players in the world.

stop thinking about basketball and felt my emotions again. Again, the tears came pouring out. After about fifteen seconds, I found myself wondering what was going to happen in the next season of *Game of Thrones*.[7] This went on for some time. It was fascinating to observe my body and my mind continue to battle. I watched myself as every time I wanted to feel and to mourn, my mind would kick in and try to stop it. I became aware of how disconnected I was from my own emotions and began to feel a sense of indignation. It was in that moment that I realized what these emotions were. It was sadness and indignation that the patriarchal society I'd been raised in had taken away from me one of the most basic methods we have for mourning and healing. I became aware of how much pain I had been holding back, not knowing how to release.

Messages like "boys don't cry," "suck it up," and "toughen up" are perhaps some of the most violent messages that we teach our young people of all genders. To force a human being to ignore and negate a part of who they are, to separate them from a core aspect of their humanity and take away such an important tool for self-healing is an act of violence.

I later found the exact quote from bell hooks's book *The Will to Change*:

> The first act of violence that patriarchy demands of males is not violence toward women. Instead patriarchy demands of all males that they engage in acts of psychic self-muti-lation, that they kill off the emotional parts of themselves. If an individual is not successful in emotionally crippling himself, he can count on patriarchal men to enact rituals of power that will assault his self-esteem.

I can think of so many "rituals of power," as hooks puts it, which I have experienced. They have not only created a gaping

---

7. A TV show on HBO. And yes, I know it is a very problematic show for many reasons.... I'm not proud to be a fan.

hole in my own soul but also a gaping valley in my relationships with other men.

Earlier, I talked about a time when I shared a childhood trauma in a group setting, and it was the first time in my adult life I cried in public. As I was breaking down, the man sitting next to me—a man much larger than me—held me tight in his arms. I had never shared that story before. I never cried like that in public. I had certainly never been held by another man like that. That kind of thing was supposed to be, you know, "gay" right?

Growing up, I was not only taught to be homophobic, but I was never given examples of healthy male intimacy. When I think back to that moment, I'm always surprised to remember how safe I felt. I never knew that crying into the arms of another man could feel so good. But that is not the type of relationship patriarchy encourages or allows. Patriarchy tells us that I can only get together with my boys to watch football games, drink beer, and talk about women. How many men have male friends they can cry with? Patriarchy has ripped away men's abilities to have authentic and whole relationships with other men.

This topic, about the ways in which patriarchy contributes to violence in our society, deserves its own book, and indeed there are many resources out there.[8] I just bring it up here, because tears are one of the most powerful tools we have at our disposal for transforming internal violence. They are something we all have access to despite some of us having been trained to believe otherwise.

---

8. Books like bell hooks's *The Will to Change*, documentaries like *The Mask You Live In* and *The Feminist on Cellblock Y*, publications like *Voice Male* magazine, and websites like www.goodmenproject.com are good places to start.

Principle Six: The Universe Is on the Side of Justice

The sixth and final principle is probably the one with the most varied interpretations. Concepts like "justice" or "the universe" mean many different things to many different people. Many people find it difficult to see how the universe is just when we see so much injustice in front of us.

For Dr. King, a Baptist minister, much of this principle was about faith. I believe that on some level, anyone who has ever engaged in the work of social change has faith in this principle—otherwise why would we do it? If we didn't believe that the work we are doing would pay off, why would we bother? Faith is a critical component in the practice of principle five as well. Hopelessness, desperation, despair, despondence are all acts of internal violence and can drive people away from a commitment to nonviolence.

Principle six is one antidote to the internal violence of the spirit that is prevalent in so many movements. Part of the practice of nonviolence is to cultivate unwavering faith that we will get there. Maybe not in our lifetime, but as Dr. King said in his final public appearance, "We, as a people, will get to the promised land." This principle comes from a longer quote in which Dr. King, in turn quoting another clergyman, said, "The arc of the moral universe is long, but it bends towards justice."[1] And we sometimes forget how big the universe is, and a lot of our sense of hopelessness comes out of that ignorance.

Back in 1999, I had the opportunity to travel to Ladakh, India, a

---

1. This famous quote, oftentimes attributed to Dr. King, was originally attributed to Theodore Parker, a nineteenth-century abolitionist and Unitarian minister.

desert plateau high in the Himalayas. It is by far the most beautiful place I have ever visited.[2] There was a moment on the journey when our bus was going up a long hill, and as we turned a corner, the road opened up into the biggest valley I had ever seen. I had no idea mountains so vast existed on this planet. I had no idea landscapes like that existed on this planet. It was breathtaking and awe-inspiring. I had never felt so small and insignificant. It was amazing. It was amongst the most humbling moments of my life. The feeling that I was such an insignificant speck of dust on such a large planet was liberating.

Years later, when I got interested in cosmology, I was reminded that even the expansiveness of that valley was one small part of one small planet in a galaxy with hundreds of millions of planets in a universe with hundreds of millions of galaxies. Yet sometimes, when I experience injustice, I end up with a belief that the entire universe is unjust.

This work is not always about us as individuals. If we believe the universe is unjust because we may not experience Beloved Community in our lifetime, then we may be overvaluing our individual experiences. This principle is about faith, but also about patience, humility, and perspective. It's a big world out there, and all we have access to is our limited bubble of perspective. We only see what's in front of us, what the media shows us, the experiences that we have lived through in our lives, and the stories we've heard. It's easy to forget how big the universe is, and how long the arc of history is. We can get into tunnel vision and forget how far we've come as stardust and as a species.

That's not to say that because the universe is just, we can sit back

---

2. There are two roads that lead into Leh, the capital of Ladakh—the highest motorable road in the world and the second highest motorable road in the world. The first was closed at that time due to an armed conflict between India and Pakistan over land rights. So we took the second and got stranded at the highest point on the path due to a mudslide. I thought I would die from altitude sickness, but it was absolutely worth being so close to the stars and hundreds of miles from any artificial light source.

and watch it do its thing. Dr. King wrote, "Human progress never rolls in on wheels of inevitability; it comes through the tireless efforts of [people] willing to be coworkers with God, and without this hard work, time itself becomes an ally of the forces of social stagnation." A commitment to nonviolence requires us to act, and it is only through our actions that the universe will bring us closer to justice. This principle is not about trusting that the universe will magically undo all evils. It is about having faith that if we put the work in toward justice, it will "roll down like waters."

We live in a shortsighted society. Every time war breaks out, every time there's another mass shooting, every time a piece of legislation moves us away from Beloved Community, we lose perspective and feel like the world is falling apart. We also live in an individualistic society. Not only do we view our experience as personal and disconnected from others, but we also live as generations disconnected from other generations. We feel like our generation has to stop all the wars, stop all the killings, and reach Beloved Community. We feel like we are on our own.

Years ago, my friend and fellow trainer Matt Guynn told me he heard that Japanese companies build five-hundred-year business plans. He later met a Japanese businessman at a conference and asked him if this was true. Hearing this, the businessman laughed in his face. "That's ridiculous," he said. "I've never heard of a business plan longer than 250 years!"

Inspired by this, East Point Peace Academy is working on developing a 250-year work plan, because we understand that this is the work of generations, not of election cycles or five-year nonprofit strategic plans. We need to remember that we are in relationship with the wisdom of those that came before us and the lives of those who will come after. In the long moral arc of the universe, there will be times we experience injustice and see things that will challenge our faith. But when we maintain a long-term, universal perspective, it becomes a bit easier to maintain faith that we will ultimately get to the Promised Land. As Dr. King taught, "We must accept finite disappointment, but never lose infinite hope."

JUSTICE AS BALANCE

In every workshop while discussing this principle, there is usually some version of a question that basically amounts to, "Prove it."

"Where is the evidence that the universe is just?" "How can you say the universe is just when you see *[fill in the blank]*." One time during a small group activity, a group wrote in big, bold letters: "The Crusades: WTF?"

For those who struggle with faith, let me provide you with some evidence that universe is just. When we hear the word justice, we often associate it with what's "good" and "right." We imagine superheroes coming down from the sky, beating up the bad guys, restoring justice to the world. But "good" and "right" are relative terms.

Do a Google image search for the word justice. What do you see? Chances are, you will see images of a scale. The scales of justice represent balance and order. So what if we look at the principle this way? "The universe is on the side of balance and order." As complex as the universe is, over time it tends to create balance and order from the chaos.

I sit back and watch the investments that our society makes into systems of violence. We invest in war, broken school systems, a broken prison system, guns, violent media, economic policies that perpetuate poverty, fossil fuels—a culture that isolates us and moves us further away from our true selves. We invest in all of these systems of violence, and when the universe gives us the return on those investments, and we see violence in our communities, we act like something is wrong with the universe.

Every time a young person is killed in the streets that is evidence that the universe is just. Every time a new war breaks out, there is another school shooting, a new species goes extinct, a hate crime is perpetrated, or there is another case of police violence, I see evidence that the universe is, indeed, just. Violence doesn't just appear out of nowhere. Everything we live with is nothing but a series of causes and conditions. Everything in this world exists because of something that came before it that gave rise to it. That is the history of conflict. As long as we invest in systems of violence, it is *just* that we get violent returns. That is the balance and order of the universe doing its thing.

What will happen when we invest in systems of peace? When we invest in our communities and invest in right relationships with each other and the earth? I believe the same balance and order of the universe will begin to give us those returns instead.

I mentioned earlier about an effort I was part of to create a culture of peace at Chicago's North Lawndale College Preparatory High School. As part of their campaign, the school got rid of their metal detectors and security guards.[3] This saved the school $400,000 a year, which they reinvested into their students and into peace education. The universe rewarded this investment immediately with a 70 percent decrease in violence. That is an example of order, balance, and justice.

While defining justice as balance can be helpful on one hand, it can also create a different problem. The criminal justice system is often represented by Lady Justice holding a scale. This interpretation of justice goes something like this: when people cause harm they skew the balance of the universe by putting weight on the side of violence. In order to restore balance, we need to punish those people and make them hurt too. The theory is that this puts weight on the other side of the scale, bringing things back into balance.

I think this is a dangerous misunderstanding of how the order of the universe works. I believe that when someone causes harm,

---

3. During an interview for an article I wrote in the winter 2012 issue of the magazine *Rethinking Schools*, the school's President John Horan told me: "Security guards don't teach peace. They teach kids to hate security guards."

weight is placed on the side of violence, and the scale gets tipped. If we respond by harming the person who committed the act, we are actually putting *more weight* on the side of violence and harm, tipping the scale even further out of balance. If we truly want to restore balance and achieve justice, I believe we need to put weight on the side of love, compassion, and understanding.[4] That will tip the scales back into balance.

ENDS AND MEANS

Dr. King, Gandhi, and many other practitioners of nonviolence taught that nonviolence is both the ends and the means. Nonviolence is not only the vision of the world that we want to create, but it is the process by which we get there.

We live in a results-oriented society where we measure everything by its outcome. As long as we meet our quota, as long as we increase our revenue, as long as we win the championship, as long as we pass our legislation, we are successful. We put very little emphasis on the quality of the process that gets us there. No matter how many relationships are forged, no matter how many lessons are learned, no matter how much we grow, if we don't accomplish our goals, then we have failed.

In a nonviolent worldview, the way we go about our work is as important as the goals we are working toward. In fact, the two are interchangeable. The spirit with which we engage in the work of transformation will be reflected in the change that we create.

When we engage in violence and hatred, when we are driven by an "us vs. them" worldview, we are planting seeds of division and those seeds will never yield a just and peaceful society. That would be like planting an apple seed and expecting peaches to grow from the ground. If we invest in violence, we will get more violence. If we invest in hatred, we will get more hatred. If we invest

---

4. I am not saying we simply hug the person who committed an act of violence. We do need to hold that person accountable, but we can view accountability as an act of love rather than punishment.

in division, we will increase division. That is the natural law of the universe. That is order. That is balance. Chris once wrote, "If we had to reduce Gandhi's nonviolence philosophy to its simplest form, ends = means would be it."

UNIVERSAL LAWS OF NATURE

The Sanskrit word *dharma* is often used to describe the teachings of the historical Buddha. But originally, it was a concept that simply described the unalterable and universal laws of nature. The teachings of the Buddha were not some religious dogma handed down by an angel or prophet. They were simply his own understanding of the universal laws of nature and the reality of the human condition garnered through exploration and observation of his own mind. Similarly, I've come to understand nonviolence as the universal laws of nature that govern human conflict.

Gravity is a universal law of nature. It doesn't matter if you believe in gravity; you are still governed by its laws. Similarly, if we understand the laws that govern our relationship to conflict as a universal law, it doesn't matter if you believe in it. You are still governed by its laws.

To me, it doesn't matter if you think you can use violence to achieve a just society. The violence you engage in will always be reflected in the change you bring about. It doesn't matter if you think hatred and resentment can sustain you. It will ultimately eat you up. And it doesn't matter if you think that love is sappy and weak. Cultivating love will fulfill you and help you achieve your potential. I believe all of those things to be true because I believe them to be universal laws of nature. Whether or not one believes them has no relevance to the universe and its ways.

In the same way that physics is the science of the laws that govern the universe, from the quantum to the cosmic levels, I see nonviolence as the science of the universal laws that govern conflict, harm, and healing from the personal to the global levels. Nonviolence isn't a naive, dogmatic, or judgmental belief that hatred and violence are bad or that love and compassion are good. Violence and compassion simply exist. Nonviolence is an exploration of the impact of violence and compassion on the human experience and an attempt to understand the laws that govern them. If we invest in systems that harm human beings, cultures that isolate people, and worldviews that divide communities, we will move away from Beloved Community. The universe doesn't care if we reach Beloved Community or not. The universe doesn't care if we fulfill our potential as a species. The universe simply exists, and its job is to continue to create balance and order. It is up to us, as a species, to understand these laws so we can move toward Beloved Community.

PART THREE
THE SKILL

CHAPTER 15

The Six Steps of Nonviolence

The Six Steps of Nonviolence
1. Information Gathering
2. Education
3. Personal Commitment
4. Negotiation
5. Direct Action
6. Reconciliation

The Six Steps of Kingian Nonviolence, sometimes referred to as "the skill" of nonviolence, has its origins in the Gandhian four-step approach to organizing that Dr. King quoted in his "Letter from a Birmingham Jail": (1) investigation, (2) negotiation, (3) self-purification, and (4) direct action.[1] This was later expanded by Dr. LaFayette Jr. and Jehnsen into its current iteration within the Kingian Nonviolence framework. In essence, the six steps are a framework through which we view the various components of organizing a campaign or a movement. However, they have deep applications to how we engage with interpersonal conflicts as well.

There was a long period of time when I believed that social change happens through protests and large-scale demonstrations. The six steps showed me that direct action was just one step within a larger framework for movement building, and that in order to make real change, we need to do much more than just protest. The six steps are not linear. They are not like steps on a ladder where you have to start with step one, then two, then three, then four. While there is some logic behind the order in which they

1. The principles are referred to as "the will" of nonviolence.

are presented, a campaign might start with step five, or you may move from step one to step two, then realize that you need to go back to step one.

The Kingian Nonviolence curriculum manual describes these steps are "coterminous," a word I had never heard before coming to a Kingian Nonviolence workshop. Merriam-Webster defines the word as "coextensive in scope or duration," which is one of those definitions that doesn't help you understand the word at all. It essentially means that each step continues throughout the course of a campaign or your response to a conflict. It's not like we do some amount of information gathering (step one) and then stop gathering information while we educate people (step two). We are always gathering information, always educating ourselves and others, etc. It's probably more accurate to see these steps as cyclical rather than straight up like a ladder.

Finally, it's important to note that there are entire books, workshops, training organizations, and fields of study dedicated to each one of these steps. The six steps as they are presented here offer a broad framework for how some of these practices can fit together. When building a campaign or a movement, it is important to have people on your team who are skilled and knowledgeable in each of these areas.

Step One: Information Gathering

In his "Letter from a Birmingham Jail," Dr. King said that the first step in any nonviolent campaign is the "collection of facts to determine whether injustice exists." In other words, we shouldn't even jump to the conclusion that the thing you are organizing against is an act of injustice. Sometimes, when we have the patience to remain calm and look deeper into a conflict, we realize there is no conflict at all. When we act without first gathering information, we act with limited understanding and a lot of assumptions. And as the old adage goes, when you "assume," you make an "ass" out of "u" and "me."

One time, my friend Rob was on break from work, sipping coffee outside a cafe near his office. He didn't have a watch, so he wasn't aware of the time, but figured he should be getting back to work. He saw a man walking past wearing a watch, so he called out to this man.

"Excuse me, do you know what time it is?"

Nothing. The stranger kept walking without acknowledging my friend.

Assuming he must not have heard, Rob tried again, a bit louder.

"Excuse me! Do you have the time?"

Again nothing.

Now Rob assumed that he was being ignored. Frustrated, he approached the man one last time, tapped on his shoulder, and yelled, *"excuse me!"*

Turns out the man was deaf.

East Point's cofounder Theresa shared a similar experience. She was in a budgeting meeting with two of her colleagues. They were crunching some numbers, and Theresa heard one of them say,

"Oh, and after this meeting, remind me to tell our vendor about this decision we made."

So naturally, Theresa asked, "Okay, which vendor?"

Her colleagues looked at her with blank faces and went right back into their conversation. Feeling a little frustrated (normal level of conflict), she simply ignored the slight and moved on. However, a few minutes later, it happened again. "Oh, and we have to make sure to get those numbers from our vendor."

She asked again, "Okay, so which vendor are you talking about? The same one as before?"

Again they ignored her and kept working (things are getting pervasive). When it happened a third time, Theresa's frustration was no longer containable. "Okay, guys, stop ignoring me! Which vendor are you talking about?!"

The two men looked at each other with puzzled expressions, and then it finally hit them. They weren't talking about "our vendor," they were talking about another colleague, whose name was Arvinder. It's easy to feel slighted or like the victim of some injustice when there is so much injustice to go around. But when we are triggered, we should stop, take a breath, try not to react from assumptions, but rather try and understand the facts from an objective place.[2]

The Indian spiritual teacher J. Krishnamurti once said, "The highest form of human intelligence is the ability to observe without evaluating." It takes a lot of practice to observe or experience a conflict and not add our own spin, but there is great value in it. When we experience conflict, most of us react from a place of habit. Because our habit patterns are reactionary, they are naturally relying on our own spin, our own interpretation of the conflict we just witnessed. But if we can learn to pause—even for a split second—and create space between the stimulus and our reaction to that stimulus, we can choose a wise and skillful response.

---

2. There is a great acronym for the word STOP, which stands for Stop, Take a Breath, Observe, Proceed.

Obviously, with practice we can get better at pausing before we react to conflict and to analyze it objectively. There is also the reality that the more time we have away from the conflict, the less emotionally triggered we are and the more objective we can be. That objectivity may allow us to see that something we perceived as a major conflict is actually a simple misunderstanding, and really there is no conflict at all. Sometimes, accusations of racism, sexism, and other forms of injustice are genuinely unwarranted.

Years before I committed myself to the practice of nonviolence, I got into an altercation with a neighbor. I got home after a long day, exhausted and a little tense. While I was in the shower, this neighbor knocked on the back door to our apartment, upset that I had taken his parking spot, even though our building did not have assigned parking spots. When I came out of the bathroom, my roommates told me that he had come down and asked, "Where is that Asian guy?"

I flipped. I stormed upstairs, started banging on his door, and immediately got in his face. "What does it have to do with me being Asian," I yelled as I shoved him against his counter. I used to think about that incident a lot and ask myself why I got so upset. After all, I *am* an Asian guy…. So why did that piss me off so much?

I think a lot of it had to do with the fact that I've been "that Asian guy" ever since I moved to the United States. A lifetime of being exoticized, tokenized, other-ized, teased for the shape of my eyes, my funny name, and the weird bento boxes that my mom would pack for my lunch made me sensitive to being seen not as Kazu, but as "that Asian guy."

There can be a level of privilege in being able to see things—particularly incidents tinged with some form of oppression—objectively. For those whose communities have historically been marginalized, we are swimming in injustice, violence, and oppression. It is easy to become sensitive and harder to view things objectively. When I say "sensitive," I don't mean that in a judgmental way.[3] The Oxford dictionary defines sensitive as, "quick to detect or respond to slight changes, signals, or influences."

Oppression is traumatic, and hypervigilance and hyper-attentiveness are common manifestations of trauma. When we are used to fighting off threats and attacks on a daily basis, we are constantly looking for the next attack, and being sensitive is an effective and important survival mechanism. At the same time, constantly looking for the next sign of danger only perpetuates trauma and does not help us heal.

When your identity is not part of US society's dominant group (white, heterosexual, cisgender, male-bodied, middle-class Prot-estant-Christian), and someone from the default/dominant group calls you out by your marginalized identity, it can feel like you are being put in a box, specifically a lesser-than box. You cease to be an individual and feel reduced to the sum of all of the negative stereotypes of your marginalized group. Over time, that can make you sensitive.

> **Constantly looking for the next sign of danger only perpetuates trauma and does not help us heal.**

Looking back on that incident, I am sure my neighbor did not mean any ill will. For him, "Asian" was probably nothing more than just a physical descriptor (he did not know my name). With the benefit of hindsight, I am able to see now that he was not intentionally being racist.

The mind is a funny thing. If you're constantly looking for something, you may begin to see things that aren't there. If our expectation is that the next harm or potential for harm is around every corner, we become more and more hyper-vigilant, which only serves to reinforce trauma. It does not help us heal.

A lot of today's social justice circles seem to have established a culture where we earn points for calling out injustice. If we see an instance of injustice and call it out, we earn credit because of how "woke" we are. And in our deeply embedded capitalist

---

3. A pet peeve: Why has the word sensitive become synonymous with weak?

mentality, we can get addicted to that currency and begin to look for it everywhere. Calling out injustice is important, but seeing it in places where it is not or exaggerating it is harmful. Oppression and violence are so prevalent in our society that it's easy to see them everywhere, but reality is hard enough without us adding extra injustice to it.

SUBJECTIVE REALITY

Of course, the burden of this work can't fall entirely on marginalized communities. Oppression and marginalization are traumatic; trauma causes hypervigilance; and hypervigilance may lead to seeing things that aren't there. Even when a marginalized person is experiencing injustice where there is none, there is also a role for those in privileged positions to understand and empathize with that person's subjective experience. Accusing marginalized people of being "too sensitive" can be incredibly harmful.

As important as it is for us to learn to see things objectively, we can't negate people's subjective experience as "not real." It is a real, lived experience that needs to be honored. Our attempts to understand conflict needs to happen with a dialectic lens, meaning we try to see the objective truth as well as honor subjective experiences.[4] During that argument with my neighbor, he accused me of playing "the race card." He accused me of being too sensitive and seeing racism where it wasn't. And you know what? He was probably right. In retrospect, I can see that I *was* being too sensitive. But that was the reality of my experience. In that moment, I may have seen something that was not there, but twenty years of mounting traumas around racism were adding up, and that day it was just too much. That was my reality, and it is an important part of the story.

As people of color in the United States, we have never had the option of "playing" this "game" called "race." It has been shoved down our throats from day one. So every once in a while, we may

4. Remember this from chapter eleven?

cough up a card and it may land on a white person's face, but it's only because we were trying not to choke on white supremacy. We don't mean for the card to land on your face. We're just trying to breathe.

How many times have we heard a man accuse women of "being too sensitive" or "acting crazy" when they call out sexism? How many times have I done that? Too many to count. Maybe some of those times I was right, but that's not the point. If all I can see is, "That person is just overreacting," then I'm not honoring their experience, and therefore I am not seeing the entire conflict.

Being a cisgender male means that I am less sensitive to sexism and patriarchy, which means I may miss a nuanced experience and not see injustice that is there. I may get defensive and stop gathering information too quickly. In doing so, I am failing again to see the complete picture.

As members of marginalized communities, our work is to heal from our traumas so we're not seeing violence where it doesn't exist and perpetuating our traumas in unnecessary ways. As members of privileged communities, our work is to understand that our position may not allow us to see the full picture, have compassion for why people may be too sensitive, and allow space for that pain and anger. This is part of the information we all need to gather about any conflict.

EMPATHY

In the summer of 2018, an American woman's African hunting trip became infamous when pictures of her posing in front of a large black giraffe that she had shot and killed went viral. In an instant, she became the personification of evil. She was labeled a "white American savage who is partly a Neanderthal," "broken and soulless," "vile ... heartless, selfish murderer," and an "idiot." Her name was shared publicly, and she received thousands of death threats.

However, once you gather more information, the story becomes more complicated and nuanced. It turns out that the specific giraffe she shot and killed was an older male who was well past breeding age. Sometimes when adult giraffes reach that age, they begin killing off younger males, thereby threatening the population of the species. This particular giraffe had already killed multiple younger bulls of breeding age. Local conservation agencies charge hunters thousands of dollars to shoot these particular older bulls in order to protect the younger ones. The money also helps to support local communities and further conservation efforts.

Personally, I don't want to support a culture where the killing of any animal is seen simply as a sport. I'm deeply disturbed that the killing of such a majestic creature can be considered "fun" for anybody. But when I read the full story, it becomes way more complex than the story that was initially being shared: Rich white blood-thirsty American kills a giraffe, threatening an endangered species. Once I gather more information, I still may not support trophy hunting or agree with this strategy for conservation, but I can see that the story is more complex than good vs. evil, with this American woman personifying evil.

After the terror attacks of September 11, 2001, many Americans jumped on the war bandwagon and Osama bin Laden quickly became Public Enemy Number One. And that's understandable. One of the warmongering narratives was, "They attacked us because they hate our freedom and want to enforce Islamic laws on the entire world." Many Americans never questioned that narrative. It was simple, and buying into a simple black/white narrative gave some people a sense of comfort, security, and stability. The reality, of course, was more complicated. Those who took the time to actually read bin Laden's two fatwas (statements declaring war on the United States and its allies), saw that the war was never about "our freedom."

Nowhere does he mention hatred toward "America's freedoms" or way of life. He does mention anger at decades of violence against Muslims all over the world, the US government's support of Israel and its occupation of Palestine, the war against the Iraqi people, and the "deterioration of the economy, inflation, high cost of living, ever-increasing debts, and prisons full of inmates"—all things he blamed largely on US foreign policy.

After reading his statements, it becomes questionable whether this was a religious war driven by a desire to enforce Islamic laws worldwide, and it begins to sound more like a political war driven by anger, pain, and a desire for vengeance. I want to be very clear that *in no way* am I condoning bin Laden's actions, his worldview, or his analysis about the cause of so much of the suffering in the Muslim world. I can't say this enough, but understanding someone's perspective does not mean agreeing with them or condoning their actions.

But understanding *why* someone hates you is pretty important information if you're going to try to solve a conflict, don't you think? If our analysis of the situation doesn't go any further than, "They hate our freedom and we have fundamentally different world views," then we are not seeing the full picture and the effectiveness of our response will be as limited as our analysis.

Almost two decades after the September 11th attacks, we see the long-term impact of short-term analysis. Bin Laden is dead, but Afghanistan remains a war-torn country, and many experts blame the US invasion of Iraq (in 2003—the most recent one) for the creation of ISIS.[5] Perhaps if we had listened, if we had actually tried to understand *why* so many people in the Middle East hated the United States, we would have found a different response.

When someone hurts us, it's easy to think it's simply because that person is mean-spirited. But the reality is that "hurt people hurt people," and once we unpack that person's story and understand what drove them to their actions, things start to make more sense.

---

5. Bin Laden witnessed the suffering and massacres of many Muslims. Right or wrong, he blamed the United States for them. We responded by invading more Muslim countries, causing the deaths of hundreds of thousands of civilians. This radicalized a segment of a new generation of Muslims, many of them who would go on to join the ranks of ISIS. Rinse, repeat.

The Art of War is a book about military strategy, written by the Chinese military general Sun Tzu, who died in 496 BCE. It has been translated and used in the fields of war, business, office politics, education, and more for over 1,500 years. So, you know there might be some wisdom in it. In the book, Sun Tzu writes about the critical importance of "knowing your enemy." Empathy is not just about being nice; it's also about being strategic. It's about understanding the perspectives of each party in the conflict, the history of the conflict, and gathering as much information as we need to understand the full picture.

I will never condone white supremacy, but I can empathize with white supremacists. To do that, I might try to understand how poverty may have played a role in shaping their worldview. I might discover they had some traumatic experience that shaped their thinking. Perhaps they came from a broken home and were recruited into a white supremacist organization at a young age, finding acceptance and community for the first time there. Or perhaps they had been misinformed by radio talk shows into believing that Mexican immigrants are stealing their jobs.

If I don't understand *why* they believe what they do, I will never understand the conflict well enough to turn their opinions around. In this case, empathizing is not about tolerating white supremacy but about acknowledging real feelings and experiences and gaining understanding about how people may have arrived at their conclusions. When we gather information, we are not doing it to prove why we are right and the other side is wrong. We do it to understand the complexity and nuance in every conflict, in every issue, in every person, so that we have the best chance at actually moving toward reconciliation.

RESEARCH AND STRATEGY

Speaking of military strategy, there is an element of information gathering that is less about understanding perspectives and more about understanding data. The importance of research, investigation, and data can be a critical step in understanding how to move forward through a conflict. I've seen many activists (myself included) rush too quickly into action without having done the necessary research to ensure that the action will have lasting impact.

During the Oscar Grant campaign, we organized an action at the BART board of directors meeting. We had a list of demands, one of which was for the BART board to fire its chief of police, Gary Gee. We brought our signs, banners, and chants and filled the room with our supporters. Later on, we found out that the BART board of directors does not have the legal authority to fire the chief of police. That power lies with the BART manager, who was not at the meeting. Because we had not done our research, we were screaming at the wrong people. Power Mapping—understanding who has the power to give you what you want—is obviously an important first step and takes some time and research.

I have had the privilege to learn from Ivan Marovic, one of the cofounders of Otpor, the nonviolent student-led revolution that brought down the dictator Slobodan Milosevic in Yugoslavia. He told me that tools like Power Mapping, Spectrum of Allies (which maps different sectors of society and analyzes how much of an ally or opponent they are), SWOT analysis (scenario planning around a movement's strengths, weaknesses, opportunities, and threats), and Pillars of Support (which looks at which institutions are propping up the larger systems you are trying to change) are among the most important tools a successful movement needs to conduct before jumping into action.[6]

He also told me that the leaders of Otpor planned, researched, strategized, and trained for a full year before launching. A full year! There are similar stories throughout history. If you've seen images of children being attacked with fire hoses in the American

---

6. There are some good online resources about each of these tools. I suggest Training for Change and Beautiful Trouble as starting points, as well as East Point Peace Academy's two-day More Than a Protest workshop (shameless plug).

South, that was during the Birmingham campaign, one of the Civil Rights movement's most successful campaigns. The leaders of that campaign planned for a full six months before jumping in with full force. The seventy-eight leaders of Gandhi's army lived in an ashram together to do the work of strategizing and spiritual preparation for 15 years before embarking on the salt march.[7] Rev. Lawson once said that, "The difficulty with nonviolent people and efforts is that they don't recognize the necessity for fierce discipline and training and strategizing and planning and recruiting and doing the kinds of things you do to have a movement. That can't happen spontaneously. It has to be done systematically."

When we look at movements from the outside, it can look like change just ... happens. One day things were unjust, the next day a movement was born, and the following day there was justice. But when we dig into that history, we see how much planning and preparation was involved. Just as we often miss the history of a conflict and only see the moment it erupts into violence, we also often miss all of

Just as we often miss the history of a conflict and only see the moment it erupts into violence, we also often miss all of the systematic work that goes into launching a successful movement.

the systematic work that goes into launching a successful movement and only see the moment the movement takes action.

When I first met Dr. LaFayette, I was blown away listening to how strategic he and his peers had been about every little detail of the Civil Rights movement. They would intentionally get arrested at 11 a.m., so the city would have to feed them lunch, which put extra pressure on the police department. Or they would get arrested at 4:30 p.m. on a Friday so they would have to be held over the weekend before they could be arraigned, creating even more cost for the city.

During the early days of the Occupy movement, I was on the phone with Dr. LaFayette, and one of the first things he told me was

7. Fifteen years!

that the movement should have started in the spring. When I asked him why, he told me it was so we would have had more warm months before winter. Those wise words came to fruition a few months later, as Occupy encampments all over the country struggled with the harsh winter weather as much as any other factor.

Dr. LaFayette has spent so much time gathering information and strategizing that those details come like second nature to him. Our responses to conflict—personal or global—will only be as effective as the quality of our information and the care we take in developing the right strategies. What kind of transformation could we bring about if invested in this step as much as the military invests in preparing for war?

BARRIERS TO INFORMATION GATHERING

There are many reasons so many people and movements struggle with this first step. Oftentimes, activists simply haven't been introduced to tools like Power Mapping or Pillars of Support. Another reason is that everything seems to be moving so fast these days. The sense of urgency can feel so overwhelming that it can feel like we don't have time to waste doing research.

There are other, more complicated barriers to gathering information. We seem to be living in extremely polarized times in which many of us are in political echo chambers that make anyone we don't see eye-to-eye with seem more and more alien. Nuance has gotten thrown out the window, and it seems like being a moderate or having some understanding of both sides of an issue is the most radical thing we can do. Confirmation bias seems to be a major barrier in our ability to understand the complexity of any issue, because so many of us only gather information from sources with which we already agree.

Our inability to see beyond a black/white paradigm is one of the biggest threats to sustainable peace. I've seen this play out in incredibly toxic ways in many circles, including a lot of progressive and social justice spaces in which it seems like saying anything not in accordance with the dominant view of that group is considered the ultimate sin. One wrong comment and you can be viewed as ignorant, oppressive, or "not woke" enough, and it's probably because you're a Nazi. Things escalate quickly, and there seems to be no middle ground. Rather than giving people space to air disagreements or different perspectives, we demonize them, shame them, and shut them down.

We are not only hurting others when we do this, but we are doing ourselves a huge disservice as well. Part of the work of information gathering within a nonviolent context is having the humility to know that we don't know everything, and there may be a nugget of truth in any opposing perspective. Even if the other perspective is 100 percent misguided, understanding it can still be a benefit. Truth is also not a zero-sum game, and understanding other perspectives does not diminish ours.

I shared before that one of my regular practices in nonviolence is to listen to conservative podcasts and watch YouTube videos of conservative thinkers. Many of my friends are surprised to hear that some of my favorite people to listen to include conservatives like Ben Shapiro and Jordan Peterson. While I disagree with a lot of what they say, when I get past my own triggers and actually listen to their messages, I learn a lot.

I believe it is healthy to venture outside of our own political and social echo chambers. The vast majority of young people now receive news from social media, and social media companies spend millions of dollars researching ways to keep us on their platforms as much as possible. One way they do this is to only show us things they think we will be interested in, including political news, analysis, and perspectives that we already agree with.

The more we live in isolated silos, hearing and reading only the perspectives that we already agree with, the more homogenous our views become, and the easier it is to dehumanize people outside of our "tribe." I see it all over society; progressives believing that all conservatives must be racist, and conservatives believing that anyone on the left is oversensitive and wants to shut down free speech.

During long periods of meditation, most people notice pretty strong sensations of pain. As someone who has struggled with back issues since I was young, there are moments—especially during long retreats—that I feel agonizing, burning pain in my back. The practice is about learning to be aware of the pain without judging it or being averse to it.[8] It's about trying to understand the nature of the pain, to not identify with it, and to watch it objectively like a scientist observing the sensation from outside your body.

This is how I try to listen to perspectives I disagree with. I try to listen without judgment, without the intention of finding holes in the arguments, without trying to prove someone wrong. I try to listen with curiosity and the intent to understand. When we can listen like this, we begin to see the true nature of their arguments. We begin to see people we disagree with as more complex than the simpleton racist, sexist, ignorant caricatures we sometimes make them out to be. It becomes easier to see their humanity and to understand that even the most ignorant views can come from a place of real fear, concern, and need. This is valuable information.

Later, we'll talk about the sixth and final step of the six steps: reconciliation. In nonviolence, all strategies and tactics should be evaluated on whether or not we are getting closer or further away from that final goal. Everything we do should build toward reconciliation. If our goal is not reconciliation, if our goal is simply to shut someone down temporarily, then understanding the perspective of the other side may not matter as much. But in nonviolence, our commitment to healing relationships *requires* that we to listen to opposing perspectives to develop empathy and understanding.

---

8. I want to emphasize that there are many different modalities of meditation, and I am most familiar with one particular tradition of what is known as Vipassana meditation. Other modalities may have other practices to respond to what comes up, and I am in no way suggesting that one is better than another.

Sun Tzu wrote:

> Know your enemy and know yourself, and fight a hundred
> battles without danger.
> Know yourself but not your enemy, and win one battle but
> lose another.
> Know neither your enemy nor yourself, and there is sure
> to be danger in every battle.[9]

Information gathering is a process of educating ourselves about the conflict.

---

9. Sun Tzu and Peter Harris, The Art of War (New York: Everyman's Library Classics, 2018), 55.

CHAPTER 17

Step Two: Education

Once we've gathered enough information to understand a conflict, its history, who the players are, each side's perspectives, and have articulated some goals, the next step is to move toward education. Part of this is about educating ourselves to make sure we can make sense out of the data and information we've gathered. Then we move toward educating and empowering the masses, as nonviolent change rarely happens on your own.

Van Jones, founder of Green for All and the Ella Baker Center for Human Rights, once said, "Martin Luther King didn't become famous by saying 'I have a complaint.'" It is by articulating a dream and a vision of a future we could build that Dr. King became the leader of a movement. Long before he gave his famed "I Have a Dream" speech, he was articulating a vision of Beloved Community and empowering the masses. The Civil Rights movement wasn't about defeating segregation, it was about inspiring people to freedom.[1] Nonviolence education is not only about the nuts and bolts of building campaign strategy. It is about inspiring hope, articulating a vision, and reminding us all of our inherent worth and power.

> **"Martin Luther King didn't become famous by saying 'I have a complaint.'"**
> **—Van Jones**

Father Greg Boyle, or "Father G" as he is lovingly known, is the founder of Homeboy Industries, the country's largest gang intervention organization. He says that when you work with young people who are considered "at risk," you can't change them by

---

1. The Civil Rights movement wasn't actually called "the Civil Rights movement" in its day. Leaders referred to their movement as the "Southern Freedom Movement."

instilling fear. You can't yell at them, tell them that they will never amount to anything, and expect them to change. You can't scare them with threats of prison sentences or an early death, because these young people know the consequences of their lifestyles better than anyone. They're not scared of it. That's why programs like "Scared Straight" have never been shown to be effective.[2]

Father G reminds us that it's by inspiring hope that we can begin to see change. And this isn't the case only with young people. Offering a vision of a different future and cultivating the belief that such a vision is possible is the best way to motivate people to stand up for change.

One strength of the early days of the Occupy Wall Street movement was that the encampments showed us small examples of what our reality could be. We were living in the type of communities we wanted in our future, and therefore we were able to see and *feel* what's possible. The encampments were powerful because we weren't just reading about a different type of society in a book. We were living it. That kind of embodied, lived experience is the most powerful form of education. That is one of the reasons the Occupy movement inspired so many.

I've long considered myself a prison abolitionist. I believe in a world without prisons and work toward that vision. But this belief didn't really crystalize in my heart until I began to observe the deep healing work that people like Sonya Shah and Nane Alejandrez are doing inside prisons.[3] I witnessed a level of healing and accountability that I could never have imagined before.

I have seen mothers advocating freedom for the person who killed their child. I have seen rival gang members who murdered each other's friends become friends themselves. I have seen survivors of sexual violence share their stories in front of men who have

2. These are horrible programs where young people visit prisons and guards and incarcerated people yell and scream in their faces as a way to try to scare them into not committing crimes.

3. To see a different way of responding to violence happening today, check out Sonya and Nane's organizations, the Ahimsa Collective and Barrios Unidos.

caused sexual harm and take giant steps in their healing by receiving deep empathy and genuine accountability from them. I have heard stories of unimaginable violence come out of the mouths of some of the most compassionate and peaceful men I have ever met.

Prison abolition was an intellectual ideal for me until I saw a real alternative in restorative justice, which is a fundamentally different way to respond to even the most horrific forms of harm. It centers on the voices of the most impacted people, and it honors the dignity and humanity of all parties. It cultivates remorse, accountability, and healing in a way that our current criminal justice system does not. Ironically, it was in prison that I witnessed what prison abolition could truly look like. It was the work, courage, and vulnerability of incarcerated people and survivors of violent crime who showed me what's possible and reminded me of something I had forgotten.

I believe that as human beings, deep down we know our own capacities for resilience and healing. We know that holding onto pain, guilt, and resentment will be a burden on our own hearts. We know the power of forgiveness and accountability. We know

We know that holding onto pain, guilt, and resentment will be a burden on our own hearts.

we are interdependent and that we will always be in relationship with those we impact and who have impacted us. We know that healing those relationships is the best way to move forward.

Nonviolent education is not about dumping information and jargon into people as if they are empty vessels lacking some critical knowledge.[4] It is about reminding ourselves first—in an embodied way—of our core nature and about what is possible for us as human beings. If we ourselves don't believe in a different future, it's hard to inspire others to work toward it.

In Buddhism, the Pali word *panna* refers to wisdom.[5] Early Buddhist texts refer to three different types of panna: *suta-maya*

---

4. Shout out to Paulo Freire.
5. Also commonly known by its Sanskrit translation, *prajna*.

panna, cinta-maya panna, and *bhavana-maya panna*. Suta-maya panna refers to knowledge gained from an external source— understanding something new by listening to someone explaining a new concept or reading about something in a book. I first learned about prison abolition this way. I read articles about it and watched lectures by people like Angela Davis.

Cinta-maya panna refers to knowledge gained through one's own thinking. It's about using your own intellect and logic to analyze and make sense of things. After hearing about the concept of prison abolition, I thought about it for myself and became critical of our current criminal justice system. I came to understand why, logically, our current system is inhumane and ineffective.

Bhavana-maya panna is wisdom gained through lived experience. In Buddhist practice, this refers to an embodied understanding on the true nature of reality, an insight gained through meditation practice, through shugyo. But you can gain such insights outside the monastery, in the experience of everyday life. It was by sitting in restorative justice circles in prison that I lived into what prison abolition could actually be.

I sometimes think of nonviolence workshops and restorative justice circles as time machines transporting us into the future to show us what a different world could look like. Because I've been there, because I've seen it, I am more dedicated than ever to bring that future to the here and now. This is what Dr. King was talking about in his powerful "mountaintop" speech, which he delivered the night before his assassination:

> Like anybody, I would like to live a long life. Longevity has its place. But I'm not concerned about that now. I just want to do God's will. And He's allowed me to go up to the mountain. And I've looked over. And I've seen the Promised Land. I may not get there with you. But I want you to know tonight, that we, as a people, will get to the promised land!

In our movement spaces, in our families, in our households—how are we educating ourselves in an embodied way? What practices are we institutionalizing to actively combat the normalization of violence in our society and to offer ourselves new ways of relating to each other? What are we doing to heal our internal violence of hopelessness and despair? What are we doing to cultivate faith in what's possible?

This is why the most successful movements throughout history heavily emphasized training. They weren't just offering political education in classroom settings. They were helping people to gain bhavana-maya panna by supporting them to embody the skills and a value system necessary to push for change.

INFORMATION "IN FORMATION"

Of course, there is always a need for intellectual knowledge as well. I also believe there can be a benefit—even a necessity—for the more traditional, top-down form of education. Sometimes there is great benefit in shutting up and listening to an elder speak. Sometimes someone simply has knowledge that I don't, and I can benefit when they are in the front of the room, downloading that knowledge. Reading books, watching documentaries, and going to lectures are all great ways to gain intellectual knowledge and expand our understanding.[6] In a campaign, there is a lot of information gleaned through step one. Once we have that information, we need to, as Dr. LaFayette often says, put the information "in formation." It's not enough to have a bunch of raw data. We need to put that data into a formation that that will connect with our audience for the purpose of education. This means we need to be mindful of who our audience is and put the information into a format they will be able to hear.

Wired magazine has a series of videos on YouTube in which experts in fields such as neuroscience, quantum computing, and

---

6. The problem is that we have created an educational system and a culture that *only* values this type of learning.

blockchain try to explain these concepts in five levels of increasing complexity—to a child, a teen, an undergrad, a grad student, and a professional. They explain the same concepts but use different language in order to reach their target audience.

Knowing our audience isn't just about changing the level of complexity though.[7] It's also about understanding people's value systems and speaking to what matters to them. Dr. King was always very aware of who he was talking to. While he was the *Reverend* Dr. Martin Luther King Jr., he intentionally toned down the religious rhetoric when speaking to the public, which was critical in his ability to connect with the masses.

I have facilitated Kingian Nonviolence workshops for second graders, middle-school students, high-school students, teachers, college undergrads, graduate students, college professors, administrators, and deans.[8] I have trained groups of homeless youth, police officers, incarcerated people, activists in radical movements, and people who have never even been to a protest. I have worked in churches, Buddhist temples, interfaith spaces, and anarchist community centers. In all these diverse spaces, I use the same exact training curriculum, but the way I talk about the principles shifts. I just put the same core teachings into different formations.

Sociologist Robb Willer has a great TED Talk called, "How to Have Better Political Conversations." Quoting the work of psychologist Jonathan Haidt, Willer explains that studies have shown that people who lean left politically tend to prioritize values like equality, fairness, and care. People who lean to the political right tend to give higher priority to values like loyalty, respect for authority, and purity.

---

7. We often underestimate the level of complex conversations we can have with young people. When we have high expectations, I've found that young people rise to meet them.

8. I feel perfectly comfortable going into a maximum-security prison and facilitating for a group of lifers, but I had *never* been so scared before a workshop as when I was about to get in front of a room full of second graders... I was terrified.

Willer and his colleague Matt Feinberg conducted studies in which people wrote essays on hot topic issues to try and sway people on the other side of the political aisle. Not surprisingly, most people made arguments grounded in their own values. Liberals tried to convince conservatives to support same-sex marriage by arguing about equality and fairness. Conservatives tried to convince liberals to make English the official language of the United States by invoking patriotism and hegemony.[9] Not surprisingly, these arguments rarely worked.

What did work, however, was when the essay writers evoked the values of the people who were going to be reading the essay—their political counterparts. When a liberal talked about environmental protection by lifting up the importance of protecting the purity of nature or framed marriage equality as the patriotic thing to do, they were much more effective.

Too often when we are in a conflict, we get into tunnel vision and can only see what matters to us. We try to convince others based on what we think is right as opposed to trying to understand what matters to them. We evaluate what's right or what's effective based on metrics that don't matter to the other side.

Step two, education, is about connecting with people on their terms, empowering them with new information, and building a base. We cannot win people over without considering what matters to them. In order to put information into the right formation, we need to understand both the raw data about the issue as well as the people we're trying to educate.

EDUCATING VS. SHAMING

Because our goal is Beloved Community, we must engage all parties in the process of education, not just the people on our side of the conflict. While shame is perhaps the emotion that people least want to talk about when we are feeling it ourselves, we live in a society quick to shame each other, especially when we perceive

9. The United States does not have an official language at the federal level.

ignorance. We are quick to point the finger, to accuse each other of being racist, sexist, classist, and not woke enough. The idea of being ignorant is loaded with judgment and equated with being immoral. But being ignorant simply means that we lack information. Objectively, ignorance is not a word that has any value judgment on it. We all lack information about countless things, and therefore we are all ignorant. Ignorance is an opportunity to learn. When people lack knowledge about something, we have a chance to engage them and expand their perspectives on an issue. If we view their ignorance as a lack of character and attack them, they will naturally get defensive, stop taking in new information, and we will likely lose our opportunity.

When I was a young teen, my friends and I used gay slurs to tease each other. I had never met a gay person at that point (or if I had, I would have given them plenty of reason not to trust coming out to me), and I didn't think much of it. I didn't hate gay people, but neither did I see any problems calling my friends gay slurs as a way to make fun of them. At that point in my life, had someone shamed me for my behavior and attacked my character, I may have stopped using those slurs out of fear, but I may also have built up resentment for those who attacked me. Or I may have doubled down and used that kind of language even more frequently.

I'm not saying ignorance doesn't need to be called out, but if the goal is education and transformation, attacking someone for their ignorance is an ineffective strategy. At that time, I didn't even know those words were hateful or understand the potential impact of using them. What I needed, and eventually got from some allies and mentors, was to be educated and then held accountable in a loving way.

If a person from a marginalized group has the choice, willingness, and capacity to educate a person of privilege, it can be helpful. But I am in no way suggesting that it should the responsibility of marginalized people to educate those in positions of power and privilege. Doing so is hard emotional labor for those who are oppressed, and it further perpetuates oppression if it becomes an expectation. No one is entitled to education at the expense of the suffering of another.

I once heard antiracist educator Tim Wise tell a story about a house he lived in during college, in which the housemates took turns making dinner for each other. One night, a housemate made a big pot of gumbo. On that night, everyone had dinner elsewhere, so the pot of gumbo was left on the stove, untouched. When Wise came downstairs the following morning, he saw the pot and thought to himself, "Well since I didn't eat any of the gumbo, it's not my responsibility to put it away and clean the pot." So he left. Unfortunately, his other housemates felt the same way, and the person who made the gumbo felt that since they made it, someone else should clean it.

So the pot was left out, and each day, the stench grew stronger and stronger from the rotting gumbo. At some point, Wise decided it didn't matter whose responsibility it was to clean the pot. The rotting gumbo was affecting everyone, and since he had some free time, he cleaned it up.

None of us created racism. But all too often, we focus on whose responsibility it should be to clean it up, rather than on figuring out who is in a position to do something about a rotten system that is negatively affecting everybody. Who has the willingness and capacity? Trying to figure out who is responsible for a conflict can become an excuse to not do something about it. We are often better served by asking who is in the best position and has the most capacity to actually help.

When educating white people about white supremacy, sometimes a white person is the best person for the job, but other times it may be a person of color. Perhaps the person of color has a relationship with the particular white person or simply feels in that moment they have the capacity for it. Sometimes I hear blanket statements like, "It's *never* the job of the marginalized to educate the privileged." This may actually disempower people from doing something they are capable of doing, or even want to do. Anyone, at any moment, can be an educator. Each situation needs to be viewed individually.

As I said before, nonviolence is not always about being calm and polite. Nonviolent education is not always going to feel nice to the person you are trying to educate. Nonviolence often requires fierce disruption.

In his "Letter from a Birmingham Jail," Dr. King unleashed his criticisms of the white clergy in Birmingham, the church in general, and white moderates.

> I have almost reached the regrettable conclusion that the
> Negro's great stumbling block in his stride toward freedom
> is not the White Citizen's Counciler or the Ku Klux Klanner,
> but the white moderate, who is more devoted to "order"
> than to justice....

Though his words sound harsh, he never questioned anyone's humanity or dignity. Rather than trying to shame, he was always trying to educate, to win people over to help take one step closer to Beloved Community.

In a nonviolent conflict, we remind ourselves that people are never the enemy. We are never trying to defeat others by shaming them into submission. Our efforts to educate aren't about proving anyone wrong but about helping each other get closer to fulfilling our potential as compassionate human beings.

Step Three: Personal Commitment

During the Civil Rights movement, the Montgomery Bus Boycott lasted 381 days. For over a year, the Black community of Montgomery walked, carpooled, went way out of their way, and made sacrifices to protest segregation on the city buses. What was meant to be a one-day boycott turned into a commitment and a lifestyle that lasted more than a year.

A famous story emerged from that campaign about Mother Pollard, a seventy-two-year-old community leader and advisor to Dr. King. Despite her age, Mother Pollard joined the boycotts from the beginning. She refused to ride the bus and walked wherever she needed to go. When members of her community offered her rides, she replied, "My feets is tired, but my soul is rested." Mother Pollard's commitment went beyond a campaign or a protest. She was committed to her own dignity and to the liberation of her people. Nonviolence had become a way of life. This is the type of personal commitment required to create transformative change. We need more than commitments to attend a one-day march or to participate for a few hours in a blockade.

As a society witnessing unparalleled levels of violence, destruction, and isolation, we need what Nane calls "long-distance runners" and "peace warriors." We need the "nonviolent army" Dr. King called for toward the end of his life. We need what Gandhi called a *Shanti Sena*, or a "peace army," with dedicated souls as committed to creating change through nonviolence as the military is committed to waging war.

We need commitment to the long-term struggle to change value systems, cultural norms, and the ways we relate to each other as a species. Similar to joining the military, civil rights activists often had to sign over their will before they were allowed to participate in some actions to demonstrate that they understood the risks. For many of them, their commitment to nonviolence went beyond even their own lives. This is a commitment not only to our own wellbeing but to the healing of past generations and the liberation of future ones.

COMMITMENT AS SHUGYO

The level of commitment this step asks for is hard to maintain. I can only imagine how many times people's commitments were tested in Montgomery during cold, rainy days. It can be easy to lose commitment to a nonviolent worldview when you are suffering, getting beaten, or humiliated. Resentment and hatred can easily begin to percolate from your heart when you witness your community being harmed.

This is why we view commitment as shugyo, an ongoing practice. It is not something we do once at the beginning of a campaign and assume it's done. We must continue recommitting throughout the campaign and throughout our lives. Ongoing practices of commitment are deeply related to the principle of "avoiding internal violence of the spirit as well as external physical violence." We need to build these practices into the strategy for nonviolence.

This is a commitment not only to our own wellbeing but to healing of past generations and the liberation of future generations.

Take freedom songs. During the Civil Rights movement, people did not sing freedom songs to kill time. It was not a hobby. It was not karaoke night. Singing was a core part of the strategy to keep people unified and their spirits uplifted to help them maintain their commitment to the cause. During the hardest moments of the movement, people would sing. They sang in churches, they sang while facing fire hoses, and they sang in jail. They used songs as training before the march, as weapons during the demonstrations, and as medicine when they were locked up. Freedom songs kept people committed. I have heard many elders tell stories about how they would not have made it through the movement if not for those songs. Singing kept them alive.

If you've ever been in a church with hundreds of people all pouring their hearts into a freedom song, knowing they are not singing just to sing, but singing for freedom, then you have felt the power of song. You understand that the unity of voices can uplift an entire building and a spirit enters everyone in it. We can practice singing a song by ourselves in the shower, but when we sing a freedom song with hundreds of fellow freedom fighters, we enter the realm of shugyo. It becomes an act of nonviolence.

Unfortunately for me, I cannot sing. I mean, I *can*, but very poorly. Even in the shower, where most people become Grammy award-winning artists, I am aware of my limitations. This may be my biggest liability as a Kingian trainer. My leading a song would ruin the spirit of the moment, and in no way could it be considered an act of nonviolence.[1] So, singing doesn't work for me. For others, even singing by themselves can help them shift their energy or the energy of an entire room. But that particular practice of avoiding internal violence isn't for me. It's important that each movement and each person find strategies that work for them.[2] Silent meditation works for me, but may not be for everyone. Some people find spiritual renewal through running—I hate to run. Some movements sing; some movements dance. Some movements pray; some movements dress up as clowns.

---

1. It could potentially be considered quite the opposite.
2. It's also worth noting that there is a fine line between resiliency practices and coping strategies. Coping strategies can keep us from falling deeper into an endless well of despair, and there is value in that. But at some point, we need resiliency practices to lift us up, help us grow, and fulfill our potential. Think about it this way—meditation is not always easy, and I don't always want to do it. But never in my entire life have I sat for meditation and regretted it at the end. On the other hand, binge-watching a TV show is easy and fun, but I often regret it at the end. Resiliency vs. coping.

Whatever they may be, strategies to combat violence to the spirit and keep people committed to Beloved Community are as important as the tactical, analytical, and intellectual side of strategy and movement building. And they have to be incorporated into our daily lives if we are to sustain nonviolence as way of life.

SELF-PURIFICATION

Once you begin to see personal commitment as an ongoing act of shugyo, you begin to get the sense that the language of personal commitment doesn't really speak to the depth of what is required of us. And you'd be correct. Because the step of personal commitment comes out of the Gandhian tradition of "self-purification." Years ago when Dr. LaFayette and Jehnsen were developing the Kingian curriculum, they applied for a grant from a secular foundation that found the language of self-purification too religious. So they changed the language to "personal commitment" and submitted the proposal. They put information in formation.

But something was lost in translation. What was lost was the seriousness and depth of what this step is asking of nonviolent practitioners. This step is about much more than committing to a campaign. It is asking for a commitment to purify ourselves of the violence in our own hearts: the violence of hatred and resentment; the violence of apathy and hopelessness; the violence of unhealed traumas accumulated over our lives that have been passed down from multiple generations; and the violence of the ways in which we've internalized capitalism, colonialism, white supremacy, patriarchy, and any number of forces that keep us from being whole. Step three asks for a commitment to healing our own souls, and that is the work of lifetimes.

In 2013, I had the privilege to participate in the inaugural James Lawson Institute, organized by the International Center on Nonviolent Conflict and overseen by Rev. James Lawson himself. Surrounded by seasoned organizers from all over North America, we spent several days studying the strategies and tactics of nonviolent civil resistance movements from all over the world. And then something happened. Something broke down or opened up, depending on your perspective. A conflict emerged. The organizers responded by creating space for us to circle up and speak from our hearts. One participant had the courage to share something deeply personal, a painful experience that served as a catalyst for them choosing this work. Inspired by their courage, I shared a pain I had been holding. As I did, I broke down in tears—or broke open my heart, depending on your perspective.

As a trainer, I often find myself being overly critical of activists who don't spend enough time developing strategy, clearly articulating their goals, understanding power-mapping, or having a clear path toward victory. And here I was, taking time during a training about strategic nonviolence to cry and share something that had nothing to do with movement strategy. Through my tears, I found myself apologizing to the group.

But just as the apology fell out of my mouth, I tried to suck it back in because I realized that this *was* strategic. Creating space to speak our pains, share from our hearts, and help each other carry the burden of our traumas *is* strategic and needs to be viewed as part of the campaign. If we can't be real with each other, show up as our whole selves, and build trusting and authentic relationships with each other, then the challenges that come with any movement will eventually rip us apart. And that's not strategic.

> **Creating space to speak our pains, share from our hearts, and help each other carry the burden of our traumas *is* strategic and needs to be viewed as part of the campaign.**

Internal violence of the spirit, which we keep in the deepest, darkest part of our hearts, often surfaces when we are tested. It can show up when we are in a deep conflict with those we love, when we are face to face with someone that hurt us, or when we are in a tense moment during a demonstration facing a social injustice. It is often our unhealed wounds that prevent us from being able to breathe, to take in new information, to see nuance, and to humanize the other party.

Hurt people hurt people. Our own hurts are what enable us to dehumanize and cause harm to others. The act of self-purification, therefore, is a strategic and critical step of nonviolence, because healed people heal people. The more we are healed, the purer our intensions, and the more ready we will be to face conflict. Ideally, we should be creating separate spaces for this kind of work. It is as important as the work of figuring out tactics and strategies, but the work of healing and deep relationship building benefits from having separate and intentional spaces with people who have the skills to lead us through it.

I once heard a group agreement that came from the Bay Area Transformative Justice Collective: *This is not a place for healing, though healing may happen here.* The potential for healing is everywhere. Any interaction could lead to healing. At the same time, if we are in a business meeting, it is not fair or even safe to bring an expectation that this is an appropriate place to process trauma.

I appreciate the fact that I live in a place that generally acknowledges the need for healing. But I have seen healing spaces and meeting spaces often get conflated. Sometimes there is an expectation that people can process their traumas anywhere, which may actually lead to people getting retraumatized.

Beyond separating out healing spaces and meeting spaces, it is also necessary to separate healing spaces from direct action spaces. Taking part in direct actions can be incredibly healing, but direct action is about healing the wounds of society. While our individual wounds may be healed through participating in direct action, we should not have that expectation. Direct actions are a way to open up the wounds of society. We should not go into those spaces looking to open up our personal traumas. While everything is interconnected, spaces for healing, meeting, and direct action are most potent when they are created specifically for those purposes.

Of course, focusing on the wounds of our society has the

potential to touch our own personal wounds as individuals. That is one reason it is so critical to do the work of self-purification, to prepare and protect ourselves from our wounds opening up in places not conducive to personal healing. The more self-purification we do in advance, the more vulnerability we can bring to resistance spaces in healthy ways. The more we heal our personal wounds, the more we can open up to heal social wounds.

Digging around in the depths of our hearts to try and heal our deepest wounds can be scary, painful, and messy work. Feeling the anger or hurt we have toward people we have not been able to forgive, looking at our deepest insecurities, and facing our own shame is not light work. But peace is messy, and nonviolence is the work of the courageous.

Step Four: Negotiation

In some ways, the fourth step is when we directly engage with conflict for the first time. A nonviolent response to conflict is about committing to a path of reconciliation, which means committing to dialogue with the other parties involved. Even if a conflict escalates to physical violence, nothing can be resolved until dialogue occurs.

Because we are so conditioned to react to conflict rather than respond skillfully to it, we often jump straight into an argument or a protest without first attempting a genuine negotiation. Sometimes, all we need is clarity about what we want, and we can simply ask for it. Too often, because we view conflict as a competition between "us" and "them," where "they" are the enemy who must be defeated, we don't even think to ask for what we want. We jump straight to making accusations and demands, escalating the conflict unnecessarily.

Just like every other aspect of nonviolence, skillful negotiation is an art, requiring training and preparation. It involves learning to compromise without compromising our principles, learning to genuinely listen to the needs of others and synthesize them with our own, and learning to be firm and assertive while also remaining flexible. Part of that preparation is self-purification, which is why that step comes before negotiation. Negotiation is often the first time we come face to face with the person with whom we are in conflict with. In many cases that person may have caused real harm to us or to our community, which can make it difficult to maintain our commitment to nonviolence.

This underscores the importance of self-purification, of cleansing or giving voice to our anger and resentment before the negotiation. Then, when we face our adversary, what comes out will be your authentic truth. Part of that truth may be some righteous indignation, but it will not be blind rage or deep resentment. There are times it may be helpful for the other side to hear and see your anger, especially when it is grounded in the intent to educate and heal. But unprocessed anger can make someone defensive, shut them down, and make negotiations more challenging.

It is oftentimes said that anger is not a true emotion but a secondary reaction that your body creates to hide your more vulnerable emotions. Oftentimes, beneath our anger lie feelings like sadness, isolation, or shame. Because those feelings can be so difficult to sit with, we externalize it as anger to protect ourselves from having to feel them. Sitting with sadness requires us to go inside and feel the pain in our own hearts. Anger is a feeling that is projected outward and can therefore be less painful to feel.

While voicing anger is often an important step in the path of healing, it should also be noted that not every space is safe or productive for that release. Not every space is conducive to healing. A negotiation session, for example, when we are facing the people with whom we are in conflict, is usually *not* that space. It's a matter of good strategy to find somewhere else—perhaps with a trusted friend or family member—to give voice to our anger. Expressing anger in a safe container can allow us to access the feelings beneath it, which can give us a better sense of what we need. Without that clarity we aren't able to ask for what we actually want, and therefore any attempt at negotiation will be limited in its impact.

In 2016, I attended a weeklong leadership retreat in Calistoga, a small town in the Napa Valley an hour north of Oakland. The retreat was organized by practitioners of Nonviolent Communication (NVC) and focused on using the lens of NVC to explore issues of justice, race, gender, and power. During the retreat, two young men of color went into town to go to the store. Orlando is a young Black man with dreads, Alvin is a Filipino man with a shaved head. Within minutes of entering the store, they were being questioned by a police officer. It turned out that about a month prior, the store had been robbed by some men of color. Orlando and Alvin "fit the description," so the manager called the police. Neither of them had ever been to that town before, never mind that particular store. Orlando had never even been to California.

When they returned to the retreat, they shared their experience with us, and all forty of us decided to go back to the store the next morning in a show of solidarity. We spent the evening planning our action. When we are engaged in a conflict, NVC emphasizes getting in touch with the feelings the conflict triggered and the core needs we are trying to meet.[1] Perhaps because we had been

---

1. I have a long-standing NVC practice myself. I've incorporated it into my life and in my work, and I think there are elements of it that are highly beneficial. At the same time, I think NVC can be problematic in some of the ways it is practiced. I once heard one elder, a Chicana teacher of NVC, say, "I'm more inspired by the worldview of NVC rather than the structure of it." I appreciated this a lot, because some practitioners get so dogmatic about the "right" way to talk and the "wrong" way to show empathy that it can become overly scripted. Ironically, "NVC speak" can feel inauthentic and can make people feel like they are having a process used on them.

In karate, there is a practice called *kata*, which simply means form in Japanese. It is a series of moves that one practices in sequence. Left punch, right front kick, step forward, high block. By practicing these sequences over and over, the individual moves gets embedded in our body as muscle memory, and comes out naturally in a real-life conflict. Wax on, wax off. But if one were to use a kata in a real-life conflict, it would not go well for them. The individual moves must come out organically, in relationship to the moves of the person you are fighting.

Many of the practices of NVC require the use of a scripted formula. *When I observe you doing [blank], I feel [blank] because my need for [blank] was not met, and I request [blank].* I've witnessed many people try to use these kinds of formulas in a real live conversation, and it naturally comes off as scripted because ... it is. It makes the conversation feel inauthentic and makes the other person feel like a process is being used on them without their consent.

These scripted practices can help someone identify the core of what they want to be communicating to someone, which is helpful. But it should be done with a supportive friend and not the person you are in conflict with. Kata should be practiced in a dojo, not in a real-life combat situation. It also assumes that there is one right way to show empathy or one right way to speak in a way that is nonviolent. This invalidates the rich cultural diversity that exists in communication.

immersed in this practice for the past couple of days, these two young men were deeply connected to their feelings and needs.

Throughout the late-night meeting, they expressed their pain. Orlando talked about being a young, formerly incarcerated Black man who had turned his life around and was now a leader in his community—an activist who had traveled 3,000 miles to deepen his study of nonviolence. And still, when he walked into a store, he was viewed as nothing more than a criminal.

They expressed over and over that their need wasn't to get the manager fired or to shut down the store. Their need was to have their pain seen and validated, preferably by the person who caused it. "We need her to know how much what she did hurt us," they said. Their clarity helped us to articulate our goals and talking points. Without clarity about our true intentions, it would be hard to know what it was we were trying to negotiate for and what strategies would be most effective.

The next morning, we all caravanned to the store with a clear strategy. We wanted Orlando and Alvin to have an opportunity to have a genuine dialogue with the manager who had called the police, and for the store to commit to some sort of process

---

I've also seen NVC used in manipulative ways—almost always unintentionally—to avoid accountability. When someone of relative privilege is being called on for something they might have said or done that was harmful, they can turn to NVC as a way to try to "hold space" for the harmed party. They use the structure of NVC to try to guess the feelings and needs of the person who was harmed and in doing so they are completely ignoring the work of looking inside themselves and holding themselves accountable for their action. "I see that you're feeling really hurt" is very different than saying, "Oh, I just fucked up and hurt you." It keeps the attention on the person who was harmed, and it keeps you from taking accountability for your actions.

Finally, there is sometimes a sense that I get from NVC communities that making "requests" is the right way to ask for something and making "demands" is wrong. While I can understand where this is coming from, again it can be harmful to marginalized communities to tell them that there is not a space for them to demand dignity, human rights, and to be treated with respect. I believe that nonviolence requires space for people to demand their freedom. Again, this isn't a criticism of NVC as a theory and a practice, as much as it is a criticism of the ways in which I've seen NVC practiced by some people. I've simply seen this play out too often to not note it here.

to combat racial profiling. And if they were not willing to do that, all forty of us would walk into the store and engage in a direct action, letting the other patrons in the store know what had happened there.

We didn't start with the protest because that was not our goal. Our goal was a dialogue in which Orlando and Alvin could be heard and could negotiate concrete steps for accountability from the store management. The manager who had called the police was not working when we showed up, but we were able to have a genuine dialogue with the manager who was on duty that day, which led to our deciding that the direct action was not necessary.

It was important that we led with a call for negotiation, rather than leading with the protest. Leading with "We need you to understand how you hurt us," as opposed to "Fuck you, you racists" likely contributed to a successful negotiation because the other side was not as defensive. We were not there to shut the store down but to open up a dialogue. Clarity about goals, as well as the energy and spirit with which we lead, can have significant impact on the success or failure of a negotiation.

It may seem at times like a movement is jumping past the step of negotiation, but there is usually a history of that conflict that puts the order of events into more context. Nonviolence acknowledges that negotiation is where conflict is always resolved, but sometimes direct action is necessary to create the conditions for a genuine negotiation.

During the movement in Birmingham, Dr. King was criticized for using direct action by a group of white clergymen, and calls were made for him to come to the negotiating table. He responded partly by reminding the clergy that the Black community had been asking to negotiate for 340 years. Time after time, calls for a genuine negotiation had been put off by the white community, and they had been forced to use direct action.

In a nonviolent context, the term negotiation has several

specific meanings that distinguishes it from, say a legal negotiation. The first difference is that a nonviolent negotiation is about creating dialogue, not debate. Second, a nonviolent negotiation strives to find a win-win solution. Finally, we believe that only equals can negotiate.

DEBATE VS. DIALOGUE

Similar to how the depth of the previous step of personal commitment can better be explained as self-purification, perhaps dialogue is a better descriptor than negotiation for what we are discussing here. And our society sucks at dialogue. We know how to debate, we know how to talk over each other, we know how to argue, but most of us never learn how to have genuine dialogue, especially through conflict. When I'm in a conflict, I know I'm right and they're wrong, so I'm not actually trying to listen to the other party to try to understand them as much as I'm listening for all the holes in their argument.

That's not a dialogue. That's two monologues, and two monologues don't make up a dialogue. It takes work to understand a different viewpoint. And the more escalated the conflict, the harder we have to try to understand the other person's perspective. When we go into classical negotiations, we often enter with a mindset of debate. We go in trying to win, and in doing so we lose our ability to listen, understand, see nuance, or take in new information from which to learn and grow.

As stated at the beginning of this section, these six steps are coterminous. We are often practicing multiple steps at the same time. Negotiation is listed as the fourth step, but it is also a way to practice step one: information gathering. It is critical that we view negotiations as an opportunity to better understand the conflict and gather more information about the other side's perspectives, motivations, and needs. Negotiation is not about who is right or wrong or which perspectives are valid.

Negotiation can also include step two: education. We may be

educating the other side about a perspective they were not aware of. If you are negotiating with the mayor of a city, you may need to educate them about the experiences of their low-income citizens. Other times, it may be an opportunity for you to educate the other side about their needs. Parties in conflict are often so caught up in their own anger or proving they are right that they're not even in touch with their true needs. Sometimes the role of a nonviolence practitioner is to help the other side articulate what needs they actually have or to offer a compromise or solution that meets their needs in a way they hadn't thought of. A commitment to negotiation in a nonviolent context is ultimately a commitment to dialogue and relationship rather than competition and separation.

WIN-WIN SOLUTIONS

In legal negotiations, our goal is often to get as much as we can from the other side. But if either side walks away from the negotiating table feeling like they lost or an injustice was done, then while the immediate issue may be resolved, the conflict won't be over. If someone now holds resentment and has the motivation to retaliate or to try to get one over on someone else to recoup what they lost, then nothing has been resolved in a sustainable way. At best, you have created a temporary negative peace.

In nonviolent negotiations, we have to find solutions where both sides walk away feeling like they gained something. At the

Nonviolence is a way to resolve a conflict without sowing the seeds for future conflicts.

very least, both sides have to be able to walk away with their dignity intact. Only then are we giving the conflict a chance to truly subside. I read somewhere once that nonviolence is a way to "resolve a conflict without sowing the seeds for future conflicts." Because we usually see conflict as a zero-sum game with clear winners and losers, we end up looking for solutions that almost guarantee resentment will surface down the line. When we try to take advantage of the other side, we are sowing the seeds of future conflict, investing in a future of conflict.[2] After months of hard-fought demonstrations during the Nashville Sit-ins, white business owners agreed to desegregate the lunch counters in Nashville. In response, Dr. LaFayette and the other movement leaders made a decision that surprised everyone. They decided not to make a public announcement. No parade, no press conference, no major public celebrations. They simply and quietly stopped the sit-ins and the boycotts.

Why, you ask? The movement leaders decided that any sort of public celebration could have been a further embarrassment for the white business leaders. While the movement won the immediate victory of integrating lunch-counters, the leaders were committed to a longer-term vision of reconciliation and Beloved Community. Winning the campaign but rubbing the victory in the faces of their opponents would perpetuate the us vs. them worldview and further the divide, taking one step forward and two steps back.

A clear winner had emerged from the negotiations. The movement had won, but ultimately, desegregation was a victory for the human race as it brought us all closer to Beloved Community. Whether the business owners saw it this way or not, desegregation brought them closer to their own dignity. The decision by the movement's leaders helped the business owners save face and prevented them from seeing the young activists as enemies. Instead of sowing seeds for future conflict, they planted seeds for reconciliation.

NEGOTIATIONS VS. CONVERSATIONS

The third key aspect of a nonviolent negotiation is that we believe only equals can negotiate. If one side of the table has more power, then we can have a conversation with them—if they allow it. We can share all of our concerns and hopes for a particular outcome,

2. This becomes the seed of the "history of conflict."

but they can simply say, "We've heard you and we're just going to do things our way." That's not a genuine negotiation.

Inequitable power dynamics are one of the biggest factors that prevent real change. What motivation does a corporate executive have to listen to the concerns of low-income workers or sharing power with them at the negotiating table when they have millions of dollars in profits at stake? Just because one side is ready to have a genuine dialogue does not mean the other side will come to the table in good faith. Sometimes, willingness to enter a dialogue is not enough. Sometimes, we need to create the power equity necessary for a genuine negotiation on equal terms. Sometimes, talking is not enough. Sometimes, we need action.

Step Five: Direct Action

Whether a loved one is struggling with alcohol addiction and is refusing to have the difficult conversation that would lead to their recovery or a nation addicted to fossil fuels is refusing to talk about climate change, sometimes assertive action is necessary to dramatize the issue, bring conflict to the surface, build power, and force a necessary dialogue. My first organized form of direct action was in eighth grade. In retrospect, I feel pretty awful about it, but at the time it felt exhilarating. At the beginning of that school year, we had a new teacher in foreign language. Not only was this teacher new, but her classroom wasn't ready in time for the semester, so her classes took place in the cafeteria. These two factors contributed to many of us feeling like this wasn't a serious class, so we decided this was the class in which we were all going to act up.

Act up is a kind way to put it. On multiple occasions, we made this teacher cry. She left the job within a couple of months. She was replaced by a stricter teacher, but by then the culture had set in. Everyone knew that foreign language was where we were all going to misbehave. Things escalated quickly. I remember once when every student in the class agreed that at a certain time, we would all throw a paper ball at the teacher. Imagine thirty-five paper balls in the air coming at you at once. Another time, we had the *entire class* singings songs, completely ignoring the teacher as she tried desperately to move through her lesson plan. Sometimes, she would pretend nothing was happening. Other times, she threatened to take us to court for assault. (To be fair, a student had thrown a stapler at the window and cracked it).

When she started with the legal threats, we decided to get her fired. The entire eighth grade planned to sit down in the hallways before first period and refuse to go to class. We didn't even know the word "sit-in" and we weren't coming from a place of righteous indignation. We were being mean-spirited brats. We were just bored and organizing this "action" felt exhilarating. We never gave this teacher a chance.

I could feel the energy, excitement, and anxiety in the hallways. Were we actually gonna go through with it? Or would we chicken out? Then I saw a few kids take a seat in front of their lockers. Then a few more. Within seconds, pretty much the entire grade had sat down, filling up the hall.[1] We had no idea what to do next. I remember watching our health teacher angrily trying to walk through and over the pile of student bodies, and I wondered out loud, "Ummm ... what happens next?"

Eventually, the principal came down and asked us all to come to the auditorium so we could talk. We didn't have any decision-making or leadership structure, so there was a momentary lapse of confusion as we tried to decide what to do. Some of us thought that going to the auditorium would mean "listening to the man" and giving up our power. But it was also clear that talking in the hallway was not logistically possible. So eventually, we went.

A couple of weeks later, the teacher was gone, and foreign language class was cancelled for the rest of the school year. We got the result we wanted. With the benefit of hindsight and all of the lessons that I have learned about direct action since then, I look back at that experience with a little bit of embarrassment and a lot of remorse. Especially now that I have a lot of educator friends, I have come to have an incredible amount of respect for the work of classroom teachers. I feel bad about how we acted that year. But that experience also taught me a lot about direct action and how to plan effectively.

---

1. A couple of students went to their first period class. Some of the teachers gave these students "get out of homework free" cards to reward them for staying in line.

UNDERSTANDING YOUR GOAL

One of the most important lessons I eventually learned about direct action is that it is never a goal in and of itself. It is a tool that you use to get a goal accomplished.

During the Occupy Wall Street movement, I was invited to Occupy Seattle to offer a workshop as well as to facilitate a dialogue between advocates of nonviolence and advocates of "diversity of tactics." The dialogue was getting pretty heated at one point, with each side making their argument about what they thought would be more effective for their movement. It was at that point that someone yelled out, "We're *all* right. But what are we trying to *do*?"

The debate between nonviolence and violence (or diversity of tactics in this case) is ancient. But oftentimes, that debate is held outside of the context of a stated goal. Without clarity and agreement on what the goal is that you are seeking, having debates about what tactics or strategies will be most effective is putting the cart in front of the horse. Without understanding the goal, it's impossible to figure out what strategies will be best in getting you there.

In my early years of activism, it felt like I was protest-hopping. I traveled up and down the East Coast, from Boston to Philadelphia to D.C. to New York, going from one protest to the next, rarely seeing any concrete changes. After a while, I realized that we would get so caught up in mobilizing and organizing protests that it seemed like organizing the protest became the goal, as opposed to using protest and direct action as tools to accomplish a goal.

For many of us, organizing and participating in direct action is more entertaining than research or negotiation. We get seduced by the excitement of a protest, the empowerment we feel when we are part of a team, the adrenalin rush of being in the streets. And we can lose sight of the goal. Protests are fun, and we're habituated to having them. It's oftentimes the first thing we rush to. It can feel like it's all we know how to do. But without strategic thinking, direct actions are reactionary and lose their power.

Dr. King articulated two reasons movements should use direct action. The first is to "dramatize" an issue, to educate the public about an injustice that may not be widely known. As long as the public remains ignorant of an injustice, it is impossible to have a conversation about it. The second reason to use direct action is to give ourselves leverage in the negotiation. In the previous chapter, we discussed how in a nonviolent negotiation, only equals can negotiate. As long as there are unequal power dynamics at the table, we can never have a real, genuine negotiation. Direct action can be used to create leverage—to balance the power dynamics so we can negotiate on equal terms. If a government official or corporate leader refuses to engage in negotiations in good faith, then one thousand people sitting outside of their office may change their mind.[2] When Dr. King was criticized by the clergymen in Birmingham for using direct action, he responded, "You are quite right in calling for negotiation. Indeed, this is the very purpose of direct action. Nonviolent direct action seeks to create such a crisis and foster such a tension that a community which has constantly refused to negotiate is forced to confront the issue."

Direct actions are largely about mobilizing people power to counter the structural power that has become barriers to genuine negotiations. They create leverage to take to the negotiating table so that we can be heard. Far too often I have been part of movements that spent significant time and resources organizing a direct action creating tons of leverage, but because we did not know how to use that leverage, have a concrete demand, or know who to negotiate with, all that leverage would dissipate and go to waste.

Occupy Oakland, for example, passed a policy to *not* negotiate with the city of Oakland. While many people made valid arguments for this, I saw this as a wasted opportunity.[3] Our

2. There are interpersonal examples of direct action as well. Parents may withhold ice cream until the vegetables are eaten; kids may refuse their car seat until an ice cream is promised. It creates leverage for negotiations.
3. Some argued that negotiating with the city would legitimize a source of power that many people saw to be illegitimate. Others argued that negotiating with

mobilizations created so much attention and leverage that we could have, for example, used that leverage to demand that the city divest from certain financial institutions or invest more in communities. But because we were unwilling to have that conversation, much of our leverage was wasted.

I have come to realize there are other reasons to engage in direct action. After the killing of Oscar Grant, a young man who had never organized a protest was frustrated at the lack of a community response. He created a flier and called people to the BART station where Grant was killed exactly one week following the shooting. An impromptu committee came together around this young man hours before the event, and we put together something resembling a plan.

Because this protest was organized so last minute, our main message was, "Come back." We announced that exactly one week from that first protest, we would gather in even larger numbers in front of City Hall. *Join us. Spread the word. We will not let this go.*

We held a ton of meetings in the week between those two events. At one point, we considered canceling the second rally because we felt we weren't ready. We expected thousands of people to show up, so we had to train dozens of peacekeepers, figure out a line-up of speakers, and write up a list of demands. Without knowing specifically where we were moving all this momentum, we didn't feel like it was strategic to call all these people into the streets.

The suggestion to cancel the protest was quickly shut down. For one, the word had already gotten out, and people were going to show up regardless. There was simply no stopping it. And perhaps more importantly, we realized this wasn't about demands or strategy, it wasn't about dramatization, leverage, or tangible outcomes. It was about relationship. It was about mourning. The community of Oakland simply needed to come together and collectively grieve.

---

the city would require representatives from the Occupy camp, which would inevitably lead to spokespeople and hierarchical leadership within a movement thought to be "leaderless."

Once we were clear about the goal of that action, we designed the specifics accordingly. Since our goal was creating a space for people to grieve, we decided to start the rally with a march so that people could move their bodies as a literal first step to processing their grief. We decided to have faith leaders standing at every corner along the route. We prioritized having enough visible peacekeepers to try to maintain a certain tone and prevent anyone getting teargassed while they were grieving. We organized a late-night poetry reading so that after the rally people had a safe place to go.

For various reasons, few of those things happened.[4] The police overreacted, people were teargassed, we did not have enough visible faith leaders, windows were broken, fires were set, and arrests were made. So yeah ... despite all our planning, it was impossible to control the flow of events.

I was at a retreat once where someone said that "anger, rage, and call-out culture is *grief looking for a container*." As organizers, we didn't do a good enough job of creating that container, so rage spilled out. But despite what actually happened, the point is that being clear on why we engage in direct action can help us design an appropriate action.

When our goal is to dramatize an issue to win more people over to our cause, we make sure our messaging is accessible and not going to turn people away.[5] When our goal is to create leverage, we engage a target that has a direct connection with our issue.[6] When our goal is to grieve, we bring in speakers and

---

4. The various reasons could fill another book. Some of it was interpersonal; some of it was logistical. We were an ad-hoc group of individuals who had never worked together as a group. Some people were brand new to organizing and didn't have any established relationships. We had less than a week to pull it off, organizing in the midst of a city overwhelmed with grief and with hundreds of people showing up to our meetings. It was a difficult time to organize.
5. Tools like Spectrum of Allies can help you design specific messaging for specific groups of people.
6. As mentioned before, Power Mapping and Points of Intervention can be helpful in identifying targets.

musicians that can hold the type of energy that is conducive to healing. Of course, the reality is that most of the time there is a combination of reasons that drive direct action. But without being clear on our primary goals and intentions, we may end up choosing tactics and messages that are ineffective for what we are trying to accomplish.

THE NEED FOR DISRUPTION

When I first learned about these Six Steps of Nonviolence, I was surprised to learn that direct action is the only step out of the six that is not a necessary component of a campaign. In nonviolence, the goal of any conflict is to find a win-win solution through dialogue, which allows us to move towards reconciliation. If we can find that without using direct action, we can move straight toward reconciliation.

That said, I'm afraid that we often fool ourselves into thinking that changes in our society can be made without radical direct action. We fool ourselves by telling ourselves that things aren't that bad. We fool ourselves into thinking that capitalism, patriarchy, white supremacy, and other forces of injustice haven't taken root so deep in our hearts and minds that they impact everything we do, every relationship we have, and every decision we make. We fool ourselves into thinking that we have hundreds of years before climate change forces us to make radical changes in our lifestyle. We ignorantly hope minor reforms actually make a dent in the overall systems of exploitation, violence, and injustice.

While the purpose of direct action is always to lead back to a dialogue, Dr. King realized that we need massive, powerful, and courageous direct actions to force society to have that dialogue in any sort of meaningful way. While we may celebrate our annual Martin Luther King Jr. holiday by watching a documentary of the movement, listening to some speeches, and performing acts of community service, we forget that the real-life Dr. King was a militant radical at the end of his life.

When Dr. King was assassinated, he was organizing the Poor People's Campaign. He was asking poor people from all over the country to come to Washington, D.C., to create an encampment on the National Mall. He was going to use this encampment to build a movement of civil disobedience that would cripple the infrastructure of the city. He was going to use that leverage to demand billions of dollars a year from the federal government to fight poverty, calling for a "radical redistribution of economic and political power."

In an interview he gave to NBC less than a year before his death, he talked about how the gains made in the previous twelve years of the Civil Rights movement "didn't cost the nation anything. In fact, it helped the economic side of the nation. It integrated the lunch counters and public accommodations. It didn't cost the nation anything to get the right to vote established." He went on to acknowledge that the movement was now "confronting issues that cannot be solved without costing the nation billions of dollars. Now I think this is where we are getting our greatest resistance." He understood that the state was not going to simply hand over billions of dollars without pressure. And he understood that this pressure was only going to come from radical forms of direct action.

There are many ways that one can practice nonviolence, but let us be real about the specific need for nonviolent direct action in today's world. Let us be real about the levels of violence we are confronting: the urgency of the climate crisis, the threat of nuclear holocaust, the depth to which oppression has sunk into our souls. Let us be real about the escalated responses required to heal from the injury to our spirit in these times.

Some communities consider themselves to be nonviolent because they love and forgive people, practice nonviolent communication, choose not to eat meat, practice yoga, and meditate every day. Those are all important aspects of a peaceful lifestyle, but privilege often allows certain communities to stick with interpersonal practices of nonviolence and avoid the risky and scary aspects of nonviolent direct action. Some people have never had to resist anything.

Some communities, on the other hand, have never had the privilege *not* to resist. As Chris often reminds workshop participants, when empire isn't knocking down your door every day, it's easy to stay within the realms of personal transformation and nonconfrontational forms of community building and not risk engaging in acts of political resistance.

We need to acknowledge that the conflicts in our society are at such a heightened, overt level that our nonviolent responses have to match their intensity. We must stop the immediate harm so that we can create space to work on reconciliation. This requires resistance.

DISRUPTION, NOT DESTRUCTION

It has been great to see efforts to reclaim the radical legacy of Dr. King over the past several years. However, sometimes I see people reclaiming Dr. King's militancy but leaving behind his undying commitment to love and Beloved Community. It is true that his politics became more and more militant toward the end of his life, but he never wandered from his

> "When empire isn't knocking down your door every day, it's easy to stay within the realms of personal transformation and nonconfrontational forms of community building."
> —Chris Moore-Backman

commitment to nonviolence.[7] I've seen people use quotes from the end of his life to suggest that he was moving away from nonviolence, but the reality is quite the opposite.

In "Where Do We Go from Here?" a famous speech he gave less than a year before his assassination, he publicly reaffirmed his commitment to nonviolence:

---

7. Dictionary.com defines the word "militant" as, "vigorously active and aggressive, especially in support of a cause."

Now, let me rush on to say we must reaffirm our commitment to nonviolence. And I want to stress this.

And so I say to you today that I still stand by nonviolence. And I am still convinced that it is the most potent weapon available to the Negro in his struggle for justice in this country.

I'm concerned about a better world. I'm concerned about justice. I'm concerned about brotherhood. I'm concerned about truth. And when one is concerned about that, he can never advocate violence. For through violence you may murder a murderer, but you can't murder murder. Through violence you may murder a liar, but you can't establish truth. Through violence you may murder a hater, but you can't murder hate through violence. Darkness cannot put out darkness; only light can do that.

In that same speech, he shared, "I have also decided to stick with love, for I know that love is ultimately the only answer to mankind's problems." In speaking of love, he said another powerful statement, one of my favorite quotes:

Power without love is reckless and abusive, and love without power is sentimental and anemic. Power at its best is love implementing the demands of justice, and justice at its best is power correcting everything that stands against love.

Claiming the militant power of nonviolence does not mean leaving love behind. There is actually great danger in utilizing power without love or cultivating love without power. Power without love becomes domination, and love without power cannot challenge systems of injustice.

If we are being true to Dr. King's legacy, then the nonviolent aspect of nonviolent direct action needs to be of the unhyphenated variety. It is not enough to avoid throwing Molotov cocktails. We need to proactively move toward healing and reconciliation as the goals of our resistance.

In 2017 I had the privilege to travel to Standing Rock as part of a delegation from the Buddhist Peace Fellowship to stand in solidarity with the Lakota, Dakota, and Nakota people who were fighting for their sovereignty and protesting the planned construction of the Dakota Access Pipeline through their lands. It was the largest gathering of different Indigenous nations in history. Thousands of people were camped out at Oceti Sakowin and its surrounding camps.

The elders there taught us something that I will never forget. As groups headed out of the camp to go to a direct action, they would remind us that we were not simply going to a protest but to a ceremony. They encouraged us to conduct ourselves as if we were going to a sacred ritual.

The purpose of direct action is often to disturb and disrupt complacency and negative peace, which can be done in ways that are constructive, that honor relationships and the dignity of all people. Direct actions may surface conflict, they may be uncomfortable, and they may temporarily hurt relationships, but we can still resist in a way that ultimately brings us closer to healing.

There may be times when direct actions do harm relationships in some way. In these cases, we need to be committed to healing those relationships on the other side of that action, and to double our efforts at reconciliation. Otherwise, we have won the battle but fueled the war.

The sit-in that got our foreign language teacher fired was a great example of a non-violent (hyphen) direct action. It was not a nonviolent direct action. It was effective in accomplishing our immediate goal but harmful relationally and actually moved us further away from Beloved Community. It severed our relationship with that particular teacher and it damaged relationships between the students and the school administration as well as some of our other teachers. And we never did anything to repair those relationships, so it was not successful in the Kingian sense. From a Kingian perspective, our responses to conflict are not successful until they lead to the final step of nonviolence.

Step Six: Reconciliation

The Kingian Nonviolence training manual states that reconciliation is the "mandatory closing step" in a campaign or conflict. Key word: *Mandatory*. It is largely a commitment to this step that separates a principled approach to nonviolence from violent approaches to conflict or from a purely tactical and strategic commitment to "non-violence."[1] In Kingian Nonviolence, a conflict is not over until there has been reconciliation.

Early in his career, Dr. King wrote: "The nonviolent resister must often express [their] protest through noncooperation or boycotts, but [they] realize that these are not ends themselves; they are merely means to awaken a sense of moral shame in the opponent. The end is redemption and reconciliation."

So what is reconciliation? Despite being god-awful at math,[2] I devised these formulas to describe it:

Grief + Empathy = Forgiveness
Remorse + Insight + Amends = Accountability
Forgiveness + Accountability = Reconciliation[3]

I've written a bit about forgiveness in chapter seventeen and about accountability in chapter fifteen, so I won't go too much further into them here, though obviously these two concepts could easily

---

1. Note the hyphen, people; note the hyphen.
2. An Asian who sucks at math. I defy stereotypes....
3. I initially had written down Forgiveness (Understanding + Grief) + Accountability (Insight + Remorse + Amends) = Reconciliation, which to me is much simpler. But I was told that adding parentheses means multiplication. I'm not trying to create a complicated formula where you add healing with liberation and multiply it with forgiveness. That makes no sense. I hate math.

fill a book on their own. Both forgiveness and accountability can be difficult, complex processes that take time, and people have to be ready for those processes. Sometimes people rush too quickly into reconciliation, and they bypass either forgiveness or accountability, but I believe both of these two elements are prerequisites for true reconciliation.

My friend Sarah had a former partner who was abusive and was still harassing her. A social worker was encouraging her to forgive him so that she could move on. While it

In Kingian Nonviolence, a conflict is not over until there has been reconciliation.

may be true in the big picture that forgiveness is needed before one can move on, if someone has not gone through their own process of healing, or is still actively being harmed, telling them to simply forgive the other person is not helpful. My friend was trying to force herself to forgive her ex—which put the emphasis on him, instead of on her own needs. She began to judge herself for not being able to forgive him.

Accountability cannot be forced either. I was suspended once in eighth grade for acting out in class.[4] The principal forced me to sit in his office and write an apology letter to the teacher. I wrote it, not because I felt sorry but because I was told to. A few days later, the teacher handed out homework assignments and on mine she had written, "I accept your apology, I forgive you."

My immediate thought was along the lines of, "Fuck you, I didn't ask you for your forgiveness." Her assumption made me more upset than ever. Maybe her forgiveness was genuine, but my accountability was shoved down my throat, so this was nothing close to reconciliation. Reconciliation has to be earned, and it's hard work, especially for the side that caused the harm. Often people try to bypass the need for accountability, especially when the side that caused the harm has an unequal power advantage.

When people say, "Let's just forget it and move on," that oftentimes ignores the pain still held by one side of the conflict and

4. It was, of course, in our foreign language class, before our infamous sit-in.

assumes we can get back to normal without addressing the harm. "Slavery was hundreds of years ago; we just need to move on." "Women are leading major corporations now; why are we talking about sexism?" "Gay marriage is legal; let's all just get past it." These arguments lead to negative peace, not true reconciliation.

NO "THERE" THERE

Of course, much like the concept of Beloved Community, reconciliation is a process more than a destination. Howard Zehr, who has done a lot of work to spread restorative justice in the United States, says "Restorative justice is a compass, not a map." Reconciliation is the same. It's a guide that points us in a direction, rather than a set of step-by-step instructions to a specific destination.

In our efforts to create reconciliation, our focus should not be on a prescribed or pre-scripted outcome, but in the strengthening of relationships over the long-term. My friend Sierra once said, "Resolution feels like the end of something, whereas reconciliation feels like an ongoing relationship." Dr. King also said that, "Forgiveness is not an occasional act, it is a constant attitude."

Toward the end of the Nashville lunch counter sit-ins, a white business owner approached the movement leaders and told them he was going to integrate his business. To his surprise, a young Dr. LaFayette and other movement leaders told him not to. They told him that if he announced he was going to integrate his lunch counter, he would receive criticism, be isolated by the white base and perhaps even the other business owners. They didn't want to see him go out of business. Instead, they asked him to continue segregating his lunch counters but begin backroom discussions with the other business owners to convince them to integrate too. This one act didn't mean that they had fully reconciled with this one business owner and certainly not with the other business owners or with the Nashville public. But honoring their relationship with him was an important step to ensure that they stayed on the path of reconciliation.

INDIVIDUAL AND COLLECTIVE HEALING

The processes of forgiveness and accountability can work independently of each other. We can forgive for our own benefit, even if we never express it to the person who harmed us, or that person can't receive it.[5] One practice that has been helpful on my own healing path is writing forgiveness letters to those that have harmed me. I have written several of these and have never actually sent them. But writing the letters has helped me to heal and has liberated me from harmful history.

Accountability also doesn't require another party. We can have true remorse and hold ourselves accountable for harms we have caused even if the specific people we harmed may never know. Many of the people I've worked with in prison are unable to communicate directly with the people they harmed or their families. So instead, they enter conversations with other people who have experienced crimes similar to those they committed. These dialogues can be healing for both sides. Many of these men continue their accountability by committing to a life of service. Some of the greatest peacemakers, restor-

Our own healing is never dependent on anyone else.

ative justice facilitators, youth mentors, nonviolence trainers, and some of the kindest, most compassionate men I've ever met have come out of decades of incarceration.[6] Of course, seeing true accountability from the person who has harmed us can be incredibly healing, and hearing that someone has forgiven us can speed up the process of accountability. But these are not

---

5. One reason someone might not be able to receive forgiveness is that they haven't forgiven themselves, and in my work, I've found that self-forgiveness is the hardest aspect of forgiveness. Of course, in this interdependent world we live in, there is oftentimes a relationship between the two. Hearing that someone has forgiven you can take you a long way on the path to your own self-forgiveness.

6. Unfortunately, too often the healing and transformation they have gone through have been despite the prison system, not because of it. Healing has taken place through the mutual support that incarcerated people offer to each other and because of the commitment of people who run programs from the outside.

necessary components. Whether we're the one harmed or the one who caused harm, our own healing is never dependent on anyone else. That said, the healing of our society does depend on our ability to reconcile conflicts *together*. We heal society not only through individual resilience, but by healing our relationships to each other. Because we are harmed in relationship, we need to heal in relationship.

RESOLVING VS. RECONCILING

Back in 2009 when I was learning to become a Kingian Nonviolence trainer, one of our trainers said that within the framework of Kingian Nonviolence, we make a distinction between conflict resolution and conflict reconciliation. It made sense on a surface level. If two people are fighting and we get them to walk away from each other, one could argue that the conflict has been resolved because they are no longer fighting. But what happens the next time those two people see each other? The conflict could erupt again. Or they may go home and take out their unresolved anger on someone else. When the underlying conflict still exists, the tension may blow up in a different interaction.

Reconciliation is not about separating people in conflict but about bringing them back together. Theresa once told me the origin of conciliation means "to make one comfortable with." So reconciliation is about making people comfortable with each other again. My understanding of reconciliation deepened when I heard one of our incarcerated trainers, Bilji, say, "Resolving a conflict is about fixing issues, and reconciling a conflict is about repairing relationships." For whatever reason, it took Bilji's voice and his particular wording for the concept to really sink in. Reconciliation is about *repairing relationships*.

I later found a book titled *From Conflict Resolution to Reconciliation* by Yaacov Bar-Siman-Tov. The author writes about how international peace treaties often are not sustainable because they are pieces of paper signed by heads of state who do nothing to heal the relationships of the nations of people who may have been fighting for years, decades, or generations. Until that happens, we will never have true reconciliation.

Too often in our society, we only go as far as fixing issues. This is one of the huge limitations of our criminal justice system. At best, all it can do is "fix" issues by doling out punishment, instituting restraining orders, or demanding financial restitution. This is also the limitation of violent or strategic nonviolent responses to conflict. They can pass a piece of legislation or change a policy.

Even in our personal lives, we often only go so far as fixing issues. Next time, *you* wash the dishes. Next time, *I* pick the movie. Next time, we'll eat at *that* restaurant. We rarely do the hard work of repairing the relationship that may have been damaged throughout the course of that conflict. And until we do that, lingering resentment or frustration could surface again later.

Chris is another one of our incarcerated trainers. Almost twenty years ago, his best friend was murdered days after Chris's birthday. Chris is currently serving time for a retaliation murder he committed. In 2013, he was transferred to a new prison where he found out that the man who *actually* stabbed and killed his best friend was serving time at the same prison, on the same yard. We'll call that man "Tony."

"For the first several weeks, I was completely stressed out," Chris shared. "I wanted to take revenge and felt that if I didn't do something my peers would look down on me. At the same time, if I did take revenge, I knew it would affect my family because I would probably never go home."

For the next few years, Chris avoided Tony at all costs. He was filled with anger and hatred, but he knew that if he ever wanted a chance to go home, he had to keep his distance. It was his attempt at keeping the peace. When he started to learn about Kingian Nonviolence, he realized how his anger was affecting him and how avoiding Tony was only creating negative peace. He says that nonviolence "helped me accept my friend's death and move toward forgiving the person who took his life. I learned about the importance of reconciliation."

So, what did he do? Something only the courage of nonviolence could drive him to do. He reached out to Tony. "Now, I'm able to sit and talk to him about our purpose in life—about the type of men we want to be when we go home." Chris told me this story after a workshop one day. He wanted to tell me because Tony was in the workshop that day. Chris had invited him.

It's said that you know that true reconciliation has happened when the two sides of a conflict are *closer* to each other than they were before the conflict started. True reconciliation is about *even more* than repairing relationships back to its original state. It's about growth, strengthening relationships, and moving forward stronger than we were before. It's about moving us all toward Beloved Community.

Our North Star

Maybe this nonviolence stuff isn't normal. Yet. Maybe it's not in our DNA to be nonviolent and loving to all people. Maybe it's in our nature to be violent, at least for now. But I believe that our destiny as a species is to evolve beyond the constraints of our social norms and our biology.

Certain things are hardwired in our DNA. We seem to always have a tendency to fall in line behind charismatic leaders, for example. We see this same trait in chimps and other nonhuman species with which we share a common ancestry. But I believe that it doesn't have to be that way forever. One major difference between humans and chimps is that we have the capacity to *choose* how we want to continue to evolve. We have the ability to be intentional about the next phase of our evolution as human beings.

In the same way that violence has been institutionalized, we can institutionalize its antidote—nonviolence. We can build institutions, structures, and policies that are constantly reinforcing a new way of relating to each other. When practices are constantly reinforcing justice, healing, accountability, forgiveness, love, and understanding, we can start changing who we are.

Beloved Community is something we have never had as a species, other than in small glimpses. In some ways, loving everyone just because they are human beings may not be natural, because fearing difference has been a survival tactic long before we evolved into *Homo sapiens*. But it doesn't have to continue to be that way. I was born in one of the supposedly more ethnically homogenous countries in the world

> In the same way that violence has been institutionalized, we can institutionalize its antidote—nonviolence.

and spent many years of my upbringing in communities with very little diversity. But it did not take me long to begin to appreciate differences—to honor them and to celebrate them.

I used to grapple with the idea that violence is part of our nature. It's a comment we get in our workshops all the time, and it was tough to argue against. Then I met Paul Chappell, a graduate of the Military Academy at West Point turned peace activist. Paul and I were both presenting at a conference and bonded over our mutual love of peace work and combat sports.[1] In his speech, Paul said that every study that has ever been conducted on violence shows that it is traumatic. Even if we only *witness* violence, it can cause PTSD, anxiety, depression, and trauma. He went on to ask, if violence is part of our human nature, why does it break our brains? Why does it short-circuit our neurons, sometimes seemingly permanently? If violence is part of our nature, shouldn't we be able to engage in it without breaking some part of ourselves?

Finally, Paul pointed out that not a single person has ever been traumatized by an act of compassion. Maybe this is enough evidence that it's the things that fulfill our potential as human beings—love, community, understanding, and relationship— that comprise our core nature as a species. Evidence that we are already on a path away from violence is out there. In his book *The Better Angels of Our Nature*, author Steven Pinker documents that despite the media narratives and our culture of fear, violence has been in steady decline over the history of our species.[2] If we are already evolving without having made that a conscious decision as a species, *imagine if we made it intentional?* What if we held nonviolence as a value, and we educated ourselves about it? What if we all decided that it is not only possible, but it is our destiny to evolve beyond violence? What if we all chose Beloved Community

1. That's right, a nonviolence activist who often enjoys coming home to watch people beating each other into submission. Balance, I suppose?
2. He writes about people perpetuating violence against other people. You could argue that violence against the earth has increased due to our technological "advances."

to be our North Star and began walking in that direction? What if we transformed our major institutions so they were facing in the direction of Beloved Community? How quickly could we heal—how quickly could we evolve?

Years ago, East Point was running a series of parallel workshops teaching Kingian Nonviolence at an Oakland high school and at the San Bruno jail. We invited the students and the men inside to write letters to each other about what they were learning. In a letter to one of the guys inside, a student wrote that he didn't believe that a world without violence is possible. Then he added, "But if we can change the heart of even one person, then it's worth working for."

This comment sparked a long and interesting conversation in the jail. Is a world without violence even possible? Is that what we are working toward? Are we being naive? It was then that one of the elders in the jail spoke up with his seasoned wisdom. "When slaves were on the underground railroad, they were walking toward the North Star as their guide," he said. "And every night, when the stars would come out, they would find the North Star again and they would continue to walk toward it. Night after night, they continued to walk in that direction.

"Those slaves *weren't trying to walk to the North Star*. They understood that no matter how far they walked, they would never get to that star. That wasn't the point. They knew that as long as they used the North Star as their guide and continued to walk toward it, they would get to where they needed to go. They would get to freedom."

The North Star is 323 light years away from Earth. Sometimes, Beloved Community can feel just as far. But the point isn't about whether or not we can get there. Whether or not we believe Beloved Community is possible, it is still our guiding star. Whether or not we'll end oppression, overcome violence, or reconcile all conflict is not the point. The point is to always be walking in the direction of freedom.

I once saw a documentary about the people of Meghalaya, a state in northeastern India. One of the rainiest places on earth, the rivers in the forests flood each monsoon season. Hundreds of years ago, the people who live in these forests created an ingenious way to cross these rivers year-round. They wove together the roots of rubber trees when they were still saplings, young enough to be malleable. They would weave them together into living bridges that span from one side of the river to the other. The challenge was that they had to wait for growth to happen. They had to wait for the roots to grow from one side of the riverbank to the other and become strong enough to support the weight of the people crossing them. This could take years, even generations.

In one scene, an old man was teaching his young niece how to tend to these bridges. He explained to her that he may never walk on this bridge, but her children and her children's children will walk on this bridge, just as he has walked on the bridges built by his ancestors. This has become a powerful analogy for how I look at the work of social change and the work of building Beloved Community. It is the work of generations, not election cycles, grant periods, or five-year strategic plans. We don't need to be weighed down with the expectation of single-handedly changing everything, because we are not alone. We have the wisdom of our ancestors and the lives yet to be lived by our descendants.

Our work is simply to learn from our elders, tend to our portion of the bridge, and pass on the knowledge to the next generation. Our work is to bridge our ancestors with our descendants, meet intergenerational trauma with intergenerational wisdom, and heal the trauma and transform it into the resiliency that we will pass onto our children so that they can cross wider and wider divides.

Maybe we'll never get there. Maybe we'll never fully evolve away from violence. But it's still the direction I want to walk in. And who knows, with the wisdom of our ancestors and the lives yet to be lived by our descendants, maybe someday our children's children will reach the other side of that river.

APPENDIXES

Nonviolence Weights

At the 2018 Arnold Strongman Classic, Icelandic strongman Hafþór Björnsson set a new world-record by deadlifting 1,041 pounds.[1] It's safe to say this was not the first time he ever tried a deadlift. He had trained for that moment.

In the history of nonviolent movements, there are countless stories of people looking death in the eye and responding with love. Whether we're talking about Jesus on the cross asking God to forgive his executioners or David Hartsough telling a segregationist with a knife to his throat that he will try to love him, these acts are the equivalent of lifting 1,000 pounds, nearly impossible without extensive training.

Some people think that they can never practice nonviolence, because they could never show kindness to the most hateful person in the world. Well, yeah, if you've never trained, that would be nearly impossible. Whether you are talking about weightlifting or nonviolence, if you have never trained in it, you have to start small. Lifting five pounds once may not build your strength, but if you lift five pounds a thousand times, the benefits add up until you can lift heavier weights.

Here are a few concrete practices to build up your muscles of nonviolence:

5–20 Pounds

· Spend a few minutes a day practicing mindfulness meditation.

---

1. Björnsson is also the actor that plays "The Mountain" in *Game of Thrones*. I swear I'm not some secret *Game of Thrones* junkie. I like the show, not enough to go out of my way to sneak this in. I promise.

The more you learn to focus on your breath, the more you cultivate your ability to focus on the present moment.

- Spend time every day intentionally focusing on the love you have for someone close to you, perhaps a child or even a pet. The more you intentionally focus on love, the more you grow your heart's capacity to hold love.

- Read books, watch movies, and have conversations about nonviolence, forgiveness, reconciliation, etc.

- Try to understand both sides of someone else's conflict. When we are removed from a conflict, it's easier to understand both sides.

- Try to understand both sides of political issues. Start by listening to podcasts like KCRW's "Left, Right & Center" or watching long-form debates like those on "Intelligence Squared."

- Celebrate the small things. We too often focus on our challenges and things we don't like. Spend time every day practicing gratitude for what you *do* like. Make a list every day before bed of a few things that made you smile that day.

- Smile at strangers as you pass them on the street. You never know who might need it!

20–50 Pounds

- Increase your daily meditations to ten to fifteen minutes a day.

- Start each day spending five minutes reflecting on your commitment to nonviolence. You will quickly notice your muscles of nonviolence getting stronger.

- Perform random acts of kindness for strangers. You can amplify this practice with Smile Cards from www.kindspring.org/smilecards.

- Create a conflict journal. Every time you experience or witness a conflict, write about it. Write down what type and level of conflict it may have been. Write how you felt as you experienced it. Explore where you felt the tension in your body. Write about how you might respond differently next time.

- Think about small conflicts that you have had in the past and try to think about how the other person may have perceived and experienced it. This is not about evaluating whether or not they were right.

- Cultivate your ability to simply sit with intense emotions rather than reacting to them. Anytime you feel intense emotions, whether positive or negative, sit or lie down and observe the physical experience of feeling. Practice letting go of thinking about emotions, analyzing them, or trying to change them.

- Practice *Metta* meditation. Metta is the Pali word for loving-kindness. Begin by focusing on compassion for yourself, then for someone you love, then for someone you have neutral feelings for, and then for someone who you resist or dislike. There are many books and online resources for Metta meditation.

- Tell a friend about a small conflict you are experiencing but from the voice and perspective of the other person in the conflict.

- Volunteer. While charity alone won't change the world, doing acts of selfless service will cultivate compassion and agape love.

- Find a friend and develop a regular, weekly, or biweekly

schedule for checking in about conflicts you are going through in your life. It can be helpful to have some structure to these check-ins. Tools like nonviolent communication or cocounseling may be useful.

50–100 Pounds

· Listen to podcasts and read articles and books by people on the other side of the political aisle.[2] While you may disagree with a lot of what they say, you may also find surprising places of commonality. At the very least, you will begin to understand a broader perspective. This is good practice for engaging in political conversations with people you disagree with in your own life. Listening to a podcast can be less triggering, so you build your capacity to listen to others and learn from them, even when you disagree.

· Next time you are in a conflict with someone, S.T.O.P. as soon as you are able: Stop, Take a Breath, Observe, then Proceed. Learn to identify when you've been triggered. Stop and remind yourself, "Oh, I just got triggered." Then take a deep breath and observe the emotions you're experiencing and your options for responding. *Then* proceed. This cultivates the ability to *respond* to conflict rather than habitually reacting.

· Reflect on larger conflicts you have had with people close to you that have never been resolved. Write about your current feelings around the conflict. Write what the other person may have been feeling. Write out your ideal outcome. What are your goals and true intentions?

2. I'm not advocating for people to listen to people like Alex Jones or Rush Limbaugh, who I believe knowingly spread lies and conspiracy theories. There are plenty of intelligent people with whom I disagree, and I look for them. For example, I disagree with 90 percent of what Ben Shapiro says, but his is amongst my favorite podcasts.

100–200 Pounds

We're now getting into lifting heavier weights that can injure you if you haven't cultivated strong enough nonviolence muscles. Be careful with this work and consider doing it with a support system, much like weightlifters working with spotters.

· Write a forgiveness letter to someone that you need to forgive or to someone from whom you need to ask for forgiveness. You do not have to send this letter. In fact, deciding in the beginning that you are *not* going to send it may give you more freedom to write from your heart. If you don't send it, create a ritual around it after it's complete such as burning it or burying it in the woods.

· Write a harm letter. This can be about a time that you were harmed or a time that you harmed someone else. Write about the incident in as much detail as you can remember. As hard as it can be to relive traumatic experiences, doing it with intention and support can be healing. Write about what would bring you healing around these harms. Again, you don't have to send it.

· Tell a friend about a major conflict you are experiencing but in the voice and perspective of the other person in the conflict. This kind of role-playing will help you gain insight into the other person's perspective.

· Intervene in a conflict that may be happening between two friends or family members. Helping to deescalate and reconcile a conflict that you are not directly involved in is great practice, in addition to the fact that you are performing a great service.

200+ Pounds

· Intervene in conflicts between strangers that you may witness happening around you, as long as you feel like you can stay safe. This could be a conflict between two neighbors or between the police and someone being targeted. Don't wait for someone else to take the lead. Tools like the Five Ds of Bystander Intervention from the organization Hollaback! are very useful in this kind of intervention.

· Attend longer meditation retreats. Ten-day silent Vipassana meditation retreats are relatively accessible if you can find the time.[3] Other retreats have specific themes, such as Metta retreats, forgiveness, retreats for people of color or queer people, etc.

· Enter into a dialogue with someone who has harmed you or that you have harmed. It may be helpful to find a mediator or a restorative justice facilitator to support you through this process. Entering this kind of process doesn't mean reaching out to the person right away. It means beginning the process of getting to that final goal. Depending on the severity of the harm, it may take weeks, months, or maybe even years before you are ready. But think about it and engage in a proactive process to move in that direction.

· Join support groups, healing circles, or restorative justice groups; find a therapist to help you look at your traumas. We all have trauma and need to work through it if we hope to help others. This would not be a one-time thing but an ongoing process with a person or a group that you trust.

---

3. They are held all over the world on a regular basis and are offered by donation. More information at www.dhamma.org.

Quick Responses to Common Criticisms of Nonviolence

Nonviolence isn't effective, especially against violent regimes.

The work of Erica Chenoweth and Maria Stephan dispelled this myth pretty convincingly. Chenoweth, an academic at the University of Colorado, was a critic of nonviolence when she and Stephan began measuring the success of violent and nonviolent movements around the world. Their findings, published in the 2011 book *Why Civil Resistance Works*, looks at more than three hundred people-led movements in the past century. They found that nonviolent movements were twice as likely to succeed as violent movements, even against the most violent regimes. They also found that nonviolent movements are becoming more and more successful over time, and violent movements are becoming less and less successful. I highly recommend everyone to read their book or watch Chenoweth's TEDx Talk, titled "The Success of Nonviolent Civil Resistance."

Property destruction isn't violent.

Here's an excerpt from an article I wrote for *Waging Nonviolence*:[1] I think anyone who believes that property destruction is *never* violent or that it is violent *period* needs to think more critically about the issue.

> The recent burning of two mosques in Texas were acts of violence. The Ploughshares movement, in which activists

---

1. The article is titled "Why Black Bloc Tactics Won't Build a Successful Movement" and can be read in full at www.wagingnonviolence.org.

sneak into military bases to dismantle weapons, is an act of nonviolence. Property destruction can be incredibly violent, or it can be an act of nonviolence. Context matters.

Writer Rebecca Solnit wrote that, "The firefighter breaks the door to get the people out of the building. But the husband breaks the dishes to demonstrate to his wife that he can and may also break her. It's violence displaced onto the inanimate as a threat to the animate." During Occupy Oakland, I witnessed a mob of people using Black Bloc tactics rush a corporate business in the middle of the day and start spray-painting and banging on their windows. I remember seeing a young child inside the business with her mom. I don't care about the window, but I do care about the impact on that girl. I don't think breaking a window itself is an act of violence. But I wouldn't be surprised if that act also traumatized that little girl—and that *is* violent.

However, regardless of your stance on property destruction, the basic fact remains that the majority of Americans seems to view it as violent. We spend too much time arguing about what we feel, and we ignore what the public feels. And if we are not including public sentiment in our calculations, we are making a huge mistake.

Generally speaking, I believe we spend too much time debating about whether or not something is violent. There is a more important question that we need to be grappling with: Are violence and property destruction effective?

Nonviolence is for privileged people.

I don't necessary disagree with this critique. Nonviolence requires action, sacrifice, and training, all of which require a certain level of privilege. But so does violence. Being able to participate in a violent resistance movement may actually require *more* privilege. It requires physical strengths and abilities, which tend to prioritize the participation of young, able-bodied men. All movements require those with privilege to use that privilege to fight for justice. Nonviolent movements allow for the participation of many more people, something else that Chenoweth and Stephan's work clearly laid out.

A related critique says that oppressed people don't have the privilege to remain nonviolent. This critique assumes that nonviolence is about nonaction. It is not. Nonviolence understood in its proper context is about acting against violence and injustice. As Chenoweth and Stephan's research has shown, it is actually more effective than violence.

Finally, this critique assumes that violence is the form of resistance more accessible to oppressed communities, which is complicated. I would argue that in less overt conflicts, nonviolent resistance is easier and more accessible to communities. However, nonviolent responses to the most overt forms of violence—such as some of the world's most violent regimes—do require more strategy, preparation, creativity, and training. Regardless of effectiveness, it is easier to pick up a gun and start shooting than to think of nonviolent ways to bring about regime change. This is why we need to institutionalize nonviolence trainings and make them more accessible.

You can't tell oppressed people not to fight back.

This criticism is rooted in a misunderstanding of nonviolence. Nonviolence is about fighting back. As I've written in this book, nonviolence is not about telling people that they don't have a right to fight back, nor is it about casting judgment on people who choose to use violence. Nonviolence is about acknowledging that if the ultimate goal is for reconciliation and the creation of Beloved Community, then violence alone will never be enough. When it seems a nonviolent response is not available, people should protect themselves as best they can. But the more we train, the more we realize that there are always nonviolent responses to conflict.

Nonviolence would never work against _____ (Fill in the blank).

Nonviolence would never work against ISIS. It would have never worked against the Nazis. It would never work against X, Y, and Z. Let's really break this down.

It's hard to conceive of a nonviolent response to the Holocaust, but we'll use that as an example. First, Hitler and the rise of Nazism was the result of violence. Hitler came to power in a Germany that was devastated by World War I. After the violence of that horrific war, there was never an attempt to reconcile with the people of Germany. There was never an attempt to bring the German people into Beloved Community. They were beaten down and left on their own—defeated and humiliated.

In that vacuum of power and pride, Nazism rose to power. When societies invest in violence for long periods of time, they leave entire communities to suffer decades of war and poverty, which breeds hatred and isolation for generations. Groups like ISIS, Al Qaeda, and the Nazi Party are the result. After generations of investment into violence, some people criticize nonviolence for not being able to immediately solve the crisis.

Perhaps if we stop investing in violence and start investing in nonviolence, we will finally interrupt these cycles of violence. Perhaps if after World War I, the nations around Germany had helped it rebuild, Nazism would never have risen to power. Perhaps if after the first Gulf War, the United States hadn't imposed sanctions that led to the deaths of up to five hundred thousand children, hatred would not have taken shape in the form of ISIS.

Second, nonviolent responses to these extreme cases have never really been attempted. We know of small-scale examples of nonviolent resistance to the Nazi regime, many of which *were* successful. While we can find these small-scale examples, large-scale examples don't exist because it's never been tried at the same scale as violent responses. We say war "works" after we invest billions of dollars and countless lives to overthrow a regime.

What if we spent the same amount of resources in a nonviolent response? What will it look like when we spend billions of dollars preparing a nonviolent response? What if tens of thousands of people risked their lives for a nonviolent response to conflict? What if entire nations mobilized massive resources towards reconciliation? We can't say that nonviolence won't work against ISIS if we're comparing a small handful of grassroots organizations to the billions of dollars that the Pentagon invests in violence.

Nonviolence could get you killed.

Yup, and so could violence.

Dr. King was successful because of the threat of Malcolm X. Gandhi was successful because of Subhas Chandra Bose. The British empire was weakened due to the wars they were fighting. Nonviolence movements wouldn't be successful if not for the threat of violence.

It's true that both King and Gandhi's movements were impacted by violence or the threat of it. Nonviolent movements don't happen in a vacuum. They happen within an ecosystem of relationships, and often violence contributes to their success. But all movements, violent and nonviolent, are impacted by world events, the influences of other simultaneous movements, the strength of the opposition based on social, political and economic conditions, and any number of other factors. This criticism is not special to nonviolent movements. It should be acknowledged as a factor in all movements.

Nonviolence doesn't work against people who have no morals.

This might be true. Nonviolence is based on an unwavering faith that the core of humanity is about belonging. Even if people have forgotten their own morals, nonviolence is about reminding them of it. Nonviolence assumes that ultimately, no one benefits from violence. Violence may get us physical and material benefits, but it will destroy our souls in the process.

While there may be a small percentage of the population who are clinical narcissists or psychopaths, there will always be nonviolent ways to keep them from causing harm while maintaining their dignity as human beings. And of course, a nonviolent society would not allow someone like that to rise to a position of power.

One point I want to make on narcissists and psychopaths, since people always want to find the most extreme examples and find the loophole. "What about in this instance? Can we use violence then?" There are fewer clinical psychopaths than people think, and we can't judge the effectiveness of something based on the most extreme cases.

I have major issues with the mental health industry and the way it pathologizes people. Some studies cite that as many as 25 percent of men in federal prisons are psychopaths. I believe that the vast majority of these people are simply acting out their traumas as opposed to there being something fundamentally wrong with them. In fact, once you start to hear the stories of many men in prison, you would imagine that something would be wrong with them if they *didn't* act out in some harmful way.

So I believe that the actual number of people who are clinical psychopaths is significantly smaller than what we believe.[2] Psychopathy is an extreme exception to the rule. And we can't judge the effectiveness of something like nonviolence based on the most extreme and unlikely of scenarios.

Are you saying that if someone was pointing a gun at your mother that you wouldn't do something to defend her?

I never said that.

---

2. The most commonly cited number is that 1 percent of the general population are psychopaths.

Selected Resources

Alexander, Michelle. *The New Jim Crow: Mass Incarceration in the Age of Colorblindness*. New York: The New Press, 2012.

brown, adrienne maree. *Emergent Strategies: Shaping Change, Changing Worlds*. Chico, California: AK Press, 2017.

Chenoweth, Erica, and Maria J. Stephan. *Why Civil Resistance Works*. New York: Columbia University Press, 2011.

CNN. *The Feminist from Cellblock Y*. 2018.

Davis, Angela. *Are Prisons Obsolete?* New York: Seven Stories Press, 2003.

DeGruy, Joy. *Post Traumatic Slave Syndrome: America's Legacy of Enduring Injury and Healing*. Portland, Oregon: Joy DeGruy Publications, 2005.

Engler, Paul, and Mark Engler. *This Is an Uprising: How Nonviolent Revolt Is Shaping the Twenty-First Century*. New York: Bold Type Books, 2016.

hooks, bell. *The Will to Change: Men, Masculinity, and Love*. New York: Atria Books, 2003.

INCITE! *The Revolution Will Not Be Funded: Beyond the Non-Profit Industrial Complex*. Durham, North Carolina: Duke University Press Books, 2017.

Kaira Jewel Lingo's official website. www.kairajewel.com.

King, Martin Luther. *Stride Toward Freedom: The Montgomery Story*. Boston: Beacon Press, 2010.

LaFayette, Bernard, and Johnson, Kathryn Lee. *In Peace and Freedom: My Journey in Selma*. Lexington, Kentucky: University Press of Kentucky, 2013.

Laloux, Frederic. *Reinventing Organizations: A Guide to Creating Organizations Inspired by the Next Stage in Human Consciousness*. Oxford UK: Nelson Parker, 2014.

Moore-Backman, Chris. *The Gandhian Iceberg: A Nonviolence Manifesto for the Age of the Great Turning*. Be the Change Project, 2016.

Radiolab podcast. "More Perfect: Mr. Graham and the Reasonable Man." WNYC Studios, November 30, 2017.

Rosenberg, Marshall. *Nonviolent Communication: A Language of Life*. Encinitas, California: Puddledancer Press, 2003.

Tariq Khamisa Foundation. www.tkf.org.

The Good Men Project. www.goodmenproject.com.

The Representation Project. *The Mask You Live In*. 2015.

Voice Male: The Magazine for Changing Men, voicemalemagazine.org.

Wing Sue, Derald. *Microaggressions in Everyday Life: Race, Gender, and Sexual Orientation*. Hoboken, New Jersey: Wiley, 2010.

Waging Nonviolence. www.wagingnonviolence.org.

Wink, Walter. *Jesus and Nonviolence: A Third Way*. Minneapolis: Fortress Press, 2003.

Zimbardo, Philip. *The Lucifer Effect: Understanding How Good People Turn Evil*. New York: Random House, 2007.

Gratitude

I've been privileged to write this book. I'm a high school dropout with no college education. Two semesters of Spanish at a community college years ago are all that account for my higher education credits. And here I am, writing a book because a publishing company *invited* me to. I have always dreamed of writing a book, and my mom always pushed me to think about it, but that's just what moms do, right?

In the summer of 2017, I was at the University of Rhode Island, helping lead a two-week certification training for new Kingian Nonviolence trainers, when I received an email from Hisae Matsuda, the then-acquisitions director for Parallax Press. She expressed interest in my writing a book and offered to meet me for coffee to talk about it. The experience of receiving that email was similar to the moment that Jun-san asked me to go with her to the temple in Lumbini. I knew in my heart the second I saw that email that this book was going to happen. I tried to play it cool at that first meeting, but I couldn't wait to get started.

On that fateful day of the Middle Passage Pilgrimage when I as a teenager decided to stay on the walk, I saw a short poem engraved on a stone by Thich Nhat Hanh. I had never heard of him before, but the quote attracted me, and soon after, I bought a book he wrote called *Living Buddha, Living Christ.* It was the first book I ever read on Buddhism and peace. It is fitting then that the first book I write is with Parallax Press, a small nonprofit publishing house started by Thich Nhat Hanh himself, who famously had a relationship with Martin Luther King Jr. and was nominated by Dr. King for the Nobel Peace Prize.

I realize I have the incredible privilege of being asked to write a book. Who gets that kind of honor? Not only that but to work with a mission-based press whose values are aligned with my own? Parallax's mission is to "publish beautiful, well-crafted books that nourish happiness and show the connection between the inner and outer work for peace and justice." *C'mon!* I couldn't find a more fitting publisher if I tried.

I'm so grateful to Hisae and the whole team—Terri Saul, Josh Michels, Earlita Chenault, Stephen Houghton, Katie Eberle, Jacob Surpin, Steven Low, Heather Harrison, and Leslie Schneider—for having faith in me and giving me this opportunity. They've made this first-time author feel comfortable throughout this whole process. I am forever grateful.

Thank you to my two sisters, Erika and Megumi, for all of the shared struggles, tears, laughter, fighting, and for sharing this journey together. There are so many memories—good and bad—that have contributed to my learning and a lifetime of memories still left to make, especially with young Jett.

Kato Shonin, the head monk of the New England Peace Pagoda, and anyone else who spent time on the US leg of the Interfaith Pilgrimage of the Middle Passage: you changed my life forever, and I have you to thank for inspiring me to write this book.

To everyone I met during my years at the Peace Development Fund: Dr. Mildred McClain, Chief Wilbur Slockish, George Galvis, Tina Reynolds, Lori Goodman, Miguel Moreno, and so many more. I am honored to still be in community with so many of you.

The Oscar Grant movement was a critical time in my growth as an activist and an organizer. Despite all of our arguments, I think back fondly on the times I spent with Dereca, Jay, Cat, Jessamyn, Tshaka, Jack, Rachel, Tony, Malachi, Krea, Theresa, Cam, Mandigo, and all of the others who helped the seeds of nonviolence sink deeper into my heart.

To all of the people who helped to make the East Point Peace Academy real and to those who were there from the very beginning: Aaron Nakai, Tye Kirk, Lauren Veasey, Beth Rosales, Bill Bank,

Chela Blitt, and of course Leah Pearlman. To those who have added to that foundation, including Sierra Pickett (who was also one of the early reviewers of this book—thank you!), Nirali Shah, Toni Battle, Julia Rose Golomb, Chris Van Breen, Melissa Crosby, Astrid Montuclard, and so many more.

David Hartsough, an old-time activist who met Dr. King at age fifteen and has been arrested more than 125 times in the name of peace since, invited me to speak on a panel discussing nonviolence vs. diversity of tactics at a packed church in Oakland at the peak of the Occupy movement.[1] David has since become a key mentor and supporter, and it is thanks to his generosity allowing me to stay in his cabin right now, getting a much-needed break from my regular work, that I'm able to type these exact words.

To others in the Kingian world: Matt Guynn, Victoria Christgau, Anne Weills, Mary Lou Finley, Joan May Cordova, Tanya Maus, Ashley Olsen, Pam Smith, Sherri Bevel, Mary Liuzzo, Thupten Tendhar, Kay Bueno de Mesquita, Laura Dussault, Gail Faris, and Kezia Curtis.

To everyone in the Ahimsa Collective, especially Maegan Willan, Rev. Samantha Wilson, Alison Espinosa-Setchko, Tye Lancaster, AJ Urriza, and Dennis Scott for sharing space with me, and to Bonnie Wills, Dave Belden, Martina Lutz-Schneider, Kashka Banjoko, nuri nusrat, Richard Cruz, and Daniel Self.

Thank you to Lauren Quan for all of the late-night conversations during some of the hardest and most inspiring periods of my activist life. We may have taken years off of each other's lives sitting in that backyard, but I also grew immensely from those talks. To Etah for being a friend, brother, and true warrior.

---

1. "Diversity of tactics" is a term many people use to articulate an agreement to use tactics that step beyond the limits of nonviolence during political action, including acts of property destruction and limited uses of violence. In my opinion, it is unfortunate framing as it suggests that there is not a wealth of diversity within nonviolent tactics. In fact, nonviolence offers more diversity and creativity than violence.

To Nicamer Tolentino and William Cooper, who rolled out the red carpet to help us institutionalize Kingian Nonviolence in the San Bruno jail. Thanks to the doors they opened, we have had thousands of men and women in the San Francisco County Jail system go through our workshops and have graduated four cohorts of inside trainers.

Lt. Roland Ramon, Clayton Smith, Captain Metcalf, Officer Morales, and many others who work within corrections who have helped our work flourish inside and have consistently shown me kindness.

I'm grateful to Shilpa Jain for accepting my challenge and reminding me how to cry, and to the late-night stargazing crew of Alvin Rosales, Darsheel Kaur, Mike Tinoco, Michelle Booth, Orlando Amsted, and others for almost emptying my reservoir of tears.

To Carlos Saavedra, one of the smartest people I've ever met. The work that you and your colleagues at the Ayni Institute do is a true service to the world, and it is an honor to learn from you.

Eric Stoner and the team at *Waging Nonviolence* have given me a platform to not only share my thoughts but explore my own beliefs and analysis through my writing, an incredibly valuable part of my own growth and training.[2] To the elders of Standing Rock for reminding me to breathe and to the Buddhist Peace Fellowship for getting me there. To Sima Savdharia for challenging me to grow even if I fought kicking and screaming the entire way. To Vishnu Sridharan for our ongoing practice together. To Honda Katsuichi for the three months we spent together studying race relations in the South. To elders and not-so-elder teachers like Michael Nagler, Rev. James Lawson, Joanne Sheehan, Miki Kashtan, Yuka Saionji, Gus Newport, Rabbi Lynn Gottlieb, Gaylord Thomas, Rev. Liza

---

2. Portions of this book are from articles that I have written for the site in the past. Check them out in full, as well as articles and analysis by other authors, at www.wagingnonviolence.org.

Rankow, Erica Chenoweth, Ivan Marovic, and so many others for being part of my journey.

As I look back on my life, I marvel at the diversity of my experiences and the many different communities I've had the honor to know. They have given me so many different perspectives on life, which are critical to understanding nonviolence. I've gone from living in a six-bedroom, multi-million-dollar oceanfront mansion to being homeless. I've gone from hitchhiking through the Deep South to living in Buddhist monasteries in South Asia; from working with people of wealth in the world of philanthropy to working with people of wisdom in the world of prisons; and from living in rural New Hampshire to traveling the world to settling in Oakland. I've lived multiple lives, and while it hasn't always been easy, I am forever grateful.

I think about how malleable we are as a species. How much our environments impact who we become. And how so much of it seems to depend on blind luck. I think about how, had things gone a little differently in my life, I could have stayed in Japan and ended up as the chancellor of a major university in Tokyo like my grandfather. I would have grown up surrounded by class privilege, likely ignorant of many justice issues. I would have worn a business suit every day and most likely would have been consumed by Japanese salaryman culture.[3] Nonviolence might have been completely foreign to me, and social justice movements would have been the furthest thing from my mind.

I think about what would have happened had I not heard about the Interfaith Pilgrimage of the Middle Passage. I was a high-school dropout getting high every day and surrounding myself with others doing the same. What if I had met a military recruiter instead of

---

3. The term "salaryman" refers to the Japanese businessman whose life is committed to his work and who lives in service to the company that pays his salary, not unlike the samurai who lived his life in service to his lord. In the deeply patriarchal culture that is Japan, women are excluded from this term and from many full-time career-oriented jobs.

Buddhist monastics? How might have I turned out if I had gone off to war? And what about after the war? Not even armed with a GED, I could have easily become a cop or a prison guard, as many returning soldiers do.[4] I might have come to glorify the use of violence instead of nonviolence and ended up becoming an abusive guard working in one of the prisons where I volunteer now. Or what if I had joined the many young people, who, without any guidance or purpose, go on to live a life knowing nothing but self-destruction? Would I have continued onto harder drugs, harder crimes, and ended up in prison myself?

My life experiences tell me that any of these scenarios could have easily happened. When I sit with men in prison, I realize that I am no different from them. I could have easily ended up in their place had my life gone slightly differently. And if I could have that understanding and empathy of those men, then I also need to extend that understanding for the prison guards. Had things gone slightly different in my life, I could have just as easily ended up in their shoes.

We like to think of ourselves as so different than "those people." We think of ourselves as almost a different species from someone capable of committing murder. We think of ourselves as inherently different from someone who could vote for *that guy*. "They're inhuman," we say. "How could people do those things?" we ask.

The answer is not that complicated. Given the same conditions, we are all capable of doing anything another human being is capable of doing. No matter how foreign certain actions, perspectives, or value systems may seem to be, the insight of nonviolence reminds us how similar we are. The privilege I have had of living so many different lives and knowing so many people from different backgrounds has deeply grounded me in this worldview.

To each and every single person who has ever been part of a training, workshop, or presentation I have given, thank you. I often

4. I did not get my GED until my mid-twenties.

say that every time I facilitate a training, I deepen my own training. Every time I present, I deepen my understanding of nonviolence because of the rich conversations I'm able to have with participants. In this way, I have had the privilege to learn from countless thousands of individuals. And in this way, I carry all of you with me everywhere I go.

Thank you all for helping me write this book.

About the Author

Kazu Haga was born in Japan and moved to the United States with his family when he was seven. At the age of seventeen, he participated in the Interfaith Pilgrimage of the Middle Passage, a walking journey to heal from the legacy of the transatlantic slave trade. This experience launched him into a lifetime commitment to spiritual practice and social change.

As the founder of the East Point Peace Academy and core member of the Ahimsa Collective, he is a teacher and practitioner of nonviolence, restorative justice, meditation, community organizing, and movement building, and he works in prisons, schools, and community settings. He resides in Oakland, California.

Related Titles

How to Fight Thich Nhat Hanh

The Idealist's Survival Kit: 75 Simple Ways to Avoid Burnout
Alessandra Pigni

Keeping the Peace: Mindfulness and Public Service Thich Nhat Hanh

Love in Action: Writings on Nonviolent Social Change Thich Nhat Hanh

Love Letter to the Earth Thich Nhat Hanh

Leading with Love Maude White

Peace, Love, Action! Everyday Acts of Goodness Tanya Zabinski

Reconciliation: Healing the Inner Child Thich Nhat Hanh

True Peace Work: Essential Writings on Engaged Buddhism Parallax Press

World as Lover, World as Self Joanna Macy

 **PARALLAX PRESS**

Parallax Press, a nonprofit publisher founded by Zen Master Thich
Nhat Hanh, publishes books and media on the art of mindful living and
Engaged Buddhism. We are committed to offering teachings that help
transform suffering and injustice. Our aspiration is to contribute to
collective insight and awakening, bringing about a more joyful, healthy,
and compassionate society.

For a copy of the catalog, please contact:

Parallax Press
P.O. Box 7355
Berkeley, CA
94707

parallax.org